To Joana.

Thanking for the
years of working
together on
broadcasting issues
Best of luck
for the future
wherever that may be!

Ted

November 2010.

'SOMETHING MUST BE DONE'

SOUTH WALES v WHITEHALL

1921 – 1951

Best wishes

Ted Rowlands MP

Ted Rowlands

November 2170

ttc

Books

'Something Must be Done'

South Wales v Whitehall

1921 - 1951

British Library Cataloguing in Publication Data

A catalogue record for this book is available from the British Library
ISBN 0953937615

Published by:

Books
First Edition 2000

Printed by: Rainbow Print (Wales) Ltd, Merthyr Tydfil

CONTENTS

List of Illustrations
Preface
Acknowledgements

Introduction by Prof. Dai Smith   10

1.   **1921 - 1934: South Wales And Whitehall**   13

- A Place of suffering - South Wales' people -
Whitehall's people - Whitehall's Policies - South Wales calls on
Whitehall - A National crisis, A National government

2.   **1934: A Turning Point**   41

'Fairy godfather of South Wales' - 'Nothing New, Nothing Heroic' -
'A Laboratory Experiment' - The Special Areas (Development and
Improvement) Act

3.   **1935: 'A Mistake'**   62

- 'Palliatives' - Return to the land - 'Crudities and confusions' - 'A
Gateway to South Wales' - Treforest - The Reopening of the Ebbw
Vale Works.

4.   **1936: 'Something Must Be Done'**   83

'Don't you say a word against South Wales ...' -
'The situation in Merthyr Tydfil ...' – ' God bless the revolution ...'
– 'Our mysterious lady known as Sara...' - Stewart's last stand -
Something must be done - 'A detour to Dowlais' - 'After South
Wales you can't let him down '

5.   **1937: 'A Second Experiment'**   108

'A second experiment' - 'A sister to SARA' - 'Blue' and 'Pink'
plans

6.   **1937/8: 'Hope Dawns On Dowlais'**   121

'Hope dawns on Dowlais' - 'The promised land' - Buttons and silk stockings - 'Working against the ring'

7.   **1939: 'A Big Gesture'**   145

- 'A large and growing family' - 'The plain truth' - The shadow factories

8.   **1939 - 1945: South Wales And Whitehall At War**   155

'Regional devolution has become vital'- Requisitioned - Reconstruction and the Advisory Council - a Princess and a Secretary of State for Wales - The Distribution of Industry Act - The New Believers

9.   **1945 - 1951: Something Will Be Done**   173

- Cripps and Warter - Treforest revisited - 'Not suitable for Industrial Development' - The Standard Advance Factory - Prams, Toys and Light Bulbs – 'A Model Factory, a Symbol of Prosperity' – 'Our Pentrebach Child' - 'Simply a matter of internal arrangements'

Postscript   190

List of Ilustrations

Dowlais during the depression
'Under the Shadow'
The Last Time He Saw Merthyr
Sir Wyndham Portal, the investigator for South Wales
Sir Malcolm Stewart – commissioner for the Special Areas
Rather early for Christmas isn't it?
'The Royal Visit; IS IT THE DAWN'
Memorandum by the King's private secretary, Major Hardinge
'A detour to Dowlais, the King's programme
The King with Captain Geoffrey Crawshay, Mr Ernest Brown and Mr Bean inspecting land tractors and lorries at Boverton
The King greeted by large crowds at Dinas, Rhondda
The King greeted by large crowds in Merthyr
The King mixes cement at Pentrebach Training Centre
The King's visit to the Merthyr Employment Exchange
The King stands amid the dereliction of the Dowlais works
The Welsh Products factory, Goatmill Road, Dowlais
Kayser Bondor
The cartoon deriding the new jobs
The ICI factory
The Hoover application to build in Pentrebach
The Hoover factory opening 12 October 1948

Preface

This book began as a local lecture at the Dowlais Library, Merthyr Tydfil. Dowlais, the home of two of Wales's greatest historians, Gwyn Alf and Glanmor Williams, had been at the very source of Britain's first industrial revolution. The great Guest iron works, established in the last quarter of the eighteenth century, had been the foundation of Merthyr's reputation as the 'iron metropolis' but Dowlais, between the two world wars, had also been at the eye of the industrial tornado that swept through South Wales. As one of a generation of post war children, I had been brought up to share my parents' vivid memories of the destitute thirties and their association with mass unemployment. My generation inherited the image and view of a National government that had been uncaring and unwilling to respond to the economic plight of our communities.

I had, however, never read an authoritative account that could quite satisfy my curiosity as to why government could have been so neglectful: why did ministries and ministers do so little to help? I chose as my lecture title, 'South Wales versus Whitehall', assuming the obvious- that this was a story of conflict between a local society and the government of the day. To illustrate my simple proposition, I decided to analyse the cabinet meetings of 1936, a year of high political drama both nationally and locally. This was the year of the great Jarrow hunger marches, which, in November, culminated in a huge mass demonstration in London, the largest of the decade. It was also the year of a fleeting royal visit to South Wales, which became a part of the folk lore of the valleys and even of royal legend. In November 1936 King Edward VIII visited South Wales and reputedly proclaimed, 'something must be done'. That visit, however, had been quickly followed by the abdication crisis, and the plight of South Wales was subsumed in the drama of the King's departure.

So how much did the plight of Merthyr Tydfil and South Wales register on the political Richter scale before the King's visit? How many times did the situation in the Valleys reach the cabinet table? For the first nine months of the year it appears hardly at all and confirms the government's inaction and neglect. Yet at the cabinet of 2 September 1936, following item 5 'Situation in Palestine', the agenda included 'the situation in Merthyr Tydfil'.

Not only South Wales, but one town had reached the cabinet. I knew from my own ministerial experience that no item reached cabinet without a trail of departmental memoranda, minutes etc preceding it. And so it proved to be. 'HLG 30/47', a fading yellow file in the Ministry of Housing and Local Government, contained the material gathered by the department from others, draft memoranda and civil servants' observations. Consideration of the situation in Merthyr Tydfil reached other departments, including the mighty Treasury. Service chiefs were prodded to respond and Merthyr's situation even reached one of the most prestigious of Whitehall's committees, the Committee for Imperial Defence. A search of the royal archives revealed the King's astonishing proactive interest in the detailed arrangements of his visit in November 1936. Clearly, the standard account of South Wales's relationship with Whitehall at this crucial time required at least further elaboration if not revision.

The year 1936 would have proved fascinating enough on its own but, irresistibly, I was tempted to extend the scope of the study. As this book reveals, the conjunction of circumstances and pressures, of which the royal visit was an important part, compelled Chamberlain to change government policy. That policy change, embodied in the 1937 Special Areas Amendment Act, has understandably attracted little more than a footnote in either Welsh or British history. It lasted little more than a year or two before being engulfed by the coming of the Second World War. However, examination of the implementation of the revised policy, the case studies which essentially form chapter 6 of this book, demonstrates a rather greater significance. Whitehall became embroiled, in a hitherto unimaginable way, in the detailed mechanics of regional industrial relocation, a process which foreshadowed the comprehensive post-war regional development policy. Fatefully, this conclusion enticed me even further, and I decided to carry forward the analysis and case studies through the war and into the first five years of a full-blooded regional policy, thus delaying completion of this study by two years.

This book seeks to offer a rather special insight into the operation of government and into the relationship between a society in distress and its governors, mandarins and ministers. As will become patently obvious, this is not a definitive study of the 1930s. I have deliberately left out the 'people's history', so wonderfully developed by others in recent times. I also only briefly draw upon the parliamentary battles, as these are more easily accessible to the student through Hansard. Instead, I have concentrated on bringing to the reader the far less accessible material, the perceptions and opinions of the 'insiders', which have survived in tatty departmental files of government. I hope this approach will lead to a better understanding of thirty of the most significant years in modern Welsh history.

Acknowledgements

So many people have kindly assisted me. Miss Elizabeth Grint, Karen Hier and Owain Rowlands gave invaluable support in the early research for the study, while Mrs Judith Jones, Miss Linda Brown, and Mr Ian Bevan have somehow managed to create order out of chaos in the innumerable revisions of the script.

I am especially grateful to Mr Colin Parker, Tydfil Training Consortium Limited and Mr Brian Roberts, Rainbow Print, who have enable me to publish and print this book locally.

Geraint Jones and Carolyn Jacobs at the Merthyr and Dowlais libraries have been constantly enthusiastic about transforming a lecture into a book. They have also kindly organised the impressive collection of photographs included in this text. Andrew Parker and the staff of the House of Commons library have shown infinite patience in dealing with my endless queries.

I am very grateful for the gracious permission of Her Majesty the Queen to use material from the Royal Archives and for the very considerable assistance of Lady De Bellaigue and the assistant keeper of the royal archive, Mr Oliver Everett.

I owe a special debt of gratitude to my 'tutor' over these last few years, Professor Dai Smith. His guidance and understanding have been inspirational. Without Dai's encouragement, I would not have embarked upon the venture. Finally, I know that there must have been times when my wife had wished that I had not. Without her perseverance and unfailing encouragement, I would never have completed it.

Introduction

The book that follows tells one of the most inspiring stories of twentieth century Welsh history: not heroic, not vainglorious, not gallant and defeated but resolute, painstaking in its detailed application and, ultimately, victorious. The inspiration is from that interwar time- how an industrial society brought to the brink of economic destitution and social collapse re-claimed its direction- and for this present time- how democratic institutions can, by internal and external pressure, be made to take a grip, through executive will via administrative means, on the material circumstances blighting individual lives.

It has been acknowledged for some time that the Second World War was the driving engine force in this process of transformation. As the author forcefully puts it:

'From the administrative upheaval there emerged a structure, singularly lacking before the war in South Wales, a regional administrative industrial machine capable of assessing manpower and factory needs and, consequentially, becoming an advocate for the area and its people. A new Welsh administration was born, and was not to be disbanded at the end of the war. Welsh administrative life was never to be the same. A new regional Welsh industrial administrative machine took its place alongside the longer standing Welsh health and education boards… War had been a watershed in terms of accepted and acceptable role of government. Whereas in 1918 there had been a consensus, even an eagerness to demobilise war time powers, in 1945 the powers were deemed essential to combat the evil of unemployment to prevent, as one junior official observed in 1943 'a depression falling on Merthyr again, a by word for all evils from which all South Wales had suffered!' A new generation of public servants had been baptised in state power. They were the new believers.

And one of those believers (a Rhondda boy born in 1940) would be the young man who became the Labour MP for Merthyr Tydfil in 1972 and has now turned his mind and pen towards answering the question why his town and constituency had not simply been shut down and moved elsewhere, en bloc, as the experts (always the experts) had advised in the 1930s. Ted Rowlands could survey the benefits of post-war industrial policy and its attendant welfare safety nets for the people he has ably represented for almost three decades but, as he confesses, he could not see why the powers available within government, and especially inside the Whitehall labyrinth, had not been utilised earlier to combat the endemic underemployment and poverty which had become the never-again

10

memory of South Wales after 1945. The national Government of the mid-1930s was undoubtedly brutal and callous in ideology but was it also blinkered and stupid in policy towards the 'depressed areas'?

So began a personal quest combined with avid intellectual curiosity through cabinet records, ministerial files, governmental correspondence and memoranda and even the Royal Archives to see if Whitehall really was the adversary of South Wales. The research has been meticulous and is now pulled together in a cool, taut prose which, nonetheless, like the cold steel emerging from the former blast furnaces of Dowlais, carries the heat of its origins everywhere with it. For this is the passionate book of a passionate man, still made angry by human waste yet mindfully tempered by inside knowledge of government of the potential that can, indeed, be released. He marshals the familiar evidence of how desperate the plight of South Wales really was and how helpless to act was a government convinced that labour 'surplus to requirements' had to submit to 'transference' before mounting his most startling revisionist coup: that the Special Areas Act of 1937 represented a fundamental change of policy, forcing a reluctant administration into dealing, in manner and detail, with the issues of industrial reconstruction in a way that foretold the experience of war, 'when suddenly the resources of South Wales, the people and their supposed limited skills, became vital for survival'.

In this revelatory work Ted Rowlands is not concerned with the 'people's history' of these years nor, yet, with the parliamentary arena, the occasional theatre for their protests and their forgotten existence. Nor is it his task to rescue reputations since most that was done for the good after 1936 happened, at the centre of things, by muddle and reaction or from political fear and calculation. But once it was begun, and effected by better sense and knowledge, the process had a logic, even and undeniable worth, that would, in the circumstances of war, prove unstoppable. In other words, its application in practice swept away the fatigue of world weary ignorance of local detail that had once masqueraded as knowledge of 'higher' things.

South Wales as a whole has been particularly fortunate that Ted Rowlands has represented its general interest so intensely and intelligently since he first entered the House of Commons for Cardiff North (1966-1970) and then succeeded the considerable figure of S.O. Davies at Merthyr on his death in 1972. Arguably, it is only with the publication of this pathbreaking book that we can see what Welsh intellectual life lost to Welsh political life's gain: though, on reflection, it would take a politician of Ted's stature and experience to ingest his research in the way he has, so compellingly, done here and it would take

11

an intellect whose mind has been shaped by the moral contusions of public life to speak so eloquently and so clearly in this century of the profound lesson for action we can still learn from the last.

Dai Smith

1

1921 – 1934: SOUTH WALES AND WHITEHALL

'A Place of Suffering'

The South Wales of the 1920s and 30s was a society in crisis. Mass unemployment followed the collapse of the coal trade and the decline of the iron industry in some areas. It was an experience made all the more shattering by the suddenness with which it struck. The South Wales of Edwardian times had dominated Britain's coal industry. The growth and youthfulness of the area's population was only exceeded worldwide by the United States. Between 1911 and 1921 population growth in South Wales of 13% contrasted sharply with that of Greater London which grew by just 4%.

It was coal, steel and tin-plate output that had underpinned the pre war growth and confidence. During this period, more than a quarter of a million miners produced more than 50 million tons of coal and even the immediate post-war period seemed to reaffirm, albeit briefly, the economic and industrial status of South Wales. The destruction of the Belgian and French coal-mining areas, the French occupation of the Ruhr Valley and a fortuitous strike in the United States allowed record export levels of 35 million tons from South Wales.[1]

There was one town in particular at the centre of both the coal and iron industries and which epitomized the confidence of the area and the period. Indeed, it must have seemed as if Merthyr Tydfil looked forward to a particularly bright future. In 1905, the efforts of Merthyr's leading citizens to turn its Klondike-style settlements into a civic society had triumphed with the incorporation of the area as Wales's fourth county borough. Armed with new civic powers, the borough embarked upon an expansive development programme of libraries, parks and schools and undertook to build and finance the great new water project of Taf Fechan. Appropriately the newly created county borough acquired Cyfarthfa Castle from the Crawshay family and that ultimate symbol of ironmaster status and power became the county borough's free secondary school.[2]

Such civic confidence had been supported by the remaining powerful coal and iron interests in the borough. The great coal combines- Ocean collieries at Treharris, Nixons at Merthyr Vale, Hill Plymouth, Crawshay's and GKN' produced some 3 million tons during the early years of the century and employed 16,000 men at thirty-four mines. The future of the

13

Crawshay iron works was already in doubt, but the mighty Guest works at Dowlais employed more than 3,000 men and continued its traditional railmaking business for the expanding world-wide railway systems. Yet within less than two decades, all the hopes and expectations of the county borough councillors lay in ruin: the Dowlais works closed, there were only two pits left and they employed less than 4,000 men. Unemployment had soared to 65%of the insured working population. The population had fallen by 20,000, consisting almost entirely of the borough's ablest and fittest men.[3]

Unemployment destroyed the purchasing power of the county borough, undermined its civic finances and created tensions within local society and between county borough and Whitehall. Half the local rate, the highest in the land, had to be devoted to public assistance for the unemployed, and this had to be paid for by fewer and fewer employed citizens. As late as 1939, the recently formed Political and Economic Planning (PEP) organisation described Merthyr Tydfil as 'the least habitable' district in England and Wales:

> 'the sole justification for a large town on this site has been the abundance of profitable coal and iron deposits and no detached person would be likely to favour going to live at such a spot after the minerals have ceased to make it worthwhile. Nor does it seem reasonable to ask the tax-payers of the rest of Britain indefinitely to pay hundreds of thousands of pounds a year in order to give large numbers of people the dubious pleasure and benefit of continuing to live at subsistence level.'

PEP's final solution for Merthyr lay in the total closure of the town and the transference of the population to a new town on the River Usk or the Glamorgan coast. Over a ten-year period, the £10 million required to relocate the whole of Merthyr Tydfil would be offset by savings in benefit and grants worth £800,000 per year paid by central government to the beleaguered Merthyr population. PEP recommended that such a solution could also be applied to 'other known and often smaller areas such as Rhymney.'[4]

Within the county borough, the township of Dowlais suffered a particularly devastating blow. As already noted, the Guest works had been at the forefront of the Welsh industrial revolution. Its Goatmill Road plant had rolled out generations of rail for the worldwide network. Yet despite the electrification of the coke ovens, the ageing plant could not supply either the quality or lengths of rail now demanded by the rail companies. In 1928, for the first time, the works failed to supply a single

United Kingdom order, and its failure to meet a life-saving order from the Egyptian government virtually sealed its fate. In October 1930, after 171 years the twenty-four Bessemer converters were decommissioned and the 30-foot Goatmill Road plant was shut down. In 1936 the 21' big mill followed until only the foundries converter and the Ifor engineering shops remained open. A total of 3000 men were immediately redundant as a result of the closures. The derelict site, a powerful image of destitution, was to catch the nation's attention in November 1936.[5] Earlier in the year and despite the appalling plight of the community, Dowlais could still sustain and send a mixed choir to the Fishguard National Eisteddford. The choir carried all before it, drawing from the distinguished musicologist, Sir Richard Terry a poignant observation

> 'I could tell as I listened that the people who were singing had come from a place of suffering. It was moving beyond belief.'

Dowlais and Merthyr shared their industrial agony with neighbouring districts in north Glamorgan and Monmouthshire. Ebbw Vale, Nantyglo, Rhymney, and Brynmawr in Breconshire reeled from the double blow of coal's collapse and the traumatic closure of the Ebbw Vale iron works in 1928. The whole of the South Wales coalfield suffered as the favourable market conditions that had led coal to be 'king' disappeared. The special role South Wales had played in Britain's coal exports now became a nightmare. Competition from Polish, Dutch and German coalfields, whose output per man per shift were 14-15 tons higher than those of the South Wales miner, together with the crippling decision in 1925 to restore the gold standard, contributed to a dramatic collapse in the export markets for South Wales coal. To add insult to injury German war reparations were paid in coal. As a result, by the end of the 1920s exports had fallen by 23% and in the following decade by a further 25% from that high of 34.9 million tons to 17.9 million tons. The situation in the domestic market was hardly any better as the Admiralty's decision to switch from coal to oil meant a fall in a market of 1.7 million tons in 1913 to just 380,000 in 1925. Economies in coal use for pig iron production and gas also depressed the market for South Wales's major product.

The consequences were equally depressing in terms of employment and jobs. In the period between 1922 and 1944, the number of men employed in the coal industry fell from a quarter of a million to 112,000. The area's dependency on coal meant that mining was responsible for more than half the South Wales workforce and in communities such as Rhondda it constituted more than 80%. In 1929, of the 83,000 out of work in South Wales, 38,000 were miners. Throughout the coalfield unemployment soared to more than 30% while the counties of Glamorgan and

15

Monmouthshire suffered a staggering decline in population - more than 390,000 during the inter war period.[6]

The collapse of coal exposed the particularly narrow base of the area's economy. It compared unfavourably, not only with the diverse and fast growing greater London or with Midlands car production towns (in Coventry and Oxford inter-war unemployment rates hovered around 4 to 8%) but also with the traditional northern industrial societies. Surveys contrasted the employment structures of Blackburn and Merthyr, Oldham and Rhondda, where communities of similar populations and, indeed, with similar unemployment rates, revealed a striking difference. The numbers in work, particularly women, enabled the northern towns to sustain a greater purchasing power. In Wales, women were to all intent and purposes excluded from the economy.[7]

The brief illusory post-war boom had in fact burst in 1924: but for a few years many clung to the belief that the collapse of the market represented just another cyclical downturn which would sooner or later correct itself. The realization that something more fundamental was occurring, carrying permanent structural consequences for South Wales, now began to shape the politics of unemployment and the relationship between the Welsh and Whitehall.

South Wales' People

The question was, who would represent the needs and concerns of South Wales to ministers and ministries? If one could talk of a South Wales establishment, it predictably reflected the essentially narrow coal and iron interests. The industrial development of South Wales had, for much of the nineteenth century, grown out of a host of family concerns, fragmented and frequently incapable of combining for any length of time to promote or protect a collective interest. The nascent coal-miners' associations of the second half of the nineteenth century primarily bound their members to a defence against the demands of labour rather than to the general promotion of the industry's interests to the world of Whitehall.[8] The inter-war years, however, witnessed a rash of amalgamations in both coal, steel and tin-plate. Concentration of ownership went further than in any other mining area. GKN and Baldwin Ltd brought all their coal interests together in 1930 as the Welsh Associated Colliery Company. The other major consolidation occurred under the Powell Duffryn combine which, finally, in 1935 amalgamated with the Welsh Associated Colliery Company to become the largest mining company in Britain. A similar process followed in steel and tin-plate, focusing upon Richard Thomas and Co. and British (Guest Keen and Baldwin) Iron and Steel Company.[9]

16

Not surprisingly, when the Bishop of Llandaf brought together a collection of the powerful and influential persons to represent the concerns of South Wales to ministers in 1935 the composition of the committee mirrored such dominant interests. Captain Leighton Davies, managing director of Baldwins, and Edmund Hahn, chairman of Powell Duffryn, led the committee along with other coal and iron interests (D.M. Evan Bevan, colliery proprietor at Neath, L. D. Whitehead of the Iron and Steel Company in Newport, Charles Gilbertson of the Pontardawe Tin Plate Works, Morgan Rees, (the Wire Rope Works at Cardiff) and Sir David Llewellyn. They were joined by the emerging civic great and the good of early twentieth-century South Wales: Rhys Williams, vice-lieutenant of Glamorgan, the ubiquitous Percy Watkins from the South Wales and Monmouthshire Council for Social Services, the coalfield solicitor, Gerald Bruce and Lady Williams, President of St John's Ambulance. Though not a member, one other prominent Welshman stalked Whitehall's corridors, Thomas Jones, Lloyd George's lieutenant in Whitehall, and after 1935, a member of the newly created Unemployment Assistance Board.[10]

As the account of the ill-fated encounter between the Bishop's committee and the Minister for Labour will reveal, the South Wales establishment exercised a remarkably feeble influence over government policy and action. Powerful as they were industrially and commercially in South Wales, they carried little weight in Whitehall. They were no 'movers or shakers' in altering government's response to the plight of the area, nor do they appear to have exercised any overt influence upon the Conservative party, the dominant force within the National government.

An alternative establishment had also emerged during the first twenty years of the century, founded upon the South Wales Miners Federation (the Fed) and the Labour party. The Fed, formed in 1898 out of the seven union district councils, thrived upon the bitter pre-war industrial disputes and especially from the Cambrian coal strike. Membership of the Fed had soared to more than 200,000 by 1921, only to suffer a corresponding collapse with the decline in coal production after 1924. After the protracted 1926 strike, membership plummeted to 100,000 before gradually climbing again to 147,000; for most of the inter-war period the Fed actually represented about a half of miners at work.

Much of its energies in that period were devoted to repelling the incursion of the rival company sponsored union. Yet the Fed succeeded in becoming a new force in Welsh and British trade unionism and Welsh politics. The Fed and later the N.U.M did much to shape political and industrial life for three generations and for nearly three-quarters of a century. Affiliation to the Labour party in 1908 had ensured a seminal role in Welsh political and parliamentary life; all but one of the MPs for the South Wales valleys were miners, most belonging to that remarkable breed of union officials, the miners' agents. Not surprisingly, the deputations to ministers, at least during the late 1920s, reflected the fusion of Fed and Labour Party that formed the nature of working-class political representation.[11]

The Labour movement's Who's Who, the equivalent of the Bishop of Llandaf's committee, formed the core of the deputations that descended upon Whitehall in the late 1920s. They comprised union president, Enoch Morrell and vice-president S. O. Davies (Labour MP for Merthyr), general secretary Thomas Richards and treasurer Oliver Harris, supported by the leading miners' agent, Arthur Jenkins (later MP for Pontypool), William Davies, EC J Thomas, G Gwent and William Mainwaring (later MP for Rhondda East). The Welsh MPs included Lt-Col. D. Watts Morgan, Will John, George Hall, Timothy Jones, D. R. Grenfell, Evan Davies and George Barker, all Fed members, and, after 1929, Aneurin Bevan. Together they constituted a formidable alternative establishment in South Wales.[12]

Underpinned by such an industrial force in a society so heavily dominated by one industry, the Labour party achieved an ascendancy in South Wales politics few would have predicted on the eve of the First World War. Our familiarity with such an ascendancy, perhaps, blunts the sense of awesome change wrought in Welsh party politics in so short a time. At the 1906 election, the Liberals held twenty-nine seats and it was they who represented the political establishment of early twentieth-century Wales. Within thirty years this number had shrunk to five, primarily Lloyd George and his extended family. At the 1922 election the Labour party's candidates attracted 40% of the vote, and in 1929 a half million votes returned twenty-five labour members out of thirty-six. This powerful core support for the Labour party even survived the implosion of the Labour government in 1931: whereas nationally the party's vote fell significantly to 30% in 1931, 43% of the vote in Wales returned sixteen Labour members out of its parliamentary total of forty-six. Twelve of the sixteen were from the Fed.

A position of almost total control over local government in the Valleys reinforced Labour's ascendancy. Glamorgan, Monmouthshire, the Merthyr county borough and a host of Valley urban district councils provided what was potentially an alternative power-base, offering a generation of working-class people an opportunity to govern and administer. This was the beginning of a whole new experience in learning the arts of debate, representation and negotiation. Their schools were the lodge and council chamber.[13] However, under intense pressure from the community, first the elected boards of guardians and, after 1929, county and county boroughs found themselves in frequent conflict with Whitehall over the administration of poor relief and the maintenance of services, especially education. The councils also, by refusing to apply a strict means testing regime, became the guardians and protectors of the people against the harshness of the regulations governing unemployment relief. Neither was tension confined to the relationship between local and central government. The inexorable rise in unemployment led to fewer and fewer ratepayers capable of sustaining local services. The poor product from a penny rate compelled councils into increases in the rate burden hitherto unimaginable, provoking rate payer rebellion and local 'vigilante' groups. As an employer, the council became the focus of intense lobbying for what seemed to be the only secure jobs in society - a job with the council. Charges of nepotism and favouritism, inevitably, arose within communities desperately seeking to maintain at least a minimum quality of life.[14]

Yet Labour's 'ascendancy' did not guarantee political or party cohesion. Within the Labour movement, the lodge, boards of guardians, councils and in the Welsh Parliamentary Labour Party, competing pressures between what may be crudely labelled the 'moderates' and the 'rejectionists' made united representations to government difficult. This crude division between those who believed capitalism was incapable of reform and those prepared to seek the pragmatic compromise ran through much of the institutional and political life of South Wales, from local government to the House of Commons. Within the Welsh parliamentary group of the 1930s a large gulf existed, for example between Aneurin Bevan who pointedly refused to attend upon the King during his visit in November 1936, and George Hall from Aberdare who was especially commended to meet and advise him. Rarely does one find, within the formal representation of Welsh Labour MPs to Whitehall, unanimity of effort. Nor was there much of a collective effort between the political parties to represent the concerns of South Wales to Whitehall. Individual Conservatives, like Reginald Clarry, member for Newport, did accompany other members in the rare attempt of 1936 by the Welsh Parliamentary Party to influence government policy. Pressure for change from within the government party actually came primarily from the larger English north-west group.

After the 1931 election, the Liberal party had become a spent political force in Welsh politics and the influence that it did exercise was wholly attributable to Lloyd George's powerful advocacy of Keynesian solutions. 'We can conquer Unemployment' (1929) and his British 'New Deal' programme in 1935 at least compelled Whitehall to devote considerable intellectual energy in rebutting the case. A comparable effort by the Labour party only really emerged from the appointment of a party commission to investigate the plight of the distressed areas. Led by Hugh Dalton, the commission's report in 1936 signalled a significant shift within party thinking which had hitherto struggled to relate or connect its socialist instincts to Keynesian solutions.

The brief twenty-year period between the two world wars redefined the nature of Welsh political and industrial life. Lodge, Fed and Labour party constituted new political structures within the community operating and promoting a very different social and political agenda. For generations, capital and labour, mine-owner and miner had belonged to a naturally powerful local society, founded upon its own mineral resources, which made a significant contribution to the greater British and imperial economy. The relationships that mattered most were between the two and they did not require government to intervene to support or prop up that society. Owners and workers made competing demands upon governments, primarily for the purpose of regulating the relationship between capital and labour. Certainly the coal-owners and iron-masters expected the state to uphold the elementary rules of law and order, as it did during the Tonypandy riots, but otherwise the power of government was marginal to the living standards of the majority of people. Yet, within the short period covered by this study, a significant shift from the primacy of coal, iron and heavy engineering to a new consumer economy, serviced by manufacturing production and no longer restricted by the geography of resources, led to a different demand upon government. At least from one side of society, the unemployed worker, came the demand that government assist in the re-creation of the local economy. It was a demand which the Whitehall of the day neither felt equipped to tackle nor considered a desirable one for government.

Whitehall's People

By today's standards the Whitehall of 1931 was small: twenty-five ministers stood accountable for a non-industrial central government of some 137,000 people. Few at the end of the First World War had argued for the maintenance of 'big' government, retaining war time powers to forge a post war society 'fit for heroes'. Indeed, much of the war time administrative apparatus had been demobbed as speedily as the servicemen. But government had been growing and those 137,000 still represented a near doubling of a pre war Whitehall of 70,000. In retrospect, the Lloyd George reforms, which led to the introduction of national insurance and pensions, proved to be the watershed in the role of the state. The creation of a national insurance commission, and the Treasury requirement to find £27 million to finance the new scheme, had begun an inexorable process. The total public service had risen during the first decade of the century from 116,000 to 282,000. The barometer of state activity - public expenditure as a proportion of gross domestic product- had registered 12% at the beginning of the century. Despite the efforts of inter-war governments to repress it, public expenditure/GDP remained stubbornly at double that level. Briefly, between 1928 and 1930, government expenditure fell by about 2.5% in money terms (from £1094 million to £1066 million), though ironically, as a result of the fall in prices, government expenditure as a proportion of GDP actually rose from 24.2 to 25.9%.[15]

Twenty-one departments made up post 1918 Whitehall. One wartime creation, the Ministry of Labour, survived the peace. Another, the Ministry of Health, was established in 1919. Lloyd George's appointment in December 1916 of the first cabinet secretary, Maurice Hankey, proved to be of immense significance to the machinery of British government. The cabinet office survived to serve successive prime ministers.

One other 'national institution' also emerged as a dominant influence in British administrative life. Our perception of the Treasury's role, the concept of Treasury 'control,' and the omnipotence of the 'Treasury view' all derive from post-First World War reform and reorganization. New war-time ministries had been created by acts of parliament that vested control over spending and staffing with the individual ministers rather than with the Chancellor of the Exchequer. To restore control, a Treasury minute empowered its own permanent secretary as head of the civil service and adviser to the Prime Minister, to recommend all senior civil service appointments. An Order in Council also gave the Treasury power to regulate the whole establishment, classification, remuneration and conditions of service, so paving the way for a uniformly trained and staffed British civil service. Ultimate Treasury control was reinforced by a minute requiring all departmental spending submissions to be put to the Treasury before going to the cabinet. Internal reorganization established three branches, home, supply (public expenditure) and establishment (organization, manpower and pay of the entire civil service).[16]

This new concentration of Treasury power was also gathered into the hands of one remarkable product of British public administration. Sir Warren Fisher, permanent secretary between 1919 and 1939, had originally been a devoted supporter of Lloyd George, but he became one of the most hostile opponents of Lloyd George's 'New Deal' plans. Repeatedly we shall find his succinct, dismissive, fountain-penned, personal minutes deriding any suggestions that government could or should intervene directly to create or promote employment. As chairman of the Industrial Transference Board, he remained committed to the policy of moving surplus labour from the 'dead' or depressed areas, backing up and stiffening the Chancellor of the Exchequer, Neville Chamberlain's, own innate instinct against all Keynesian-style solutions. Closely associated with Chamberlain, Sir Warren Fisher's influence during the 1930s extended beyond immediate Treasury concerns, and his personal philosophy of administration and service imbued the whole of the inter war civil service. It was he, more than anyone, who fostered the culture of the gifted generalist. It was not 'the business of permanent heads of departments to be experts'. 'They are general managers. A man who has been running one of these huge businesses can run any of them!' He fostered the idea of 'musical chairs' among the top positions, overseeing a uniformly trained and highly centralized bureaucracy.[17] As Thomas Balogh has argued,

> 'From the post war reforms a new corporation arose, vastly more important in the life of the nation than any other. As the bureaucracy grew stronger they grew bolder. Yet by that time the problems and needs of the nation had completely altered leaving it with an outdated and rather unsuitable bureaucratic organisation. It became a vast, completely centralised service facing its ever growing responsibilities with increasing insistence on a lack of expert knowledge..'[18]

Certainly between the wars 'the problems and needs' of South Wales 'altered' only to be met at all levels with a remarkable uniform response. The views of Chamberlain and Fisher were shared by all who served the Treasury and, indeed, by most of the Whitehall departments and decision makers. Fisher's deputy and successor, Sir Richard Hopkins, controller of the supply division, later second secretary, exercised the greatest operational influence over depressed area policy within the Treasury. Hopkins personified the best ideals of the superior civil servant: the classics scholar from Cambridge who had entered the Inland Revenue and become chairman of the Revenue Board before transferring to the Treasury. He commanded a powerful intellect and was much respected; but he was no innovator. His great capacity was that of the model senior civil servant of the day: 'to take in, and then express in simple and compelling terms the complex ideas of others.' It was Hopkins who challenged Keynes and his theories before the Macmillan committee on finance and industry in 1930, achieving (according to the chairman, Lord Macmillan) 'a drawn battle'. Hopkins served Chamberlain industriously and skilfully, but unlike Fisher he never became overtly personally associated with him and thus suffered nothing when Chamberlain fell from power in 1940. Two years later Hopkins succeeded Sir Warren Fisher as the permanent secretary to the Treasury.[19]

The same could not be said of the third knighted mandarin who formed the triumvirate of senior policy advisers on distressed areas. Sir Horace Wilson, a personal confidant and adviser to Chamberlain, held the post of chief industrial adviser. The prosaic title of his position belied the persuasive influence he exercised. One contemporary described him as enjoying the power of a 'Cardinal Wolsey'. The Duke of Windsor considered that he 'carried great weight in the daily evaluation of high government policy'. That was clearly true in respect of distressed areas policy for, as chairman of the official interdepartmental committee, he channelled advice to cabinet committees and cabinet ministers. Unusually for such a senior civil servant of the time, Sir Horace was not a product of public school and Oxbridge. His father had dealt in furniture and his mother was a Bournemouth boarding house landlady. He attended a local board school, and entered into the second, executive division of the civil service before rising to such an astonishing position of influence. This rather different personal background and experience, however, did not result in a different attitude or contribution to Whitehall policy. Sir Horace Wilson shared, articulated and prosecuted the common assumptions within the administration of the 1930s that 'nothing new or heroic' could be done to create employment by government action.[20]

As chief industrial adviser, Wilson co-ordinated the input of the core departments dealing with these issues - Treasury, Trade, Health and Labour. Others - Education and, with the beginning of rearmament, the Services departments- also contributed.

If there was a lead department it was the relatively newly created Ministry of Labour. The establishment of this ministry had been the Labour party's price for support for Lloyd George's war-time coalition government. The department's original primary function had been envisaged as that of an industrial reconciliation service, a function which withered rapidly amid the increasingly bitter industrial conflicts of the inter-war years. It was a department that became increasingly absorbed with the changing structure of the unemployment benefit regime, and its preoccupations eventually culminated in the establishment of the Unemployment Assistance Board. With its network of employment exchanges, the ministry emerged in the 1920's as the second largest department. Burgeoning unemployment relief costs raised the departments budget to £78 million, a fifth of net public expenditure, until the newly created Unemployment Assistance Board assumed responsibility for relief in 1935.

Sadly, for much of the inter-war period, the ministry and its senior officials defined their role narrowly. The employment exchange, Whitehall's only local intelligence service on employment, contributed little to policy formation. It was a department with no regional structure which could have co-ordinated regional experience or need, or which could have acted as the voice of the distressed areas. Indeed, the government in general did not have a regional dimension during the inter-war years. Senior officials rarely travelled; occasionally if a particularly tricky problem arose an official was sent to enquire and report. The department of health covering local government did control a network of inspectorates reporting on health and local government financial issues. Most unfortunately, in the case of South Wales, the reports of particular local officials were, as we shall see, uniformly critical and unsympathetic to the plight of the locally unemployed. It has to be said that such officials only reflected an amazing conformity of view held by civil servants from the lowest to the highest levels. One searches in vain for meaningful dissenting advice from within or between departments.

Nor were there any meaningful differences between officialdom and their political masters. Baldwin and Chamberlain became the controlling influences of the National government of 1931 and both showed an intense and instinctive dislike of intervention. They were dismissive of Keynesian programmes or 'New Deals' of the kind promoted by the American president F. D. Roosevelt. Baldwin 'dreaded Roosevelt's experiments' and forecast 'an appalling mess in the United States as a consequence'. Chamberlain was more brutal 'The Yanks' were 'barbarous ' and Roosevelt 'a medicine man'. If Ramsay MacDonald, as head of the National government, occasionally dared to suggest an alternative approach, he was quickly sidelined and isolated, lacking any support from a ministerial team increasingly influenced and chosen by Baldwin and Chamberlain.[21]

Whitehall's Policies

The collapse of the coal trade came as much as a surprise to ministers and Whitehall as it had been to miners and mining communities. Indeed, an illusory economic boom from 1918 until the summer of 1920 during which prices and wages rose and unemployment was negligible, prodded the government into action to keep 'the boom' in check by means of high bank rates and credit restriction. The sudden slump and significant rise in unemployment in the summer of 1920 compelled the cabinet to establish a committee for unemployment and to introduce relief works such as road-building. The Unemployment Grants Committee was empowered to give grants to local authorities for public works in areas Whitehall defined as 'necessitous'. These modest efforts were, however, undermined by the contradictory pressures by the Treasury for an economy drive, making it impossible for any local authorities to take advantage of job creation schemes.

The alternative remedy of trade protection, espoused in 1923 by the Conservative government, fell with that government at the 1924 election. The Labour government that followed briefly addressed the problem by further public works and setting up juvenile employment centres. However, the centre of economic policy attention was shifting towards the Treasury's fundamental goal of returning to the gold standard achieved in 1925 - a decision which compounded the problems of the coal trade as exports became even more uncompetitive. Matters were further exacerbated by the prolonged strike of 1926. A cabinet committee on the coal trade acknowledged in 1927 that the industry suffered from 'structural' unemployment, and that a revival in trade would not be sufficient to restore meaningful levels of employment. A 'surplus' of labour existed in the mining communities and this would have to be transferred elsewhere

Transference, namely the removal of the unemployed to more prosperous areas, became the centrepiece of government policy for a decade. The shift in policy that ultimately took place in 1936 was, in part, the result of the dawning realization, even within government, that transference could not be the only solution. In the late 1920s, however, the notion commanded a certain consensus and even Labour acknowledged the necessity when confronted by the size of the 'surplus' working population in mining communities.[22]

The Industrial Transference Board had been the recommendation of the Ministry of Health and its minister, Neville Chamberlain, and it was chaired by Sir Warren Fisher. Initial assessment of the total 'national surplus' of labour, eventually defined as being some 200,000 men was made by the ministry's district inspectorate. The ministry's man in South Wales was a James Evans, whose stream of reports and observations shaped and coloured Whitehall's view of the area.

Evans' report in February 1928, on the six poor relief unions covering the most depressed areas, represented the first of a cock-shy assessment of surplus labour. The Bedwellty and Crickhowell Union, including Abertillery, Bedwellty, Ebbw Vale, Nantyglo, Blaina, Rhymney and Tredegar constituted 'a bleak and barren spot allowing nothing other than agriculture, mountain sheep farming.' The bulk of a population of 24,515 were dependent upon the principal employers, the Ebbw Vale, Tredegar

Iron and Coal and the Powell Duffryn companies. Evans concluded that 'the continuance of the great bulk of these people cannot be justified by its own industrial potentialities'. It would be a great relief to these two Unions if 3,000 working units apart from any dependants could be transferred from the area within the next year or so!

In the much larger Merthyr and Pontypridd Unions (a population of 500,000), Evans detected a measure of hope in the future. Pontypridd held 'virgin coal,' while GKN, Powell Duffryn, D. Davies, and 'more recent financiers, Sir D. R. Llewellyn and Lord Buckland, offered enterprise and investment to the area. Evans was, of course, writing two years before the calamitous closure of the GKN Dowlais works. Even in 1928 he calculated a surplus of at least 6,000 'working units'.

The third group, Bridgend and Cowbridge and Neath, enjoyed newer seams of coal, had works which had prospered during the war and was more favourably situated in regard to its recuperative powers. Evans, nevertheless, could not 'help thinking that the removal of 2,000 men in the near future would be an advantage.' The inspector's estimate of surplus colliery workers covered the top range of 50,000 to the lowest of 20,000 of whom some 11,000 could be 'migrated to districts or emigrated to the Dominions.'

These area assessments presaged a concentrated, if flawed, effort to make transference policy work. In the brutal opinion of officials such a policy had to be accompanied by an unyielding view of unemployment benefit and poor relief.

> 'The only hope for the South Wales area is a redistribution of population which can be effected only by economic pressure. Unemployment benefit and poor law relief have up to the present time tended to postpone the operation of this pressure and it would be fatal to introduce further measures for the relief of distress'

Implementation of the transference policy fell to the Ministry of Labour which, through its local employment exchanges, canvassed vigorously for vacancies in prosperous regions. Free travel and a list of lodgings were provided and if the transferee achieved secure employment, arrangements were subsequently made for the transference of his family.[23]

Within the United Kingdom some 100,000 individuals and 6,630 households were transferred between August 1928 and December 1930, though throughout the period of the Board's operation very many more from the distressed areas left unaided to find work. As we shall see, the limitations of such a policy gradually emerged. The response of employers to the high level appeals of ministers (Baldwin contacted 166,000 employers in July 1928) was less than full hearted and the appeal raised only 4,000 vacancies. Many jobs proved temporary leading the disillusioned miner to return home, thus often discouraging others from leaving. Hostile reaction from workers in the 'reception' areas also grew. The establishment of the Industrial Transference Board, however, tacitly acknowledged (despite Treasury misgivings) that the high level of unemployment constituted a structural problem rather than a temporary cyclical phenomenon. It also meant that the problems required policy remedies, an uncomfortable challenge to a Whitehall naturally averse to intervention.

The notion of organized transference of labour also focused greater national attention upon the plight of the mining community. Three articles in *The Times* in the spring of 1928 portrayed to comfortable Britain the condition of 'these strange mining townships straggling snake-like up the mountains where people have nothing to live for'. *The Times* correspondent observed that 'despite an apparent cultural poverty' the miner was all too 'ready to debate with anyone the efforts of the Dawes plan on the Welsh coal trade', but apart from his own industry he knew 'little of the world outside the valleys and nothing of its feelings ...' He was 'genuinely astonished if anyone should suggest that the actions of his Federation in 1921 and 1926 were responsible for what prejudice there was against mining communities'.

The Times articles brought home to a wider audience the rippling consequences of the collapse of the coal trade, not only upon jobs and family life, but also upon local government finances and the dilemma of ever rising local rates deterring any alternative commercial activity. 'Only philanthropists would dream of choosing one of the distressed areas for his factory '. Emigration had been an option 'less popular with the young fellows than a year ago because men who had gone to Canada without any sort of preparation had come back with reports that it was impossible to get work there either'. There remained, however, 'a strong stream flowing out to Australia and Canada '

The Times correspondent dismissed the Labour party's more radical proposals; superannuation and pensions for the over-60s, and the raising of the school leaving age. He commended the more modest proposal to expand juvenile training centres and noted that 'employers in the rest of the country had to be told seriously to consider the claims of the unskilled but useful man'. For these older men and their families, the correspondent urged a more sympathetic regime of relief for a family of four dependent upon 16s a week. The day-to-day needs of 'people who are wasting away required national as well as local measures for clothing and boots and sustaining the health of the population'

The Times correspondent claimed that it was not the miners who were mainly to blame for their present distress. The future happiness of the coal industry rested with the owners. Individual mine-owners had been reluctant to amalgamate and face the challenge of internationally competitive mining. But the miner, too, had himself to become integrated in any new developments within the industry through pit committees:

> 'the coal valleys bear the marks, psychological as well as physical of having been arenas for a scramble by everybody high and low for quick money. The miner, still intensely religious, especially on Sunday, has lost his light heart and taken to politics. Now the country needs to make its coal industry, so long a source of profit to itself, a source of credit too.'[24]

South Wales calls on Whitehall

The year 1928 witnessed a major attempt by South Wales to engage Whitehall in a detailed dialogue upon the plight of the area and its people. On Wednesday 20 June 1928, a deputation of eleven Labour members, one Liberal and two Unionists pleaded with the Chancellor of the Exchequer, Winston Churchill (accompanied by the Minister of transport and secretary for mines, Lt-Col Wilfred Ashley and Commander H. Douglas King) to introduce immediate rating relief for the South Wales coal export trade. This meeting itself was following up an earlier private meeting with the Prime Minister. Time, the members pleaded, was not on the side of the area, not only old pits but new collieries were closing. George Barker, MP for Abertillery, vividly recounted the state of the Ebbw Vale Company and its twenty collieries working for a month or two before closing and reopening. The company's shares had fallen to 3s. Preference shareholders had received no dividend for five years and the company was 'in the hands of the bankers'. Members repeatedly refuted an earlier comment by Churchill portraying the coalfield as 'derelict'; many of the modern collieries were idle, flooding of one colliery threatened neighbouring pits.

While commending the very temperate and able memorandum which concentrated on the case for freight relief for export and blast furnace coal, Churchill feared that the proposal was little more than an emergency export subsidy. Such a subsidy would be attacked 'by a good many people who would say "you are actually selling this coal for foreigners at less than it costs you"'. The Chancellor doubted the value of such a remedy. If it pulled the South Wales coalfield round for two or three years it could be well worth doing; but in Churchill's view the effect would have been temporary relief for a small part of the field, in which case it would be very difficult to persuade the country to agree such a remedy; 'a 5% remedy'.[25]

Welsh MPs received little joy from Churchill. Interestingly these and, indeed, most subsequent representations confined their appeal to a host of 'remedies' for the coal industry. Little was made of, and no case pressed for, the creation of alternative non-coal-related jobs. Understandably, given the dominance of coal for so long, the notion that future South Wales employment might be created by manufacturing automotive parts for the fast growing car industry, let alone by those industries manufacturing radios, fridges, irons or light bulbs, was never canvassed. The word 'factory' never passed the lips of the Welsh deputations of the late 1920s and early 1930s.

Most MPs and union representatives had other and more immediate preoccupations. The burgeoning numbers of unemployed men, and the length of time that they remained unemployed meant huge pressures on the finances of the local boards of guardians which administered poor relief. Tension had grown between Whitehall and the local guardians who were under pressure from the community to bend or ignore the demeaning means tests for relief. Increasingly anxious Ministry of Health officials had been issuing warnings and threats to a number of boards and ministers had gone to the length of disbanding the Bedwellty board.[26] In October 1928, a powerful deputation of Fed officials and Labour MPs brought to ministers and senior civil servants the mounting collective concern of a society in distress. The 'extraordinary and increasing' levels of unemployment had, they claimed, made meaningless any notion of the 'seeking work' test for benefit. Thousands had exhausted their entitlement to benefit and had been driven to apply to the local boards of guardians who themselves were finding it impossible to sustain the system. The limit of £1 a week maximum for relief bore down tragically upon families. The Pontypridd board, for example, operated a scale of relief which gave 19/- a week to a man and wife and three children and this was in a district with an average rent of 12/6d a week.

The members of the deputation accompanied their plea for a more generous relief system with a call for a local public works programme, 'works of utility'. This was at a time when Government departments had done the opposite. The Board of Education had cut down the school-building programme; the Minister of Health had refused to sanction the erection of buildings required for the treatment of the mentally deficient in Glamorgan.

Responding for the government, the Minister of Health, Neville Chamberlain acknowledged the 'unprecedented situation' and felt 'deeply disappointed that no improvement, as he had hoped, had occurred within the coal trade.' They had to accept that many miners who had in the past enjoyed 'a conspicuous and comparatively high standard of living' would never again do so. He had been forced to the conclusion that 'the industry could no longer afford them a livelihood ...' Unfortunately, however, 'the process of transference was proving more difficult and slower than had been hoped' The number of men and boys transferred amounted respectively to 2500 and 100 and every week over 400 men were leaving mining areas.

While it had been difficult to get people to leave, once individuals found alternative employment 'a natural channel' was formed by which others would follow. In Birmingham one half of the trainees were miners, 90% of whom had come from South Wales. The Minister of Labour, Sir Arthur Steel Maitland, also welcomed the president of the Fed's agreement with the principle of transference overseas. A recent 'harvesting scheme' had been 'an amazing success'. 'A real endeavour would be made next year to arrange both temporary and permanent emigration ...'

Chamberlain was much more anxious to resist immediate pressures upon the poor relief system. While offering to investigate the individual cases brought by the deputation, he stressed that his own enquiries had not confirmed 'the most extreme view'. It had been impossible to trace any case of anything resembling starvation. 'Admittedly people were at a low ebb and such hardship was a necessary consequence', but he asked the deputation to put themselves in his place. He knew what a temptation it would be if one board of guardians relaxed their standards. It was his duty 'to avoid a landslide.'[27]

Ministers conceded nothing to the deputation. The case 'fairly' and 'moderately' put by the Fed president, Enoch Morrell, prompted Sir Arthur Robinson, the permanent secretary to minute his ministers upon the difficult judgement they faced. Mr Morrell's express statement that 'the situation was becoming dangerous had weighed upon his mind'. So Robinson continued:

'So far as we are concerned, the issue is whether the screw may not
have been turned too tight in some of the bad South Wales areas,
as a result of our attempts at once to secure the administration of
relief on sound lines and to induce local authorities in South Wales
to cut their financial coat according to the available cloth...'

Reports from the ministry's local inspectors and a summer visit to the area
by a ministry official had found nothing calling for special action, though
very much that was distressing:

'But a bad winter could be a serious thing in such conditions of
depression and worklessness ... If anything untoward should
occur in these places, and much more, if there should be
an outbreak of disorder as has, at such times, occurred
in South Wales, not only should we be subjected to serious
blame but there would be risk of panic action minatory
to the whole of recent poor law policy ..'

On the other hand, the risks of offering further relief were obvious: 'the
boards of guardians of South Wales, if given an inch will be apt to take an
ell.' Transference policy would be made more difficult and Treasury
money would have to be in grant form. Sir Arthur's proposal for 'special
action' confined itself to a high-level enquiry led by another senior official
Sir Arthur Lowry 'to get in touch with actual conditions of the people in
their homes.'[28]

Throughout the next decade, the high-level, special enquiry became
Whitehall's stock-in-trade response to political and public pressure. These
surveys and investigations, supplemented the regular reports and advice
received by the Ministry of Health's inspectorate. In the case of South
Wales, Whitehall was primarily dependent upon the reports of Mr James
Evans who, as we have already seen, offered his own highly individual
perspective upon the South Wales scene. Clearly Evans was close to the
local mine-owners and he was able to give Whitehall detailed assessment
of the coalfield. His comments, however, were frequently accompanied b y
an impressionistic view of the miner and mining communities. Having
reviewed, for example, the prospects of the coal industry in the Merthyr
valley once the 1926 strike was over, he could not resist the additional
personal observation:

'It is difficult to believe when moving about Merthyr that a
strike is in existence. Holiday-makers are much in evidence in the
crowded charabancs heading for more agreeable resorts. The men
do not want to return to work. It is stated by those in the best
position to see that the miners are extremely satisfied with
conditions which provide their children with meals and clothing
and their households with relief money sufficient to give a measure
of enjoyment and pleasure. The non payment of rent and
rates rather follows automatically. Whatever happens in
other parts of the country I think it can be assumed that
the South Wales miners will be among the last to return to work'.

Evans was no less damning about the state of local government. A little
later, backing moves to hold a public inquiry into the Merthyr county
borough, he argued that 'the doctrine which all governments are reluctant
to assail that local authorities, popularly elected, if they do wrong, can be
got rid of by the people who elect them, should not be considered
"sacrosanct"'.

'The electors are so largely composed of persons who are
dependent upon public assistance of some form or other it would
be idle to expect they would want to turn on their paymasters.
Some members of the council are themselves in receipt of
transitional payments.[29]'

Such brutal truths or prejudices informed Whitehall attitudes and
responses, occasionally perhaps feeding an innate antagonism towards an
area which was considered by its very nature to be industrially and
socially militant. A flurry of minutes upon a possible visit by Edward,
Prince of Wales, to the distressed areas, offers a revealing insight into such
attitudes. From the ubiquitous James Evans came both a warning and
solution. In his view a visit by the Prince expressly to see the distressed
places would not be a wise thing to do at that moment, 'We Welsh are
highly emotional and a special visit by the Prince might emphasise the
feeling of depression and tend to make people give into adversity ...'
Evans' solution was a simple one. If the prince's visit could coincide with
the rugby international between Wales and Scotland, during which he
might visit a few districts, then such objections could be overcome.
Whitehall officials were equally apprehensive of such a visit. As one
senior official observed.

'Of course the Prince is the Prince of Wales but unless he is very carefully brigaded any visit of his to the distressed areas is likely to do much more harm than good, except perhaps to his own popularity'

Chamberlain thought James Evans' solution of a low-key visit coinciding with an international worthy of passing on to the palace. These modest exchanges anticipated the much more contentious royal intervention seven years later.[30]

A National Crisis, A National Government

The brief but traumatic interlude represented by the minority Labour government of 1929-31 scarcely carried policy issues forward. The 1920s had found the Labour party struggling every bit as much as the Conservatives to come to terms with the drastically changed conditions within the coalfield and the leadership had acknowledged the necessity of transference of the surplus working population. For much of the decade, Labour leaders assumed that depression was a temporary deviation caused by the war and that capitalism would restore itself to generate revenues which, properly redistributed, would make social reform possible. The leadership of Macdonald and Snowden, suspicious of the theorists of the left, sought legitimacy for the party by presenting a respectable orthodox line. Its 1928 programme, 'Labour and the Nation', fell far short of the more radical Lloyd George call to conquer unemployment, although, behind the scenes, the party did prepare an emergency programme.

Although the question of unemployment dominated the 1929 election, the Labour party took power at a time of apparent economic recovery. The general election result was received with equanimity by the business community. There was no sudden financial or currency crisis as a consequence of the Labour victory. That crisis was triggered by the Wall Street crash of 1929. At the beginning of the Labour Administration, unemployment was 1.1 million, but by October 1930 it had soared to 2.2 million and represented nearly 20% of the insured work force. The government had assisted public works programmes which, by the 1930s, directly employed more than 60,000 people at a cost of £44.3 million. Some £140 million worth of schemes had been approved by September when the newly appointed lord privy seal, Vernon Hartshorn, MP for Ogmore and president of the Fed, successfully persuaded the cabinet that there was little scope for any further public works. Ministers had already rejected Oswald Mosley's alternative programme, a £200m public loan for home development.

The Treasury had disliked the expanded public works programme, but it had grown even more fearful of the public expenditure cost of soaring unemployment. The 1927 Insurance Act was intended to place unemployment insurance on a permanent non-controversial basis. The claimant would qualify for benefit on the basis of 30 contributions in the previous two years, although he remained subject to the 'genuinely seeking work' test. However, even before the 1929 election, the Baldwin government had been compelled to offer a transitional benefit from the fund to those who could not strictly qualify. Some of the earliest decisions of the Labour government had been to abolish the genuinely seeking work test, and to increase the state's contributions to the Unemployment Fund. The Exchequer had assumed full responsibility for the cost of transitional benefits. As a consequence of the massive and immediate rise in unemployment, Exchequer liability rocketed. Between 1928 and 1932 the state's contribution to the fund rose from £11.8 million to £16.48 million. Borrowing to maintain the fund more than tripled (£11.4 million) which, however, still could not cover the fast growing debt of the fund (£25 million to £115 million). The Exchequer liability for transitional relief rose to £32.3 million.

The cost of unemployment broke the minority Labour government. 'Work or adequate maintenance' had been a fundamental plank of Labour party policy. The Royal Commission on Unemployment Insurance, and another committee, the May Committee on national expenditure, both highlighted the burgeoning costs of unemployment benefits. Even the Treasury considered that the May report exaggerated the budget deficit, but Whitehall and Bank of England officials were not averse to using such evidence to frighten ministers into axing unemployment expenditure.

The Labour cabinet broke up over the proposed 10% reduction in unemployment insurance benefit, nine members refusing to support the cut. On 24 August 1931, the National government began its term of office led by Ramsay Macdonald and four Labour, four Conservative and two Liberal MPs immediately approved the reductions in unemployment insurance, increased contributions, placed limitations on entitlements, and applied a means test to transitional benefits. It also brought and end to employment creating expenditure. This package, accompanied by severe cuts in public service salaries (teachers' salaries were reduced by 15%) was intended to stabilise sterling and reassure foreign creditors. It failed miserably to do so and the new National government faced its own sterling crisis within a month of coming to office.

'A mutiny' among naval ratings, over the rumoured cut in pay followed by cabinet concessions, unnerved the markets. Behind the scenes, a crisis within the Indian government and a banking crisis in Amsterdam led to further haemorrhaging of reserves. Ironically, savings from the unemployment cuts were being eroded by rising unemployment (2.8 million in September 1931 and a forecast of 3 million in 1932). On the weekend of 19 and 20 September 1931, the Bank of England conceded defeat, decided to suspend gold payments and presented ministers with a *fait accompli*. Without official Labour opposition, the government pushed through, in one evening, the Gold (Standard) Bill, accompanied by concessions to the public services in moderating the pay cut. Suspension of the gold standard and the relative calm with which the market received the decision paved the way for a general election from which the National government achieved the greatest electoral victory of the century, 554 out of 615 seats. The Labour party was left with 46 (six other ILP candidates were elected), although the number of seats belied the popular support maintained by the Party: 6.6 million or 30.9% of those who voted.

The newly elected National government also brought a new ideological fervour to the debates on job creation and unemployment. Ministers, especially Chamberlain as Chancellor, made non-intervention an article of faith. Whereas in the previous decade officials and occasionally ministers had deployed the case against state intervention, now they offered a coherent and vigorous rebuttal of all Keynesian-style solutions. The government adopted the standard Treasury view of the economy: there was only a fixed amount of potential productive capital in the economy at any given time. Market forces would best determine and direct such investment into the most efficient and profitable projects. Public investment could displace an important percentage of such investments, lowering efficiency and consequently raising costs and prices.

This, essentially pessimistic, view was combined with a fatalistic cyclical analysis of the economy. A general 'improvement in trade' would address the short term unemployment consequences of the depression. The record of public work as employment measures demonstrated their low quality and marginal value and were expensive per capita. The National government wound up the Unemployment Grants Committee and Central government restriction on local borrowing led to a significant fall in public capital formation (at constant prices a fall from £198 million to £152 million by 1934). A thousand road schemes were postponed, leading to the laying-off of 20,000 labourers. Fortunately, the full rigour of the cuts was not felt until 1934 when, at least nationally, the economy and employment began picking up.

Yet three million unemployed remained a very costly burden to the state. Benefits and public assistance totalled £110 million of a budget of £800 million. Ministers, however, preferred this burden to the alternative of public works. A cabinet committee of 1932 concluded 'that by far the most important direct contribution of the state towards assisting the unemployed must for some time to come consist of cash allowances[32]. Tightening of the means test, nevertheless, caused tension, resulting in demonstrations and, in the autumn of 1932, serious riots in several cities, and thus compelled the government to relax the rules on relatives' incomes in assessing relief.

Indeed, the government's general hard line was not politically pain free. Some of its own backbenchers had expressed anxiety over the harshness of the means tests. Outside the House, the National Unemployed Workers Movement (NUWM), the Labour party and the Trades Union Council mounted campaigns and marches and made a sufficient impression to create rumbles within the government. In the autumn of 1932, a new cabinet committee on unemployment was constituted, but carried little weight in the absence of key ministers and the Chancellor of the Exchequer. Its recommendation reflected the modesty of the committee itself, grants to the National Council of Social Services to establish a network of occupational centres. In November, another and rather different committee for trade and employment including Baldwin, Chamberlain, Betterton, Minister for Labour, and Hilton Young, the Minister of Health, met to respond further to the unemployment crisis, advised by a panel of industrialists (including Duncan, chairman of the Central Electricity Board, and Lord Weir representing major engineering interests). Their recommendation to consider large capital projects, such as a channel tunnel or railway electrification, was promptly rejected by Chamberlain and the industrial adviser, Sir Horace Wilson, as were all other schemes mooted, including those by MacDonald during the course of 1932 and 1933.

The government's non-interventionist stance at the height of the depression established its tough reputation, a reputation spiced by a strong sense of 'treachery' associated with Macdonald's desertion of the Labour party. Yet in other aspects of the economy this was no *laissez faire* government. Following the suspension of the gold standard, the Treasury assumed responsibility for exchange and interest rates and, through a newly established exchange equalization account, it proceeded successfully, to 'manage' a devalued pound. Interest-rate policy did not, however, preoccupy officials or ministers on a weekly or monthly basis. Rates were driven down to 2% during 1932 and remained so for the seven years until the threat of war!

The protectionist policy which accompanied devaluation and cheap money inevitably drew government into a new relationship with business and industry. It ushered in a period of 'industrial diplomacy', which created a range of informal contacts between civil servants and leading industrialists. A core of such industrialists became semi-detached advisers to government. Import duties legislation and imperial trade agreements, following the Ottawa conference, shaped this new political/industrial relationship. The Treasury hoped that protection would rebuild company profitability and promote rationalisation and efficiency especially in the staple industries, shipping, coal, cotton, iron and steel. It was for the most part to be disappointed.[31]

Behind the wall of protection, and spurred by low interest rates, the British economy did, however, begin to grow again. Unemployment tumbled from its 3 million high to half that level by 1938. Low interest rates triggered off one of the greatest housing booms in British history in the greater London area and the south East. The age of British consumerism was born - light bulbs, radios, fridges, the vacuum cleaner and cars. Production at the Morris works doubled between 1926 and 1936. It may not have been to John Betjeman's taste:

> 'Come friendly bombs and fall on Slough
> To get it ready for the plough'

but it meant jobs and a measure of prosperity.

However, for the remaining quarter of Britain and especially for South Wales there was no such relief. Unemployment was to be as high in 1936 in blighted Merthyr Tydfil as it had been in the wake of the Wall Street crash. The 'general improvement in trade' upon which Chamberlain and his fellow ministers rested so much of their case did not reach the benighted coalfields of Scotland, the North East, Cumberland and South Wales. It was obvious to those living in 'places of suffering' and gradually became obvious to a wider public and political audience. This brought pressure upon government to change policy. At the heart of this study is the story of how the changing relationship between South Wales and Whitehall wrought that change of policy. It is a change that proved to be of rather greater significance than most historians of the period have so far acknowledged. It constituted an important 'U' turn of policy which began, begrudgingly, as early as 1934.

'*A Place of Suffering*'

1. The size and character of the coal industry and population growth are recorded in numerous secondary sources. I have drawn predominantly on Colin Baber and Denis Thomas, The Glamorgan Economy, 1914-1945, *Glamorgan County History*, Vol. 5, ed. A.J. John and Glanmor Williams (University of Wales press).

2. For an account of Merthyr civic history, Margaret S Taylor, *County Borough of Merthyr Tydfil 1905-1958, Fifty Years of Municipal Progress,* (Merthyr Tydfil Borough Council 1959).

3. A detailed, internal Whitehall analysis of Merthyr's decline, P.R.O. H.L.G. 30/53.
    Edgar Jones, *The History of G.K.N.* (Macmillan, 1985), vol 2, 113-129.

4. Political and Economic Planning (P.E.P), Location of Industry, 1939, pps 247-251.

5. Edgar Jones, G.K.N. vol II, 120-126.

6. Baber and Thomas, *The Glamorgan Economy*, 1914-1945, pp 521-527, 538-540.

7. Location of Industry op.cit. 130,131.

'*South Wales' People*'

8. L.J Williams, Was Wales Industrialised? *Essays in Modern Welsh history* , (Gomer, 1995). 97-122, 123-150.

9. Edgar Jones, G.K.N. vol II, 120-126.

10. The membership of the Bishop of Llandaf's committee, LAB 18/38.

11. On Union and working class leadership: P.Stead, Working class leadership in South Wales 1900-1920, Welsh Historical Review 6,(3), 1973; H. Francis and D. Smith; *The Fed*, Lawrence and Wishart (London 1980), R. Gregory, *The Miners and British Politics*, Oxford University Press, 1968.

12. The deputation to Whitehall: H.L.G. 30/63, T172/1614.

13. The best account of local Labour politics; Chris Williams, *Democratic Rhondda, Politics and Society*, 1888-1951, University of Wales Press (Cardiff 1996).

14. Clashes between central and local governments and the local Boards of Guardians: Sian Rhiannon Williams. The Bedwellty Board of Guardians and the Default Act of 1927 Llafur, vol.2 no 4 (spring 1979); for the clashes between Merthyr County Borough and Whitehall H.L.G. 30/30, H.L.G. 12/15.

Whitehall's People

15. The standard work on Whitehall, D.N. Chester, F.M.B Wilson, *The Organisation of British Central Government*, Allen and Unwin, (1957), more recently, Peter Hennessy, *Whitehall* (Free Press 1989). On public expenditure, Leo Pliatzky, *Getting and Spending, Public Expenditure, Employment* (Basil Blackwell).
For the early years of the Ministry of Labour R. Lowe, *The Role of the Ministry of Labour in British Politics, 1916/1939* (OUP 1986).

16. G.C. Peden, The Treasury as a Central Government Department 1919-1939, Public Administration (1983), 371-385.

17. J.Greenaway, Warren Fisher and the transformation of the British Treasury 1919-1939, Journal of British Studies 23, (1985), 125, P. Hennessy, Whitehall, 75.

18. Quoted in P. Hennessy, Whitehall, 73.

19. G.C. Peden, Sir Richard Hopkins and the Keynsian Revolution, Econ. Hist Review, 2nd series, xxxvi, (1983).

20. R.Lowe and R.Roberts, Sir Horace Wilson, the making of a Mandarin; Historical Journal, 30, 3(1987), 641-662.

21. Quoted in R. Lowe, Adjusting to Democracy, 26.

Whitehall's Policies

22. W.R. Garside, *British Unemployment, A Study in Public Policy* (CUP 1996); R. Lowe The Erosion of State Intervention in Britain, 1917-1924, Econ Hist Review 2nd Series xxi (1978), 270. Cabinet memorandum on the Coal Trade, CAB 27/3741.

23. The various official assessments can be found in:H.L.G 30/47, H.L.G 53/176,
    H.L.G 30/4, H.L.G. 30/63.

24. The Times articles, A Stricken Coalfield, 28,29,
    March, 2, April 1928.

'South Wales Calls on Whitehall'

25. Minutes of the deputation to Churchill, T 172/1614.

26. Sian Rhiannon Williams, The Bedwellty Board of Governors and the Default Act of 1927, Llafur vol 2, no 4(spring 1979).

27. Minutes of the Deputation to Neville Chamberlain, H.L.G. 30/63.

28. Sir Arthur Robinson's minutes and the subsequent surveys and reports H.L.G 30/4. 63, MH 79/304, MH 79/331, and ED 50/83.

29. H.L.G. 33/171.

30. H.L.G. 30/63.

A National Crisis, A National Government'

31. This section draws extensively upon P Williamson, *National Crisis and the National Government, British Politics, the Economy and Empire, 1926-1932*, Cambridge University Press.

32. Quoted in Frederick Miller, The Unemployment Policy of the National Government 1931-1936: Historical Journal (1976) 453-476.

Dowlais during the depression

UNDER THE SHADOW

Mr. Chamberlain. "YES—NOW THAT OUR ATTENTION IS DRAWN TO IT, IT CERTAINLY DOES SEEM MORE FORMIDABLE THAN WE THOUGHT."

'Under the Shadow'

2

1934: A TURNING POINT

1934 was a turning point in the government's handling of the South Wales' crisis. At the beginning of the year the omens for any change could not have been poorer, yet by its end the first piece of regional legislation had been placed on the statute book. At the start of 1934, Whitehall was busy dismantling the last vestiges of a public works programme by winding up the Unemployment Grants Committee. A university of Cardiff survey on the needs of South Wales, commissioned by the Board of Trade and published in 1932, had been quietly shelved.[1] New legislation could not have been further from official or ministerial minds. They were still absorbing the consequences of the reform of unemployment insurance and the establishment of the Unemployment Assistance Board, (The UAB). The government had always seen unemployment benefit as a more cost effective way of alleviating distress than any public works programme could provide.[2]

Within Whitehall, the cabinet committee on unemployment, which had found so heavily against any form of direct intervention, had been disbanded. Prime Minister Ramsay Macdonald made a vain attempt to revive the machinery or, at least, promote a new initiative. The response from his ministerial colleagues only exposed his ebbing influence over policy and illustrated the essentially negative attitudes prevailing within government. In February 1934, Macdonald wrote to Labour Minister, Sir Henry Betterton, suggesting that a committee be appointed 'off your own bat composed partly of businessmen' he had met at a recent industrial fair, and 'partly of the best advisers within Whitehall' with terms of reference to include new industry for the depressed areas and 'land cultivation'. The reply sent to the Prime Minister, a fortnight later, conveyed the essentially do nothing attitudes of ministers and officials. After consulting his colleague, Walter Runciman at the Board of Trade, Betterton warned that they should not raise hopes of direct financial assistance which would be impossible to fulfil. In 1932, new enterprise had only created some 12,000 jobs in the distressed areas and less than 45,000 nationally. The minister even doubted the effectiveness of the government's most cherished alternative, transference. He counselled against 'a new drive in its favour' 'Industry is only now beginning to dig itself painfully out of the slough of the last four years'. Employers and working people were 'so preoccupied with their own concerns that they would not welcome the task of absorbing transferees. The time was not ripe'. Yet within a month of these exchanges major new investigations had been launched

41

into four identified distressed areas, including South Wales, and, by the end of the year, the first piece of legislation addressing the needs of the distressed areas had been passed.[3]

This apparently sudden shift in policy reveals something of the nature and character of the National Government. Despite it huge majority, the government remained peculiarly sensitive to shifts in national moods. The government rarely initiated, instinctively sought to minimise government intervention but, periodically, felt the need to respond to public and parliamentary pressures. It did so reluctantly and often grudgingly. The change in policy in March/April 1934 was typical.

A series of Times special reports (21, 22 March 1934) on the plight of the unemployed in Durham (written by the same correspondent who had covered South Wales in 1928) aroused public and parliamentary sympathy. They also created agitated discussion among ministers. The correspondent described the pessimism and resentment of 'the derelict' as opposed to 'distressed' communities of the north east, 'derelict' because the only industry in the area was 'defunct and could never be expected to be reopened'. Two portentous Times leaders endorsed their correspondent's analysis and prescription. They dismissed the possibility of the recently created Unemployment Assistance Board fulfilling the need. (Chamberlain had made a reference to the UAB's possible role on 22 March). The problem of the derelict areas were 'non-recurrent and highly localised', requiring 'special machinery - the appointment of a director of operations supported by local advisers. Why does the government not see to it that some authoritative person or persons consider these problems now?'

The themes of *The Times* articles were to fuel the parliamentary debates during the session.. George Daggar (Abertillery) spelled out the dramatic decline in the purchasing power of South Wales and the multiplying dependence upon assistance and free meals. Whereas in 1920 £4 million had been paid out, the benefit bill had risen to £15 million in 1933. Wages in South Wales had fallen from a 1924 high of £46 million to £23 million. 'There were districts of England and South Wales whose plight no amount of general trade recovery could ever cure because their sole industry was not depressed, but dead' [4]. *The Times* articles and the parliamentary debates underlined the growing dilemma facing Whitehall. The slump of 1929-1931 had created large scale nation-wide unemployment. The gradual improvement from 1932 began to expose acute regional disparities. As this painfully became more and more obvious between 1934 and 1936, the demand to do something for 'derelict' areas reached out beyond the communities most affected to a wider, sympathetic audience.

More immediately, the publicity generated by *The Times* articles created a debate within Whitehall. Hastily convened, informal ministerial meetings endeavoured to devise an adequate public response. Macdonald and Baldwin buttonholed the Minister of Labour, Betterton, to impress upon him 'the importance of doing something to meet *The Times* leaders, and the growing chorus in the Commons'. Taking up *The Times* proposal, they pressed him to consider appointing a commissioner. Macdonald had already received a volunteer, the newspaper publisher, Cecil Harmsworth. Betterton's and the ministry's reactions demonstrated an unsure political touch as well as a deep seated reluctance to endorse instant initiatives. Betterton warned colleagues of the 'potential dangers of such an appointment that would arouse anticipation of definite action probably involving expenditure on a considerable scale.' 'Were ministers prepared to offer any new financial inducements to firms?' Any enquiry into the derelict areas would stimulate demands for further rates relief. The Minister of Agriculture would come under pressure to expand allotments and small holdings: the Board of Education would be confronted with questions of malnutrition among children at school. Betterton prophesied that the suggested commission would 'stir up a great deal of trouble for the government if they entered lightly on these investigations without first counting the cost of the consequences'

The Ministry of Labour preferred a low profile investigation of the distressed areas led by departmental under secretaries or, if it was felt that the government had to go further, the creation of a commission along the lines of the industrial transference board. The cabinet, and especially the Chancellor of the Exchequer, Neville Chamberlain, were anxious for more instantly politically attractive initiatives. Rejecting, at their meeting on 28 March, a commission, the cabinet preferred the appointment of four outside investigators, though paradoxically, considered it undesirable that the investigators' findings should be publicised. Under continuing pressure from Chamberlain, ministers agreed the announcement to appoint investigators for South Wales, Cumberland and the North East even before agreeing a name for the fourth to cover the Scottish distressed area. Chamberlain minuted, 'the more we can demonstrate that we are getting on with business the better the effect especially in the districts'. Amid this frantic instant policy making environment of April 1934, Sir Wyndham Portal was appointed to undertake an investigation into the distressed coal field areas of South Wales.

Portal and his fellow investigators, however, did not embark upon their enquiries without a measure of 'guidance' from Chamberlain and the Ministry of Labour. Chamberlain, at least, had no intention of endorsing every expensive option in circulation to deal with the problems. 'Local government in the districts should be examined to discover how far it is performing its function and is the cause of failure'. 'To what extent are high rates a deterrent?' Is the tradition of local government extravagance partly to blame?'. The investigators might 'point to the setting up of some joint executive body representing the authorities of the district or even their temporary supersession by some new body'.

If this set of questions reflected a bilious Whitehall view of local government, others were to be directed at the unemployed themselves: 'Had it been brought home to these people that the prospects are hopeless if they stay where they are?' Would authoritative pronouncements on the importance of transference 'accelerate the movement of the unemployed away from the hopeless areas?' Chamberlain considered it 'important that there should be evidence of interest in the unemployed population, that they should be made to feel that there is something for them to do other than sitting or standing around'. 'In this connection attention should be paid to occupational centres, training centres for domestic servants, provision for allotments, organised games and improvement of the outward appearance of the area'. Chamberlain, ultimately, counselled against a detailed questionnaire of the kind proposed by the Ministry of Labour. 'It read too much like a school examination paper'.

These internal exchanges illustrate prevailing ministerial attitudes. The appointment of investigators was meant to be a limited exercise designed more to reinforce existing policy - transference - than to shape new policies. Ministers had acted to defuse the immediate press and parliamentary pressures, offering what they consider to be the minimum required to relieve such pressures and aimed at producing minimalist solutions. Betterton, Minister of Labour, had cautioned colleagues, realising more than most ministers that such an appointment might become the focus of greater demands and the investigators themselves might produce uncomfortable recommendations. That was to prove unerringly perceptive in the case of the South Wales investigator, Sir Wyndham Portal.[5]

'Fairy Godfather of South Wales ...'

The haste in appointing the investigators appears to have precluded the usual process of Whitehall appointments. No files or correspondence reveal how ministers discovered Sir Wyndham Portal. The Portals, a Huguenot family, had fled persecution in France in the late seventeenth century to set up in Hampshire a papermaking business, specialising in bank notes for the fledgling Bank of England. The Portals had enjoyed nearly two hundred years of the closest possible contact with city and banking circles (the Bank of England held a significant shareholding in the company). The South Wales connections may have been forged when Sir Wyndham became chairman of Wiggins Teape with its substantial paper mills in Cardiff. Portal had also become, by 1934, a director of Great Western Railway.[6]

Portal was one of the early twentieth century breed of socially conscious industrialists, a believer in trade protection and a supporter of industrial planning. Extraordinarily he had given a measure of public support to Oswald Mosley's minority labour manifesto. In December 1930, he wrote to *The Times* that 'it would take us a step nearer a settled national policy which gives industry the protection it needs with some guarantee it can plan ahead with safety'. He reaffirmed his support for 'planning as well as the need for business' broader social responsibilities' at a Cardiff meeting of the League of Industry (1st October 1934). Portal reminded his audience that 'in the prosperous days of South Wales people flowed into the region'. 'Those who amassed fortunes in a particular district should remember they have are responsibility for the people in the place where those fortunes were made '. He favoured 'trying by every means to have some sort of economic planning for labour'.

> 'Do not let us become robots in industry. Business by itself
> is a sordid thing and you can only get an inspiration in
> business by taking in those who have helped to
> make your business a success ...'[7]

Portal stands apart from the other investigators appointed in the spring of 1934. From his very first days, he signalled his intention not only to report but to pursue his conclusions and recommendations. Within days of his first meeting he had produced a confidential preliminary report and was badgering officials to discover whether 'his suggestions commended themselves to the government '. He delivered his final report ahead of the others, and, immediately, sought to address both the interdepartmental officials' committee and even the cabinet committee that had been established to receive the reports. He twice attended the officials' committee but failed in his bid to reach the cabinet committee.

He was not averse to applying press and public pressure upon Whitehall. After delivering his report, but before its publication, he told a Cardiff audience in October 1934:

> 'I cannot tell you what my recommendations and
> conclusions are but if those conclusions were torn
> up you would not see a quiet persuasive chairman
> standing here and talking now '.

Later he used the opportunity of his maiden speech in the Lords to express both impatience and exasperation at apparent government inactivity. Yet Portal was no outsider. He became a masterful player in the Whitehall game. His influence over national policy grew, especially in the making and implementation of the second Special Areas Act (1937). There would be times when Whitehall waited upon Portal. His assiduous promotion of industrial development for South Wales was to win him the honorific recognition of the freedom of Cardiff and of Merthyr Tydfil, and in 1939 a national newspaper's epithet - 'the fairy godfather of South Wales '.

Within a month of his investigation, Portal delivered 'a strictly private and confidential' preliminary set of observations. His hitherto, unpublished, memorandum, delivered to officials bears all the hallmarks of Portal's personal modus operandi, testifying to a hectic round of meetings, deputations from local authorities and business groups, calls to be made upon the chairman and chief executives of major companies, ICI, GKN and Barclays, besides the government's chief industrial adviser, Sir Horace Wilson. From the very beginning, Portal strove to engage Whitehall in a detailed dialogue on the needs of South Wales, drawing unwilling officials into greater involvement and even commitments. His private memorandum notified officials of his intention to concentrate on 'an area extending from the eastern valleys of Monmouthshire to Port Talbot, bounded in the north by the Breconshire border, but excluding towns such as Cardiff and Swansea.' These areas were the home of 88,000 unemployed and 22,000 only working intermittently. His later report defined the communities of greatest distress - Blaina, Brynmawr, Rhymney, Merthyr and Senghenydd while Ebbw Vale stood in a separate category, totally dependent upon the re-opening of the works.

Portal's initial observation that 'such things as public works' were only an expensive palliative chimed with Whitehall's approach, while his scathing dismissal of any large scale housing programme dismayed many local authorities:

> 'I am definitely of the opinion that this is in most cases
> merely a waste of money as the houses compared with
> the north of England are good, and with an ever declining
> population no valid reason can be put forward for building
> any new houses ...'

Portal identified the obvious central cause of the distress, the collapse of the coal trade and the closure of the Dowlais and Ebbw Vale works. The Italian, French and South American coal markets had dramatically shrunk, partly as a result of trade restrictions and quotas while an ever decreasing domestic market for Welsh steam coal compounded the industry's difficulties.

Portal's preliminary confidential report identified three possible markets for coal:

1. The erection of Cardiff Dowlais works which would
    provide work for 2,000 but also absorb coal from the valleys.
    He intended to meet the GKN board within a few days.

2. A hydrogenation plant converting coal to oil creating
    some 3 - 4,000 jobs, half of whom would be miners.
    Such a plant would require approximately 170,000 tons a year.

Portal was planning an immediate meeting with ICI to discuss the feasibility of such a plant.

3. The re-opening of the Ebbw Vale Steel Works which
    would prove the greatest benefit to all.

> 'Everyone's energies should be concentrated upon seeing these
> works re-opened, converting the £5,000 a week, £1/4 million a year,
> paid out in relief and benefit to idle workers into
> productive employment.'[8]

Portal's final report carried little of the passion of his private pleading to ministers though much to their great irritation, his call to re-open the Ebbw Vale works remained. The published report balanced harsh home truths with endorsement and support for a number of pet South Wales projects.

The unemployment analysis made the grimmest reading. Within the most derelict communities more than 80% had been out of work for a twelve month, 55% to 70% out for more than two years and a third to a half over 3 years. Portal drew the chilling conclusion that 39,000 men (of whom 20,000 were between 18 and 45) and 5,000 boys had become 'surplus to requirements'.

Consequently, he advocated a policy of 'transference on the largest scale' accepting that 'the cream of the population' would have to leave. The transference policy should, however, be accompanied by the expansion of training programmes through instructional or 'reconditioning' centres. A preparatory centre should be established in either Merthyr or Tonypandy to accommodate transferees who 'lacked or have forgotten the elementary rules of arithmetic etc'.

Portal, however, balanced these unpleasant remedies with support for a series of South Wales' demands, including a massive coal drainage programme capable of creating 2,000 jobs, the use of government contracts to attract development, the relocating of a government arms factory into the area, a programme of afforestation and the expansion of allotments and small holdings, alongside a more ambitious scheme to resettle unemployed miners in a series of land 'colonies'. There remained throughout the 1930s a sentimental belief that miners could return to the land from which their families had once come.

Besides reaffirming his earlier plea for the re-opening of the Ebbw Vale works, the development of the Llanharry ore mines and a sugar beet factory in Pembrokeshire, Portal offered a rather idiosyncratic suggestion to help the coal industry; the appointment of 'a liaison officer'.

> 'Owing to the present attitude of both the South Wales coal owners
> and miners representatives such an appointment would be of
> great assistance in planning and setting ideas upon the adoption
> of new scientific methods in the case of coal and would give the
> necessary impetus to the problems of marketing coal
> upon progressive lines ...'[9]

Officials found such an appointment out of the question.

One other Portal recommendation did however, gain respectable circulation within the ministries - the creation of cheap credit provision for companies willing to invest in the distressed areas. It became something of a personal crusade which was realised in 1936. His report stressed the difficulties of establishing new industries in the Welsh valleys by 'normal methods'. A financial adviser should be appointed to consider the capital needs of small industries, to put them in touch with companies such as Credit for Industry Ltd. Portal amplified these thoughts in a later part of the report: 'the one or two existing organisations were not sufficiently of a national character to provide capital for smaller enterprises'. 'One requires a Trust Company with four or five of the larger industrialists working possibly without remuneration.' Local boards should report to a central board of a new "Industrial Trust Company"'. Portal's idea for an industrial trust company eventually found its way into Chamberlain's 1936 budget proposal to create the Special Areas Reconstruction Association (S.A.R.A.)[10]

Portal's assiduous and approachable manner impressed South Wales. Local authorities sent in a stream of memoranda and organised numerous deputations. From the county borough of Merthyr Tydfil, arguably the most distressed of the distressed areas, came a weighty submission. Unemployment exceeded 60%. The burden of public assistance and historic loans had led to rocketing rates, the highest in the country. 'Here is a borough visibly withering away', 'twelve thousand people vegetating in idleness with no hope in their lives all taking place in a borough rich in industrial experience and skills with sites capable of attracting new industries such as leather, cleaning and dyeing, concrete plants and brick works'. There were 1,000 acres awaiting afforestation - all, of course, on top of its coal and iron tradition. Portal acknowledged Merthyr as a special case.

'The conditions and circumstances which influenced South Wales were generally seen to be gathered together and epitomised in this single district'.

He concealed from the borough, however, his confidential recommendation that its county borough status was no longer sustainable, 'a status too onerous to bear'.

An equally impassioned plea came from a very different quarter. Sir Herbert Merret, managing director of the Blacnavon Company and representative of the Welsh Associated Collieries, drew Portal's attention to the high quality coals of Blaenavon, Tirpentwys, Viponds and Mynydd, ideally suited for a coal to oil plant sited at Cwmbran. Portal may not have been able to bridge the fundamental divisions between capital and labour in South Wales but he was able to relate to both. Through the intense process of consultation, a degree of mutual empathy was created between him and the area. Portal was clearly moved by the commitment of so many local political leaders and impressed by their acute political consciousness. In a letter to the Minister of Labour, Betterton, introducing his final report, he contrasted his experience of South Wales councillors with his knowledge of those in English areas. 'They spoke on their subject without any reference to their permanent officials trained in a political atmosphere unlike my experience in any part of England ...'.[11]

'Nothing New, Nothing Heroic'

Whitehall was less impressed. Sir Warren Fisher's, permanent secretary to the Treasury, brusque dismissal of the investigators' reports as containing 'nothing new or heroic' reflected not only a hard line Treasury view, but a general Whitehall sentiment. An interdepartmental committee chaired by the government's chief industrial adviser, Sir Horace Wilson, began co-ordinating the collective Whitehall view to submit to a newly constructed cabinet committee. Departments were universally condemnatory of the key findings of the investigators' reports. Anything that smacked of subsidy or inducements to persuade enterprise to set up in the distressed areas was peremptorily dismissed. Subsidies would lead either to surplus capacity or uneconomic competition, invoking governmental interference in industry to an extent which otherwise would be neither desirable nor necessary. Raising the school leaving age or early retirement schemes also fell foul of standard Whitehall objections. 'Neither desirable nor necessary' became the Whitehall motto. In peacetime a government should not compete with or apply compulsion to private enterprise. Any support to the private sector would involve the state in 'embarrassing question of management'.

This principal objection to intervention particularly applied to Portal's passionate pleas to re-open the Ebbw Vale works. His championing of this cause created a maximum degree of irritation not only with officials but especially with Chamberlain.[12]

Whitehall paid rather more serious attention to Portal's case for a cheaper credit system for industry. Portal, along with Mr Gibson Jarvie, of Credit for Industry, had attended a specially convened meeting of the interdepartmental committee at which officials pressed the company to establish an advisory board in South Wales similar to that existing in Scotland. Mr Jarvie initially resisted such a proposal as 'hardly necessary' and one which would only lead to an additional charge on the resources of the company. Under pressure, he did agree to reconsider, though on the basis of Jarvie's general advice, the interdepartmental report concluded that no credit agency was required. Such an agency would 'either attract custom from existing agencies owing to the better terms it could offer or be left with unsound schemes which others would not touch'. Again things were best left to the market. Already two private companies were advancing loans to 'sound enterprises' at 4.5% to 6.5% and, if successful, there would doubtless be 'imitators'.

This persistent scepticism, which coloured so much of Whitehall thinking even towards such pragmatic proposals as favourable credit facilities, became increasingly unpalatable to ministers facing growing parliamentary and public criticism. Portal's plea for cheaper credit which fell on deaf years in 1934 became a budget proposal in 1936.

Sir Horace Wilson's covering minute to ministers, summarising officials' assessment of the investigators' report, acknowledged the bleak prospects facing South Wales. Everything depended upon a substantial recovery of the coal trade, but which at best would be a slow process. The area was unlikely to be chosen by private enterprise for the location of new industry. Even Portal's land settlement proposals would lead to agricultural over production while everyone doubted the efficacy of a large afforestation programme. Officials were equally doubtful about any visionary alternative uses for coal such as hydrogenation and coal gas drawn vehicles. They were, however, drawn into detailed negotiations on coal tariffs and quotas which arose from the government's protectionist legislation. While ministers regularly stressed that coal agreements were, the responsibility of the industry itself, they accepted a duty to bring all possible pressure upon countries which were traditionally large importers of Welsh coal, Belgium, Egypt, Brazil, Uruguay, the Gold Coast and especially France where Welsh coal accounted for 59% of the market. Some coal agreements took the extraordinary form of barter deals. The Secretary of State for the Dominions, J.H. Thomas, caught South Wales by surprise by announcing at the beginning of 1935 an Anglo Irish Coal for Cattle Deal. He claimed that it would create some 5,000 miners jobs in Monmouthshire and boost trade at Newport Docks and upon Great Western Railways. The irony of such state intervention did not go unnoticed. During a debate (3, December 1934) the new Minister of Labour, Oliver Stanley, ruefully observed:

'On broader ground is it not true that we
are all planners now? Everyone votes for a tariff
or quota, or supports a marketing board, to a greater or lesser extent
is urging some form of national board for general industry ...'. [14]

That was certainly not the message conveyed by officials to ministers in their interdepartmental report. 'Planning' in the distressed areas was the last thing being contemplated. As Sir Horace Wilson concluded his advice to ministers:

> 'None of the policies here can give big results.
> The situation seems to be one that can only be dealt
> with - alleviated would be a more correct word - by
> persistent attempts to a number of minor remedies ...'.[15]

Whitehall was prepared only to offer South Wales minor 'remedies'. Much of Portal's report contained ideas and projects which had been mooted previously. It was as much a distillation of favoured schemes regularly promoted from the area. They were to reappear in the commission of special areas reports, Lloyd George's 'new deal' and Professor Marquand's 1937 'plan for South Wales'. The Portal report contained no rigorous strategic economic analysis. Perhaps none was necessary. The South Wales crisis was not a complex one - just disastrous, and for which Whitehall had no instant remedy.

Whitehall, in the autumn of 1934, still clung, Macawber like, to the hope that somehow a general improvement in trade would resolve the crisis of the distressed areas. What if, however, that general growth did not reach or revive the areas? The question was initially rarely asked and certainly not considered by officials in their interdepartmental study of the investigators' reports. They may have justifiably criticised a lack of rigour and analysis by the investigators, but their own assessments betrayed the nature of Whitehall decision making. That was undertaken by gifted generalists with little professional, economic or industrial understanding, and even less practical first hand knowledge of the areas. Whitehall did little travelling to the regions. One is struck by the variable quality of advice which poured into Sir Horace Wilson, at the centre of Whitehall operations, in a series of polished hand written minutes. Where there existed in the region a well established administrative service, the local medical officers at the Welsh Board of Health, the Welsh education and agricultural departments, Whitehall received a certain amount of authoritative analysis. The absence of any regional industrial equivalent meant that Whitehall remained distant from and disinterested in economic development. At least one consequence of establishing the commission for the special areas was that such advice began to impinge upon Whitehall and enter the policy making process.

'A Laboratory Experiment'

A shamefaced chief industrial adviser, Sir Horace Wilson, had to admit to ministers the obvious, that his interdepartmental committee's report was hardly likely to meet public expectations aroused by the appointment of the four investigators. Chamberlain and the cabinet concurred. The cabinet had agreed, in early October, to establish a ministerial committee for the distressed areas. Chaired by the Chancellor, it first met to discuss the reports on 11, October 1934 and then on four other occasions. Chamberlain dominated the committee from its very first meeting. He remained the committee's chairman until its disbanding on the outbreak of war.

Chamberlain had been unimpressed by the investigators' reports, hoping for 'something bigger in conception'. The reports 'covered ground already covered thoroughly'. He reiterated to the committee the government's well rehearsed view that 'transference' remained central to any solution for the distressed areas. 'The question was how to increase the outflow of the population. 'There were few young outstanding figures in the distressed areas capable of leadership'. Chamberlain did not conceal his irritation with the reports which, in his view, confused what should have been the simple message of transference. He called upon colleagues to review the arrangement in place for receiving transferees. Older and less mobile men could possibly be settled on the land. The alternative of intervening in the location of industry was unthinkable, except possibly where the government owned the industry. Chamberlain did discuss the possibility of utilising the relocation of armament factories, such as the Woolwich arsenal, to address distressed areas' needs. He and the Treasury were to fight a protracted battle with the War Office and service chiefs on armaments relocation policy.[16]

This ministerial canter around the issues served only to bring home to ministers the necessity to come up with something better. They returned to a remedy proposed in the March *Times* articles, ' a director of operations' or commissioner for the distressed areas. A ministry memorandum prepared on the eve of the second cabinet committee meeting (18, October) described such a commission as 'vested with wide powers and a considerable degree of independence, having a substantial fund to carry out schemes for economic development and social improvements of a kind which a government department would hesitate to advise ministers to embark upon'. A commissioner could exercise 'flexibility' and 'a willingness to try new and risky things'. The same memorandum, however, reflected all Whitehall's qualms about such an initiative. How would such a commissioner relate to government departments and local authorities?

> 'Would he be empowered to finance the construction of roads, houses, playing fields? It would be a striking departure for ordinary state and local administration, raising issues of ministerial and parliamentary accountability. Parliament would not easily be persuaded to extend undefined powers to a commissioner however eminent'.

Ministerial/commissioner relationships would be particularly problematic. The government could not fail to be identified with commissioners' policy and 'would have either to defend it or take some steps to alter it'. The commissioner would then become 'little more that an adjunct of the ministry.' Officials optimistically hoped that these tensions would be resolved by a close working relationship between commissioner and ministers. The commissioner 'would take pains to avoid an activity which might embarrass ministers'. Finally, the shadow of the parliamentary accounts committee could fall over the poor commissioner. While no doubt the PAC would 'allow reasonable tolerance of errors,' the very threat of a PAC investigation would 'induce a spirit of caution.' The answer to the parliamentary conundrums, officials concluded, lay in drafting the commissioner's powers vaguely.[17]

Ministers, reluctantly, agreed to such an appointment. For a profoundly cautious Chancellor it was as far as he was prepared to go. Within Chamberlain's terms it was a 'revolutionary step', though as he informed ministerial colleagues 'one had to be revolutionary sometimes'!. Expectations had been raised and the appointment of a commissioner was the least the ministers could do to respond to them. Chamberlain sought to play down the significance of such a shift in policy. He insisted that it should not be considered a precedent or a breach of the government's non intervention philosophy - more of a 'laboratory experiment', an experiment that he hoped would have an important psychological effect and which would demonstrate that the government had the plight of the distressed areas very much at heart. Chamberlain and ministers agreed to emphasise the 'experimental' and even temporary nature of the appointment of such a commissioner.[18]

'The Special Areas (Development and Improvement) Act'

At the 18th October and subsequent cabinet committee meetings the principles of the new commission and the first piece of regional development legislation were shaped. Chamberlain overrode the Minister of Labour's suggestion of a £3 million lump sum, proposing instead an initial £2 million fund. He explained that, as a general principle, the new commission should not be hampered unnecessarily by lack of funds, though one should not encourage the commission to launch into rash and ill considered schemes. Officials had advised that it was vital not to convey the impression that what was being provided was 'a sort of financial hosepipe designed to pour assistance into the districts'. Drafting the bill exposed the potential awkward demarcation lines between the new commissioner, government departments and local authorities. As officials confessed, the bill could have originally prohibited the commissioner from exercising powers already possessed by government departments and local authorities, thus tying 'the commissioner's hands almost completely'. Sections 3 and 4 of clause 1 reflected a compromise by placing a duty upon the commissioner 'to make suggestions to and to co-operate with government departments, local authorities and other bodies'. The commission was also invited to make recommendations to government departments and local authorities 'as for the removal of difficulties which appear to the commission to prevent or hamper measures which might be carried out under their statutory powers'. Consent, however, would have to be sought to do anything which any other government department was required or authorised to undertake. Any inducements to private enterprise were forbidden, while the commissioner was expressly prohibited from making a contribution to any local authority towards the cost of any works for which a specific grant was payable by government departments. These uneasy caveats and conditions reflected a general Whitehall ambivalence to the whole project. Nevertheless, the bill charged the commission with the task of:

'initiation, organisation, prosecution and assistance
of measures designed to facilitate the economic
development and social improvement of the depressed areas.'[19]

The creation of a new commission, inevitably, put some noses out of joint and none more so that the newly established Unemployment Assistance Board (the UAB). The UAB had wanted nothing to do with the investigators' reports or Whitehall's follow up. Now it faced a potential competitor. As UAB chairman, Henry Betterton himself only recently the Minister of Labour (elevated to the peerage as Lord Rushcliffe), heavily reminded officials and ministers that the board had itself been charged with 'the promotion of the welfare of the long term unemployed'. If a commissioner was appointed to look after the long term unemployed in four areas would not the question be asked:

> 'If for some reason the Board cannot deal effectively with
> the long term unemployed in these areas what reason is there
> to suppose that if can act effectively on behalf of the long
> term unemployed elsewhere in the country?'.

Rushcliffe feared, with some justification, that the UAB would appear 'to be no more that a mere dole distributory agency'. Treasury officials were also aware of the odious comparison that could be drawn between the 'soulless bureaucracy of the UAB' and the 'Santa Claus commissioners.' Rushcliffe's solution to the dilemma lay in making the new commissioner answerable to the Minister of Labour via the UAB, an unpalatable suggestion for ministers bent on presenting their new policy as a bold experiment. A cosmetic compromise to assuage the UAB was devised in the form of Clause 1 (3) of the bill, allowing the commissioner to act 'in association' with the Board.[20]

The bill received a cool press and a rougher parliamentary reception, especially from the members representing areas it was supposedly designed to help. Chamberlain had announced the decision to appoint a commissioner during a debate on the investigators' reports (14, November) when his disparaging remarks about the lack of men of stature and leadership in the areas had angered everyone. S.O. Davies M.P. for Merthyr Tydfil, denounced the slur;

> 'for the last one hundred years not a single
> person either owner or part owner of any works in the
> constituency has ever identified himself with
> any kind of public service ... or even taken
> the trouble to live in the constituency ...'.

Aneurin Bevan derided the appointment of an unpaid amateur and staff to cover the whole of England and Wales as a substitute for the disappeared generation of leaders. Elected members would demeaningly have to 'make appointments with him several weary months before trying to get his attention knowing that the whole thing was, an idle, empty farce'. Clearly referring back to the establishment of the UAB, Bevan complained that the government's only solution to a major problem was just more administrative machinery.

All members contrasted the modesty of the bill to the size of the problem. Life in the distressed areas, according to Bevan, was 'like living in the middle of a graveyard and spending most of our time reading the inscription on the tombstones.'. The bill offered mere 'palliatives'. All the commissioner could initiate was 'a bit of colour washing colliers' cottages'. They had already colour-washed Brynmawr, but it had not attracted new industry. The commissioner would be reduced to organising 'skittle matches'. Will John (Rhondda West) found a darker purpose and philosophy in the bill. It encapsulated the government's attitude to the unemployed, with their preoccupation of keeping the unemployed 'active', physically fit rather than creating real jobs. 'The unemployed might, indeed, be occupied in learning the noble art of self defence but we could not develop the notion of the good citizen by training unemployed boxers'. And he issued a stark warning. 'If the commissioner intended just to promote more voluntary, charitable schemes with unemployment benefit and a few sandwiches, there would be the greatest agitation against him'.

Opposition to the bill was not confined to the Labour benches. Lloyd George, admitting that an amendment he had prepared was the first he had moved in thirty years, also damned the bill as a 'patching' and 'peddling hope' in restoring an old and discredited economic machine. The government had just not grasped or understood that 'something catastrophic had happened in the economic system of the world'. 'You couldn't possibly feed the multitude with two commissioners and five sub-agents'.

Indeed, the luckless Minister of Labour, Oliver Stanley, and his junior, Hudson, found themselves caught in cross party fire. Government supporters from Lancashire and Teesside complained that their areas had been excluded from the bill's benefits, meagre as they may have been. A young Harold Macmillan, matching the mocking skills of his parliamentary adversary, Aneurin Bevan, denied that he sought to belittle the bill:

> 'At no stage have I attempted to
> minimalise the importance, which I
> believe to be great, of the bill: but
> in a comparison with the problems
> before us this is a mouse, a nice
> mouse, a good little mouse, a
> profitable and helpful little but
> a ridiculously microscopic
> Lilliputian mouse ...'.

A 'mouse of a bill' it may have been, but ministers were still left with the task of explaining how the commissioner would fit into a relationship with central and local government and exactly what he would or would not be able to do. A barrage of questions only exposed the difficult grey areas, the ambiguous demarcation lines between them, those ambiguities which Whitehall itself had identified in drafting the bill. Would the commissioner, for example, be able to finance the great coal drainage scheme recommended by Portal? Or would such a scheme be considered as profiting private enterprise and, thereby, prohibited under the bill? The Minister was uncertain.

So what could the commissioner do? A flustered Stanley explained the commissioner's role as clearing the slag heaps, improving local amenities, giving local volunteers sites and tools. He would be a kind of 'liaison officer' between government departments and local authorities, but certainly not a promoter of 'public works or a channel for giving contributions to local authorities for their ordinary duties. Under such pressures ministers acknowledged the modesty of the proposal. Stanley did not pretend that the miners were offered a complete or even a major solution. It was by way of 'an experiment' which he begged the House to try.

Despite the volume of criticism, the bill passed all its stages within a month, and with only minor amendments. Stanley accepted the possible need to appoint a deputy commissioner (in response to the Welsh demand for a separate commissioner). One was never appointed. At the very last minute the government also accepted, in the Lords, a change to the title. The people of Tyneside, it was claimed, had objected to the term 'depressed', which disparaged the spirit and character of the people. They were not 'depressed', just 'special' areas. Thus, at the end of December, was passed the first Special Areas (Development and Improvement) Act.[21]

South Wales shared Harold Macmillan's verdict that the 1934 act was a 'mouse' of a measure. Set against the continuing appalling levels of unemployment, declining purchasing power and burgeoning cost of public assistance relief, the commission's powers to apply 'minor remedies' and useful local works seemed marginal, if not irrelevant. Even so, the immediate damning verdict masked the potential significance of the shift in Whitehall and government policy. Within the prevailing context and confines of policy thought of early 30s Whitehall, the 1934 act represented a first 'U' turn. At the beginning of 1934, Whitehall had been busily dismantling all remaining instruments of intervention. At the end of the year, a novel commission, with a high profile personality as its commissioner, had been appointed and rapidly became the focus for the demands of the distressed areas.

The commission had been a concession to political pressure. Whitehall had relented not with any particular good grace. Chamberlain may have fondly hoped, as he had done so in establishing the Unemployment Assistance Board, that the issue of unemployment as well as unemployment relief could be taken out of politics by such a commission acting dispassionately and rationally in dealing with the needs of the distressed areas. 'Organised recreation and physical exercise and wherever possible a bit of ground' would suffice for those who were compelled to remain in the derelict coalfield areas, 'the untransferable ones.' Chamberlain and ministers, indeed, never quite worked out whether they wished to present their new legislation and appointment as a 'bold' experiment or as a modest pragmatic alleviation of immediate distress. This ambivalence had surfaced in the drafting of the legislation, and in the grey ill defined area of activity accorded to the new commissioner. It was to become even more evident in the fractured relationships between the newly appointed commissioner, Sir Malcolm Stewart, and Whitehall. Ministers and officials were to rue for the next two years, the appointment of Sir Malcolm. Distressed area policy including the relations between South Wales and Whitehall, was, in part, to be shaped by the deteriorating relationship between commissioner and government.[22]

1934: A Turning Point

1. Board of Trade: Industrial survey of South Wales (London 1932); Background to and preparation of the survey LAB 14/18.

2. Frederick Miller, The Unemployment Policy of the national government 1931-1936: Historical Journal (1976),453-476.

3. Ramsay MacDonald's role in the national government: D. Marquand, *Ramsay MacDonald,* Jonathan Cape 1977, ch 29;Ministerial exchanges LAB 18/28.

4. HC Debates, 22nd March, 25 July, 15, 26 Nov. 1934.

5. Ministerial exchanges over the investigators' role and the guidelines LAB 18/28.

'Fairy Godfather of South Wales'

6. The Portal Family: private family publication, Oxford University Press 1962.

7. The Times, 30 Dec, October, 1934.

8. Portal's exchanges and submission to officials, BT55/14, HLG 30/51.

9. An Investigation into the Industrial Conditions of Certain Depressed Areas: South Wales and Pembrokeshire Cmnd 4278 HMSO (London) 1934 hereafter called the 'The Portal Report'.

10. The Portal Report, 189.

11. Submissions to Portal, BT 55/14, the unedited Portal Report' CAB 27/577

'Nothing New, Nothing Heroic'

12. Treasury views on the reports T161/831/S39260/01,2. The officials interdepartmental report, cabinet committee minutes and conclusions, CAB27/577-579.

13. Discussion on cheap credit, CAB 277/577-579.

14. Sir Horace Willson's minutes and official assessments; CAB 27/577-579, Coal trade, POWE 26/28; HC Debate 3 Dec, 1934.

15. CAB 27/577-579.

'A Laboratory Experiment'

16. CAB 27/ 577-579.

17. HLG 30/13.

18. CAB 27/577-579.

The Special Areas (Development and Improvement Act)

19. The Special Areas bill papers BT 55/14; T161/714/S39260/01, 2; LAB 16/30.

20. The UAB's position AST 7/34, T161/631/39620/01.

21. Debates, 14 Nov, 1934, 3,6,13, Dec 1934.

22. Sir Malcolm Stewart's appointment; LAB 8/18; T172/1827.

The Last Time He Saw Merthyr

Rather early for Christmas isn't it?

Sir Malcolm Stewart, commissioner for the Special Areas

Sir Wyndham Portal, the investigator for South Wales

3

1935: A 'MISTAKE'

'I am afraid we have made
a mistake in our commissioner and
I anticipate more trouble ...'

Neville Chamberlain, 22 Jan. 1935

The appointment of a commissioner for the special areas inevitably raised hopes in South Wales. Local authorities now beat a path to his door, as they had to Sir Wyndham Portal's. Stewart endorsed most of Portal's recommendations. But for the vast majority of the unemployed of South Wales in January 1935 some future hope of a job inspired by the new commission appeared irrelevant or marginal compared with their immediate predicament: the unexpectedly savage cuts in benefit that accompanied the establishment of the new Unemployment Assistance Board (the UAB). The introduction of the new rates in January 1935 triggered some of the most powerful public protests witnessed during the decade. On the weekend of 3/4 February, an estimated 300,000 people in South Wales took to the streets: 60,000 in Aberdare addressed by George Hall and the President of the South Wales miners federation, James Griffiths: 20,000 in Pontypool Park addressed by Ernest Bevin. More dramatically, on Monday 5 February a procession of 1,000 Merthyr men and women marched, upon the UAB offices where stones were hurled, and the area office windows smashed.[1]

The agitation had also been quickly transmitted to the Commons where the hapless Minister of Labour, Oliver Stanley, was forced to concede and withdraw the new scales, thus imposing a standstill which allowed claimants to choose either the new or the old terms, whichever were the higher. The Board and Whitehall had totally miscalculated the impact of its new rates, especially on the much reduced rent allowances and benefits for dependants. Chamberlain could only lament privately to his diary of Labour Minister Stanley's cowardice and junior minister Hudson's disloyalty but had to advise the Cabinet that they had had no choice other than to bend under intense parliamentary pressure, as much from north west government members as from the opposition.[2]

Relations were not much better between ministers, officials and their newly appointed commissioner. Sir Malcolm Percy Stewart had appeared to be an inspired choice, the ideal person to bridge the divisions between capital, government and working class communities. He was a rare creature for the 1930s, a model paternal employer. He and his father had made their money in bricks and cement. The family had acquired a financial interest in a Bedfordshire brick and cement works company, B. S. Forders which also absorbed the London Brick Company. When, in 1912, Forders was taken over by British Portland Cement, Sir Malcolm became managing director of what was to become the Blue Circle group. As employers, the Stewarts pioneered new management/labour relations, a welfare and pension scheme for workers, joint consultation, profit sharing and holidays with pay. The family had converted the hamlet of Wooton Pillinge, Bedfordshire into a model workers' village: low rent, modern housing, a school, canteens, recreational areas, a memorial hall and a swimming pool. Some of Stewart's recommendations to ministers were inspired by the family and company experience.

Such experiences, however, did little to assist the fractious relationships between the commissioner and Whitehall. As early as January 1935 Chamberlain minuted that they may, indeed, have made 'a mistake' in appointing Sir Malcolm Stewart. For his part, Stewart from his very first days fretted at the limitations upon his office. During the passage of the Special Areas bill he had pleaded with the Chancellor to extend his role to allow road construction:

> "While I shall have power for what I may call palliatives,
> social services, allotments, to make a real success I must be
> able to put a fair number of men in work of real value.
> In due course I aim to be able to persuade some employers
> to open new industries in the depressed areas,
> but it will take time ..."

Chamberlain considered this smacked of 'public works'. In a swift and graceless rejection of Stewart's plea to amend the bill, he reminded the commissioner that 'the government did not regard public works as providing any real help towards the solution of the depressed areas'. Powers to intrude into such responsibilities had 'serious and taxing consequences' for the exchequer and local government.

Stewart sullenly accepted Chamberlain's refusal for the time being. However, he added in his reply that

> "unless there is adopted with regard to the depressed areas what
> I deem a reasonably benevolent attitude and the government
> vote in their favour in borderline cases involving expenditure
> I fear little progress with regard to justifiable works can be made ..."

Stewart could not resist the temptation of pointedly drawing attention in his first report to the nine limitations upon his powers and responsibilities, including ministerial control, the inability to supplement a specific grant made by government departments (a reference to road building) and the prohibition upon financial assistance to new industries. A furious Chancellor dismissed these complaints as 'flimsy' while expressing to ministerial colleagues that repeated allegations of this kind would damage the government's policy.[3]

Stewart next confronted the recently appointed Minister of Labour, Oliver Stanley. They should have been natural political allies. Although the eldest son of the Earl of Derby, Oliver Stanley had always belonged to the radical wing of the Conservative party, closely associated with Harold Macmillan, and co author of a 1927 book on Industry and the State. Then Stanley had pointedly observed that under a laissez faire system 'clearly there would have been no place for a Ministry of Labour'; but in the post war world 'the ministry was needed to correlate economic facts and social aspirations to ensure that labour is employed under conditions corresponding to the standards set by the conscience of the community.'

It was, therefore, richly ironic that the earliest clash between Stewart and Stanley centred on the issue of labour conditions. Stewart wrote to Stanley:

> "It has been brought home to me very forcibly during the
> last two weeks that voluntary labour is extremely unpopular
> in most depressed areas. To adapt it could arouse trade
> union antagonism and I am told in South Wales it could
> almost damn any possibility of securing goodwill ..."

While he promised to do everything to encourage voluntary labour, he had concluded that schemes undertaken had to be on 'a wage basis'- otherwise men would be 'playing at work'. Stanley felt obliged to remind the commissioner that government policy had discontinued the costly, ineffective relief works. Voluntary schemes were of primary importance and should be maintained and extended. Stewart refused to concede and raised the temperature further by hinting that, not only should he encourage waged labour, but that it should be paid at a slightly higher rate to persuade people back to work. A Treasury official exploded at the suggestion: 'Enhanced hourly rates would lead straight to relief work and encourage the unemployed to spin the job out'. Stewart dropped the idea.

Stewart and Stanley crossed swords over one other demarcation line of responsibility. The Minister of Labour accepted that the commissioner should proceed with sewerage, water supply schemes, and clearance of derelict sites of 'economic value'; but he drew the line at 'swimming baths' and still more at 'making up back alleys'. It was Stewart's turn to explode. Thanking Stanley for replying 'so promptly' to his letter (it had taken three weeks), the commissioner tartly reminded the Minister that he had 'practical experiences regarding the provision of swimming baths for workers' and could 'unhesitantly say that of all the facilities which he had given to workers none had proved so definitely successful for promoting friendly social contact':

> "It is found that those who live near one another but do
> not become acquainted make helpful friendships in the baths,
> thus creating a better mental atmosphere as well as
> affording physical improvement and better health"

These early and increasingly bitter exchanges with Whitehall determined the character and tone of Stewart's relationships with Whitehall for the duration of his office. They had also centred upon his attempt to draft what, in today's terms, would be called a 'mission statement', a statement eventually published at the end of January 1935. The statement outlined the eventual compromise areas of activity agreed with Whitehall. While the Treasury reluctantly agreed that is was 'by no means a bad statement' and contained much that was' virtuous and reasonable', officials remained extremely nervous about the budgetary implication of an expensive commission. They urged Chamberlain to see Stewart to tell him in confidence that there were 'not countless millions available out of cash revenue'[4]

Despite these differences, administrative arrangements for the commission were quickly put in place. Staff were drafted from a variety of departments, answering to a secretary to the commissioner, Mr Frank Tribe. Tribe brought a particularly appropriate Whitehall experience to the fledgling commission. As principal private secretary to three Ministers of Labour during the 1920s, he knew more than most about the tensions at the interface between the politicians and the administrator. Prior to his appointment he had also acted as secretary to another non-governmental advisory body, the National Advisory Council for Juvenile Employment. Tribe attempted to act as conciliator between his commissioner and his Whitehall colleagues with only limited success.

The commission's four divisions reflected the areas of activity Stewart expected to promote and investigate; agriculture, industry, health and recreation, labour transference and training. The decision to establish district commissions in the four special areas proved to be particularly significant for South Wales. The appointment of Captain Geoffrey Crawshay brought back to centre stage a member of one of the great nineteenth century industrial families. The family's Merthyr Cyfarthfa works had effectively been closed before the first world war, contributing to the town's depression and adding to its extensive areas of dereliction. An assiduous man who gained the respect of the community, Crawshay became an advocate for Merthyr's regeneration.

His small staff processed the numerous applications for grants garnered at meetings with, and deputations from, local authorities. Crawshay's office played a rather greater role than the size of his staff might indicate. Its role became crucial in the symbolically important decision to undertake the large scale clearance of the derelict Dowlais and Cyfarthfa works in Merthyr Tydfil - the first commitment to bring jobs and industry into rather than transference out of Britain's oldest industrial communities.[5]

"Palliatives"

Commissioner Stewart's modus operandi revolved around his two main functions: to identify and authorise the schemes which fell within his scope, and to submit to ministers, reports on the needs of the special areas. Stewart had despaired of extending the practical assistance he could offer, and had been confined to what he had described to Chamberlain as little more than 'palliatives'. The most modest of these included small grants for a voluntary amenity schemes: construction of a children's playgrounds, football pitches and putting greens, tennis courts and community centres, and open air swimming baths. The commission supported the establishment of occupational centres for the unemployed, instructional training places for the younger unemployed, which offered some form of minimal training. There was, however, little meaningful industrial retraining undertaken under the auspices of the commission, or, indeed, at all, within South Wales during the late thirties. While Whitehall increasingly bemoaned South Wales's low quality labour, it did little to correct the problem. The lack of skills within the area remained an alibi regularly invoked by the War Office and other departments to resist demands to transfer armaments production to South Wales. Under the emergency of war, a remarkable number of men and women were to respond with great rapidity to the challenge of semi and skilled war time production.

The government did respond to a more basic identifiable need in time of war - a physically fit population. Mounting concern about the physical

66

state of the male population led to the passage of a physical training act, and the commission paying for physical training classes in almost every valley community. In 1937/8 more that 5,000 men enrolled; for example 473 in Aberdare, 499 in Merthyr Tydfil and 84 in Pontlottyn. Rather more substantially, the commission also began underwriting an expansive infrastructure programme to renew the worn out nineteenth century sewerage and water systems, as well a series of culverting and flood prevention schemes. As Stewart observed in his second commissioner's report (February 1936), 'renovation of sewers was not spectacular work; it is mostly underground and there is little to show for it outwardly'. Yet the programme constituted a useful and important part of local regeneration. It embraced a series of major schemes : £210,000 for the Penybont main sewerage board, a string of culverting and storm water drainage schemes for the Rhondda, Nantyglo and Blaina to the smallest of £480 in Crickhowell.

Stewart and the commission progressively pushed forward into one other area of considerable community need: the provision of health and hospital facilities. The first set of authorised schemes included a £250,000 new Glamorgan general hospital of 300 beds (the recently closed East Glamorgan hospital) and an extension to the Hensol Castle mental hospital (£150,000). The programme emphasised maternal and child welfare needs, reflecting the agitation from local medical officers of health about the state of children's health in distressed areas: maternity and child welfare centres at Gilfach Goch, Beddau, Ystrad and a new maternity block at Bridgend infirmary. As the commission identified, infant mortality rates in South Wales at 78.3 deaths under 1 year per 1,000 births compared sadly with a national average of 64 deaths per 1,000. Stewart, however, never claimed that the succession of infrastructure schemes represented a direct response to the needs of the unemployed, despite the possibility that there would have been some modest fall-out in terms of local contract employment. No jobs figure was attributed to the sewerage, culverting or hospital projects. Indeed, Stewart repeatedly denied that they constituted an employment works programme. He reiterated in his second report (February 1936) that the act did not make provision for 'expenditure on schemes primarily to give immediate employment' The 'artificial creation of employment was not attempted' - except in one respect, the host of schemes to encourage miners to return to the land.[6]

Return to the land

There remained throughout the thirties an almost touching belief that one of the solutions to unemployment lay in a return to the land. In retrospect, it seems a quaint notion, though it was widely supported between the wars. Contrary to its usual stance on relief schemes, even the Treasury enthusiastically underwrote such proposals both for agricultural and forestry holdings. Chamberlain and the cabinet committee agreed. Land and forestry schemes were part of Lloyd George' new deals, while the mayor of the beleaguered county borough of Merthyr Tydfil made a passionate plea that 'hundreds of our men could be employed in afforestation'. We have a large area of land between Merthyr and Brecon which could be planted. Experts have proved that 'the growth of trees would be good'.

Enormous administrative energy was devoted to the task by both Whitehall and the commission for the special areas and especially by the South Wales district commissioner, Crawshay. He, initially, demanded a comprehensive survey of the agricultural land available. The ministry of agriculture felt it knew the availability sufficiently, but co-operated fully in the expanding programme of allotments, group and small holdings as well as the most ambitious scheme of all - the Boverton Co-operative. Crawshay circulated county councils encouraging them to expand their programmes of group holdings (1/4 to 1/2 acres) and the 5/10 acre smallholdings, offering to cover salary and travelling expenses of an expert supervisor, the provision of seeds, manure and tools and even modest working capital. The commissioner agreed to bear 12.5% of any additional cost incurred by county councils. This new smallholder would continue to receive unemployment allowances for the first twelve months. Preference would be given to married men of 35 years and over.

The centre piece of the commission's effort was a 650 acre Boverton co-operative at Cowbridge to be managed by a newly established Welsh Land settlement trust. Trustees were to be distinguished Welshman, for as Stewart accepted 'national sentiment is very pronounced' and the scheme 'will be more likely to be successful if it is predominantly Welsh in character and is centred in the Principality'. Crawshay recommended that the trust included the clerk to the Anglesey County Council, Walter Jones 'one of the ablest men in Wales, with a lifetime knowledge of smallholdings and rural housing,' Alderman Arthur Jenkins prospective Labour candidate for Pontypool '(assured of election) and undoubtedly one of the ablest and sound men in the Labour Party,' as well as David Davies of Llandinam 'landowner, philanthropist, chairman of Ocean Colliery Co Ltd.' Ultimately the Trust included two major Welsh politicians, D R Grenfell and Lloyd George.

The Boverton scheme illustrates Stewart's vision and experience in building the model garden village. In his second report Stewart envisaged that, initially, the Welsh Land Trust would employ on the estate at agricultural wage rates before gradually converting the scheme into a co-operative conducted on a profit sharing basis, all employees being entitled to a share of the profits. Some 65 families had settled at Boverton by the end of the decade and a total of 278 (1151 persons) in the new smallholdings schemes and co-operative farming projects.

The Treasury greeted with some enthusiasm proposals for afforestation and forestry holdings. The Forestry Commission, however, approached a special areas programme with rather greater caution, for its programme had been a major victim of the National government's spending axe in 1931. Its 1929, 10 year £9 million, 350,000 acre and 300 forestry holdings programme had been shrunk to a five year £450,000, 20,000 acre and 20 forestry holdings programme. Forestry commissioners sought assurances of specific additional treasury funding, and emphasised the difficulties of getting going a South Wales programme. Much of the possible planting land in Glamorgan was held in common. Mining working and surface subsidence impeded large scale planting and industrial fumes and the atmosphere was 'inimical to plant growth'. The concept of forestry holdings, by which miners were granted a cottage, ten acres and a promise of 150 days a year work in the forestry, had not been much of a success. Miners were 'unused to the life' and their wives objected to the isolation. The Forestry commission, nevertheless, agreed with the Treasury a new £1/2 million special programme for the distressed areas of England and Wales. In 1937/8 that programme included 5,000 acres in South Wales, and a planting of 1,900 acres the following season. Thus, the large post-war programme of afforestation of the South Wales valleys and the surrounding Brecon Beacons had its modest beginnings in the activity of the special areas commission.

Whitehall, nevertheless, rejected one other visionary scheme especially mooted by Captain Crawshay, the development of the Welsh National Park. Crawshay's vision was not confined to a glorified afforestation scheme but drew upon American national park experience - properly laid out camping sites, complete with water supply, lavatories and sleeping huts. An American style park would 'cater not only for the masses, but for the middle class and richer members of the community in wooded sleeping shack bungalows'. The new style park would create considerable summer employment which could be redeployed in winter in forestry work. Women would revive rural crafts and weaving which would consequently preserve 'ancient Welsh crafts and industries from disappearing'. Crawshay recommended that the new park be sited not within the confines of South Wales and the Beacons but rather, 15,000 acres at Rhandirmwyn, five miles from Llandovery, Camarthenshire, 'a glorious tract of mountain land in which the river Towy rises', and within 2 _ to 3 hours from Birmingham and the Midlands. Whitehall and ministers sadly spurned such imagination. They remained unconvinced it would be of much benefit to the special areas; 'the employment value was somewhat problematical', only seasonal and requiring 'labour of a type not always easy to find in the mining areas'. The cabinet committee agreed. Wales had to wait until 1949 for the creation of the Welsh national park, and then not based on the American style envisaged by the inestimable Captain Crawshay.

For all the administrative energy and agonising, the back to the land policy produced meagre results. Commissioner Stewart increasingly confessed publicly not only to the modesty of the schemes but also to their inappropriateness. 'Agriculture is a vocation calling not only for a high degree of skill but also for special characteristics not associated in general with an industrial outlook'. Chamberlain and Whitehall were content, at least, in these early if difficult months of 1935, to confine the commissioner's activities to promote such schemes to return to the land which fitted neatly into their perception of support for the unemployed. As Chamberlain reminded colleagues yet again in mid 1935, government action could only marginally influence levels of unemployment. In transference of the young and fit to areas of employment lay the only substantial hope. Government, otherwise, should endeavour to make life as comfortable as possible for the older long-term unemployed and unemployable. 'The unemployable residuum should be kept as contented and happy as circumstances permitted'. Allotments, smallholdings and forestry work comfortably fitted into that approach.[7]

'Crudities and Confusions '

The cabinet committee for the distressed areas' meetings only served to reinforce that message when it considered the first major report from Sir Malcolm Stewart. He had continued to exasperate Neville Chamberlain. As far as the Chancellor was concerned the report contained 'crudities' and 'confusions', was 'too apologetic' and understated the value and success of the government's 'experiment'. Ministers had a point. The 1935 commission report recycled much of the earlier reports by Portal and his fellow investigators. Stewart had received the similar deputations from South Wales, visited the same local authorities and heard the same representations and prescriptions. They were part and parcel of Lloyd George's new deal and were to find their way into Professor Hilary Marquand's 1937 South Wales Plan.

The Whitehall official interdepartmental committee's report to ministers consigned many of Stewart's recommendations into the category of 'suggestions which seem open to serious objection'. Into this category went recommendations for a shorter working week, holidays with pay, preference for the unemployed in local and government contracts and the more radical idea of a levy served upon industries that left the distressed areas. A proposal to introduce early retirement with a modest pension for older miners was at least aired in ministerial discussions, and attracted a measure of support from the Minister for Labour. If confined to older miners who had been out of work the scheme would have taken 200,000 off the 'live register'. Chamberlain speedily squashed the idea. The fall in the birth rate held consequences for the future labour force. There 'ought, therefore, to be no payment to induce the elderly to leave industry'. Instead the committee was attracted to a proposal for compulsory practical physical training of the unemployed under 21 and a medical examination for unemployed juveniles. Officials had also found practical objections to the development of a hydrogenation coal to oil plant in South Wales. ICI's pilot project at Billingham, Teesside had not yet proved the viability of hydrogenation, while it would be necessary to find out more about a new German 'natural' temperature process which would allow much smaller units than that at Billingham to be worked economically.[8]

Mid thirties' debates on the political economy have, understandably, focussed on the titanic confrontation between the interventionists, Lloyd George and John Maynard Keynes and a Treasury and Chancellor's commitment to market forces. While such a fundamental divide existed, some flexibility and nuances could be found within Whitehall. At the beginning of 1935 Sir Richard Hopkins, Treasury deputy secretary, who, within Whitehall was the greatest influence upon distressed areas' thinking, presented Chamberlain with a persuasive minute: 'The state of the general recovery' he argued, was one at which 'an expansion of public borrowing would be useful for keeping up the impetus'. 'Borrowing must in the main come from local authorities and other public or quasi-public bodies rather than the state itself.' Hopkins, however, explained that paradoxically the need for new public works fell primarily in the greater London area where little provision had been made 'for a large and continuous flux of population'. The distressed areas were probably those least in need of public works 'though where the immediate employment value of such works was greater'. He offered Chamberlain 'a rough illustration' of a programme that should be launched under a new act to authorise the appropriate government department to give grants towards the interest and a sinking fund on moneys borrowed by local authorities and other public and statutory bodies: railway electrification (£15 - £20 million), renewal of bridges (£5m) land drainage (£5 million). From the 1935 debates and discussions two significant schemes of value to South Wales emerged as contenders for

71

such Treasury backed productive public works. The first became one of the most influential industrial infrastructures of the late thirties. The second became a sad saga of missed opportunities.

'A Gateway to South Wales'

The story of the Severn Bridge became one of the saddest sagas in Welsh public infrastructure development. Mooted first during the 1840s, the bridge was eventually completed in 1965. For generations the Severn estuary had attracted the dreamer and the schemer. The legendary Brunel dreamt of a remarkable canal combined with a high timber swing bridge at Awre to carry across to South Wales the London/Gloucester railway. During the 1870s as many as six different schemes were launched, including a combined road and rail bridge, before, eventually the Great Western Railway's bill for a tunnel cleared all parliamentary hurdles. The rail tunnel was opened in 1886.

The 1920s witnessed a revival of interest in alternative crossings. The GWR itself proposed a new rail/road bridge to ease the growing congestion at the Severn tunnel. That was, in turn, overtaken by the much more visionary concept of a barrage. The barrage attracted a measure of government support. The Ministry of Transport considered it could 'open up a vision which is little short of a revolution in the industrial life of the West and the Midlands'. It would effectively solve the problems of congestion of all traffic between South Wales and the West of England, and bring 'within reach of all classes of the community the blessings of light, purity and power'. An official committee to investigate the barrage concept eventually reported in 1930, but cast fatal doubt upon the feasibility of the scheme.

Commissioner Stewart resuscitated a bridge scheme by backing in 1935/36 a joint Gloucester/Monmouthshire County proposal. In October 1935 he exercised his power of recommendation under section 2 (3) of the Special Areas Act to urge the Ministry of Transport to grant 75%, some £2.5 million, towards the construction of a bridge over the Severn at English Stones. The bridge, he claimed, would 'open a new gateway to South Wales,' which would assist the economic recovery of the Welsh special areas, while also finding for work 'a fair proportion' of unemployed miners. The Severn Bridge scheme even found favour with the Chancellor, the Treasury and the cabinet committee on the distressed areas. Reviewing a number of major public projects (the Thames tunnel, the Humber, Forth and Severn bridges), they concluded that the Severn scheme represented 'an attractive' economic prospect which would also provide work for South Wales. The Ministry of Transport announced a 75% grant in December 1935.

Tragically, the bridge scheme foundered on the rocks of the arcane parliamentary private bill procedure. The Gloucestershire and Monmouthshire bill promoted before the three man bill committee was confronted by a powerful collection of alternative interests. A host of South Wales local authorities lined up behind the two county councils, while the ports of Bristol and Gloucester, the Newport harbour board and borough council, and the Severn ferry company petitioned strenuously against the bill. A number of objectors played heavily upon the rate burden to finance 12.5% of the scheme (the remaining 12.5% being collected in tolls). The most powerful lobby against the bridge, the GWR, countered the economic case presented by Professor Hilary Marquand. The rail company sought to sow fear of 'considerable and incalculable damage to the structure of the existing rail tunnel'. Water might enter due to fissures created by the construction of the bridge. The company's docks at Newport, Cardiff, Penarth and Barry would be further adversely affected by the 'physically unsound, uneconomic and unnecessary' project. The GWR were particularly opposed to a scheme 'expressly designed to benefit their competitors' This powerful lobby prevailed before the committee which, after the initial hearings, peremptorily dismissed the bill. Astonishingly, considering the significance of the scheme, the Commons accepted the committee's findings without as much as a parliamentary peep. Desultory parliamentary efforts to revive the scheme in 1937 and 1938 were easily parried by government ministers who invoked the more urgent immediate expenditure priorities of national defence.[10]

Treforest

In March 1937 a Board of Trade official minuted:

> 'Sir Malcolm had been pressing for some time for government approval for his proposal to establish his estates. When the government came to draw up the election programme for the 1935 election they wanted some proposals in regards to special areas. The legal difficulties setting up the estate under the Special Areas Act which had been previously insurmountable were overcome and the provision of trading estates approved in the election programme ...'[11]

The prospect of a general election, as much as Sir Malcolm Stewart, shaped government attitudes towards unemployment during the second half of 1935. Whitehall had initially greeted Stewart's recommendation for government financed trading estates with a familiar scepticism. Sir Horace Wilson had sounded out in 1931 the two successful private estate companies (Slough and Trafford Park) to expand their activities into the depressed areas, only to receive a negative response. They were 'unlikely to prove economic'. When Mr Tribe, the secretary to the commission, informed the Board of Trade officials in mid 1935 that Stewart might press such a case, they had reacted scathingly. 'It was improbable that such an inducement would be sufficient to overcome objections which might be present in the mind of industrialists'. 'It was hopeless nowadays to expect private enterprise to extract gold from sea-water'. Officials, nevertheless, cynically concluded that it might be preferable to go along with 'the experiment' which was, at least, open to much less serious objection than the use of government money in direct assistance to competitive enterprise. They decided to frame their response in the least objectionable way. When the issue came before the cabinet committee on distressed areas, Chamberlain backed the idea as 'constructive' though a lively debate led by a recently appointed additional minister to the committee, Lord Eustace Percy, doubted whether trading estates 'in one of the mining valleys would ever be successful'. Percy argued for the extension of the special areas to include Cardiff and the Glamorgan coastline where there could be hope for development. Chamberlain countered by indicating that the existing legislation would allow the commissioner to spend upon development in the Cardiff area.

The go ahead was given by Stewart for the first government trading estate at Team Valley in the North East of England. He delayed proceeding in South Wales because there 'was already a company planning a trading estate on novel lines' and he wanted to avoid the embarrassment of a competing scheme. When, by 1936, that scheme had fallen through, Stewart authorised site investigations by Alexander Gibbs and Partners. Their initial reports made gloomy reading. 'An even more impenetrable gloom lies over South Wales than the north East, which together with the prejudices in the mind of the ordinary businessman regarding the type of labour hampers efforts to persuade industry to come west'. 'Cardiff and South Wales may be 100 miles nearer London and the South East but it seems at the end of the Great West Road'. The North East with its excellent Tyne coastal service made it possible 'to locate production in proximity to markets'. South Wales without the Severn Bridge was only 'in proximity to its labour'.[12]

74

Despite these prognostications and after consideration of other alternatives, Dowlais, Cyfarthfa, Panteg and Cwmbran, a suitable site at Treforest was identified. By December 1936, work had begun upon a 150 acre site to house some 75 factories at the cost of £450,000, linked by a railbridge across the Taff which would allow four fifths of the tenants to have private sidings to their factories. Local materials were to be used whenever possible while contractors recruited 500 men through the Pontypridd employment exchange, drawn from the surrounding districts proportionately to the percentage unemployed in each area. The 'Roads Beautifying Association' had been called in to set out the roads, recreation grounds and factory forecourts with trees, shrubs and flowers. A booklet was prepared to promote the estate. Stewart had formed a new non-profit making company, the South Wales and Monmouthshire Trading Estate Company Limited, to develop the site, financed from a commission loan of £800,000 at 4%. Its chairman, Colonel Gerald Bruce, a member of a major local solicitors' practice Morgan, Bruce Nicholas, was accompanied by seven other directors appointed by Stewart (including Crawshay) and one government appointed director H J Bostock. Thus, the first South Wales trading estate was established to be run by a company which, for the following twenty five years led the process of industrial regeneration.[13]

The Re-opening of the Ebbw Vale Works

Chamberlain and Baldwin privately feared the electoral consequences of high unemployment much more than they ever admitted publicly. With the knowledge of hindsight of the comfortable election victory in November 1935, such concerns now seem curious; they were very real at the time. Despite the rigid public adherence to the party and government line over 'inducements' and government intervention, the prospect of a general election prompted a new pragmatism. Chamberlain skilfully manipulated the jobs implications of the rearmament programme. On the eve of the election, his speech to the Scottish Conservatives linked unemployment and rearmament. Increased armaments meant more hope for the depressed areas, securing employment on cruiser, aircraft and small arms construction projects. His election broadcast in November underlined falling unemployment (40,000 in October) but also unveiled a five year £100 million roads programme. More 'goodies' followed: the Cunard White Star Liner, Olympic, was to be towed and broken up at the redundant Palmer's ship year in Jarrow, creating eighteen months work for the unemployed shipyard workers and £100,000 in wages. The Admiralty announced, on 31 October its new construction programme of one leader and eight destroyers, reversing previous government policies of choosing the lowest tenders by directing work to Clydeside, Tynemouth and Birkenhead. On the same day, 31 October, Richard Thomas and Co announced the acquisition and reopening of the Ebbw Vale Works.[14]

The omens for Ebbw Vale could not have been poorer at the beginning of 1935. Portal's pleas in 1934 had fallen on deaf ears within Whitehall. Indeed, his persistent representations had alienated the Chancellor, and had probably cost him the chairmanship of the Unemployment Assistance Board. Chamberlain had considered his arguments as 'crude' and, perhaps, had been further peeved by Portal's attempts to go over his head to Macdonald. Portal had written to the Prime Minister as 'a personal friend' and to one at whose 'instigation he had gone to South Wales'. Sir Wyndham reported that he had to date been offered little encouragement from either the Ebbw Vale company or the chief industrial adviser, Sir Horace Wilson. The works were 'in the wrong place and not well planned'; but they were for Portal 'so critical' that 'something must be done' A plan for the works had to be formulated. He felt it would be necessary 'to put forward his views in the very near future to Betterton, the Chancellor and yourself'.[15] Macdonald's reply had offered no encouragement. 'It might be useful for you to know that your suggestion about subsidising the works in South Wales has upset some folks here'.

'It could not be confined to South Wales and cuts across the pressure that is being brought to bear on that industry to reorganise itself ...'. 'It is not considered sound, moreover, on its own merit.'

Reorganisation, the need for investment in new American style continuous wide stripmill techniques, pointed not towards re-opening at Ebbw Vale but to an accelerated closure programme of a host of small south and west Wales tin-plate works. To meet US competition, Sir William Firth, chairman of Richard Thomas, proposed that the industry co-operate in building on a new greenfield site at Redbourne, Lincolnshire a plant capable of 150,000 tons a year at an annual saving of £200,000. Such a project would have not only demolished any hopes of re-opening Ebbw Vale but jeopardised the rest of the south and west Wales industry. A deputation representing commercial, trading and industrial interests from Llanelli to Cardiff impressed upon the President of the Board of Trade and the Minister for Labour on 23, October 1935 the seriousness of the threat to the industry. A 40,000 petition from the joint interests of commerce and industry of Monmouthshire made the same case.

The re-opening of the Ebbw Vale works was a politically and electorally inspired decision. Nothing else explains Sir William Firth's abrupt abandonment of his Redbourne works scheme. Indeed, a queue gathered to claim the credit for the decision including a Prime Minister, a commissioner for the special areas as well as the company chairman. Commissioner Stewart (in his second report) offered a lengthy apology and explanation of his own efforts and involvement. He had commissioned a steel expert, Mr Brassert, to prepare a reconstruction scheme, had got in touch with several financiers 'of the highest standing' and had gained the sympathy of Sir Andrew Duncan, chairman of Britain's Iron and Steel Federation. Prior to the successful announcement in December 1935 he had been 'in constant touch' with Sir William Firth.[16]

Others were quick to claim the credit and none more so than the Prime Minister himself. At a speech in Newcastle (12th November) Baldwin welcomed the news, as an illustration of the government at work bringing back hope to neighbourhoods and the result of tariff support given to the steel industry. Baldwin claimed a personal involvement: 'I have helped quietly out of the limelight to do my best in pushing it along". He had been 'very unhappy' with the proposal 'to move a great portion of one of the staple South Wales' industries way up into Lincolnshire'.

> 'I felt that it was wrong for responsible people not to
> recognise their responsibilities to the people who had
> worked for them in an area that was beginning to have bad luck ....
> I rejoice to think that the men who had contemplated this
> change on thinking it over, have accepted that view of mine ...'

Locally, Aneurin Bevan felt under certain pressure from the politicking around the re-opening. He admitted to his wife that 'Lady Firth, wife of the M.D.' was 'stirring up a much trouble as she can. It is much more difficult than we expected'. His Conservative opponent, Miss F.E. Scarborough, had also made some attempts to capitalise upon the situation, inviting Bevan to join with her in making representations. Sir William Firth, the chairman of the company, however, gave the whole credit for the reopening to the National government. He roundly denied that either the commissioner for the special areas or Mr Aneurin Bevan could claim any credit. In a bizarre press interview, constructed in the form of a mock imaginary interview between Sir William Firth and 'a Socialist', Firth claimed that Stewart and co. had erred in concentrating on negotiations with motor car manufacturing, not realising that motor car consumption of steel at 100,000 tons a year was far too little to sustain a plant of 300,000 tons. Stewart just 'didn't know anything about the steel industry. That's the trouble when you put the right man in the wrong place.' The credit was 'due, not to Mr Malcolm Stewart, not to Mr Bevan, not to Richard Thomas and Co. but absolutely and entirely due to the National government who had given protection against foreign tariffs.'[17]

If electoral policies had played a significant part in the re-opening, industry politics subsequently contributed to the troubled reconstruction which nearly destroyed the Richard Thomas Company. Sir William Firth continued to follow an erratic industrial path. In April 1936, the company floated another programme to establish a stripmill near Corby in Lincolnshire. Firth claimed that 'it would be absurd to build a modern works in South Wales.' Northamptonshire and Lincolnshire were undoubtedly the natural centres for economic production of British Steel. 'Welshmen must be prepared to live where production could be most economically effected rather than protest that where they live was where employment should be provided', thus embroiling himself in another political row.

Firth's critics and competitors sought revenge over a 'rebel'. Adverse financial comment on the company's cash problems, an indifferent debenture issue in early 1937 and frightening escalating costs at Ebbw Vale nearly brought the works to a stop and the company to its knees. Only temporary refinancing of the company on humiliating terms saved the reconstruction. In return for an extended £6 million loan, negotiated with the support of the Bank of England, control of the company passed to a committee of bankers. Three leading steel industry chairmen were added to the board. Sir William remained notionally as chairman. Production at Ebbw Vale eventually began in September 1938 and by April 1939 the plant was operating at 70%, employing 3,500 men, rising to 6,000 at the outbreak of war.[18]

The re-opening of the Ebbw Vale Steelworks became one of the few pre-war victories achieved by political pressure. South Wales, nevertheless, remained politically marginalised. The Labour party in Wales gained a greater percentage of the vote during the 1935 general election than the National government but remained a poor second in Great Britain. Unemployment had not seriously threatened the National government electorally. It fell in 1935 below the 2 million mark for the first time since 1931. The 1935 budget had restored the salary cuts imposed upon the public services in 1931, had offered tax relief for wage earners who had also enjoyed real increases over the four year period. The selective, politically astute use of public expenditure, especially on the rearmament's programme blunted opposition appeals on unemployment. Even in Jarrow, following the re-opening of the Palmer's Yard, Eleanor Wilkinson, the new Labour candidate, could only scrape home. In Scotland, the Labour party could only capture 20 of the 71 seats, while in the north west, Bolton, Oldham, Preston, Stockport and Salford failed to return a single Labour MP. More suprisingly, in the north east Sunderland Stockton and Hartlepool were held for the government.

In 1931 the National government had run a poster of an unemployed worker pleading for a job. In 1935 the poster was updated to bear the message: 'they kept their word and gave me a job; help them to keep it for me.'[19]

'A Mistake'

1. UAB's Problems: R.Lowe, *Adjusting to Democracy; The Role of the Ministry of Labour in Britain, Politics 1916-1939*, 154-190: On the benefits crisis, F Miller, The British Unemployment Assistance Crisis of 1935, Journal of Contemporary History 14 (1979).

2. Lowe, *Adjusting to Democracy*, 176

3. The Chamberlain/Stewart exchanges: T161/669/S39853/1; MH61/2; Stewart's first report, July 1935, Cmnd 4957.

4. Stewart's exchanges with Stanley and officials: HLG 30/13; BT55/14,15; MT61/13; T172/1821; Stewart's policy statement, BT55/15; MT61/13

'Palliatives'

5. The commission's organisation and staff; LAB 12/58; BT55/14.

6. The commissioner's reports list the approved schemes. Crawshay's survey of the South Wales district, the commission's 4th report 1938, stated that £1.2 Million had been spent in water and sewerage services £720,000 in hospitals and healthy care and 15 open air swimming pools had been authorised. Approved schemes exceeded £2 million.

Return to the Land

7. Whitehall's discussion and memorandum on the return to land policy: MAF 70/175, 70/133; F18/182; T172/1828. Stewart's support for the Welsh Land Trust, his second report, Feb 1936 Cmnd 5090,60. The establishment of and records of the Trust and Co-operative; MAF70/133-139, 143, 187,192,194; MAF Welsh Dept MT70/85,86. The cabinet committee's discussion on Crawshay's American style national park, CAB27/578.

'Crudities and Confusions'

8. Stewart's visit, for example, to Merthyr Tydfil LAB 23/75. Discussions on the 1st report, CAB27/578.

9. Treasury and Sir Richard Hopkins' view T172/1828.

'A Gateway to South Wales'

10. The various attempts to bridge the Severn; BD30/13, MT95/164. Severn barrage proposals; BT63/106,192. The three member select committee, Sir David Reid, Mr Ben Smith, Mr Brocklebank, minutes of proceedings of the select committee. H.L.R.O, Thursday 23 April 1936.

'Treforest'

11. BT6411/IMI981.

12. Discussion on the establishment of trading estates; CAB 27/578,579.

13. BT 194/32.

14. For details of the 1935 election campaign and Chamberlain's public works programme. T. Stannage, *Baldwin Thwarts the Opposition: The British General Election, 1935*, Croom Helm, 1980.

15. Chamberlain's reaction to Portal's representations N C2/23A, The Chamberlain Papers, Birmingham University: Portal's correspondence with MacDonald, PRO 30/69/680/2.

16. Stewart's support for the reopening of Ebbw Vale, second report, Cmnd 5090, paras 21-32.

17. Baldwin's Newcastle speech *The Times*, 13, November 1935, Michael Foot, Aneurin Bevan, 1, 217-219. Sir Williams Firth's interview, Western Mail, 13 Nov 1938.

18. Sir William Firth's disputes with the Bank of England, Bank of England Records, SMT2/162-166

19. The best analysis of the 1935 general election, J Stevenson and Chris Cook, *Britain in the Depression, Society and politics, 1929-1939*,

(Longman 1994)

Election results in Wales: Labour polled 46.59% winning 18 seats.
The National Government polled 44.02% winning 11 seats.
(Conservative 7, Liberal Nationalists 3, National Labour 1) The Liberals
won 6 seats.

In the United Kingdom the National Government polled 45.7% of the
vote and won 435 seats (Labour 154, Samuelite Liberals 19,
Communist 1, Irish Partitionists 2).

4

1936: 'SOMETHING MUST BE DONE'.

The euphoria of the general election victory rapidly evaporated. 1936 proved to be an increasingly uncomfortable year for the government. The unemployment benefit demonstrations of 1935 gave way to the hunger marches, and, especially, to the great Jarrow march, culminating in November 1936 in the largest unemployment demonstration of the decade. The distressed areas' case reached a much wider and more sympathetic public. It became obvious that 'the general improvement in trade' served only to emphasise the gulf between the distressed areas and the rest of Britain. The commission for the special areas' own figures underlined how little government policy and action had dented the remorseless levels of unemployment in South Wales. In Glamorgan, 33% were out of work, the figure rose to 60% in Merthyr Tydfil - while the British average was 12.9%. A total of 123.052 Glamorgan men, women and juveniles were wholly unemployed in September 1936.

Agitation in the streets fed into Westminster where a vocal group of northern government members threatened rebellion. Within Whitehall, the debates between commissioner Stewart and officials became progressively more acrimonious and came to a head with the completion of his third and most critical report, which coincided with his resignation on personal ill health grounds. Stewart called for 'a second experiment', new inducements to attract industry into the special areas and restrictions upon the booming London and South East. It was an unpalatable message to send to Chamberlain and officials for it challenged basic tenets of government policy, and also, because it was delivered at a peculiarly sensitive moment.

The phrase 'something must be done', reputedly uttered on at least three occasions by King Edward VIII during a two day visit to South Wales in November 1936, has become a part of valley folklore and royal legend. From the government's point of view ,the untimely visit only added to the pressure. In response, Chamberlain unilaterally overrode the overwhelming official objections to Stewart's new 'inducements' and on the eve of the King's visit to South Wales, rose in the Commons to announce his 'acceptance of the commissioner's report and a second experiment'.

'Don't you say a word against South Wales ...'.

Accumulative political and public pressure forced a shift in policy during the course of 1936. That pressure came not only from the politicians, but from a host of ad hoc non political groups that mushroomed in the thirties. One such group was the bishop of Llandaf's committee. The bishop had written to Baldwin in July 1935 to explain the origin and purpose of the newly formed committee. He had taken the step of calling together a private, entirely non party conference of the principal leaders of industry in South Wales and Monmouthshire, 'with the view to discovering whether local knowledge and experience' might not 'supplement' the efforts of the commissioner for the special areas and to discover 'solutions to the problems of reviving the endurable prosperity of Wales'. Comprising prominent industrialists, church and academic leaders, the committee appears to have been primarily motivated by objections to the commissioner's first special areas report. Stewart's 'pessimistic advocacy of compulsory transference' angered the bishop's committee, causing 'anxiety mounting to consternation in South Wales'. The bishop warned the Prime Minister of 'the serious consequences if it came to be generally believed the policy of the government is one of abandonment rather than the revival'.

Revival of the South Wales economy required the appointment of a commissioner exclusively for the area, with a £2 million budget. Such an appointment, would 'go far to allay the profound anxiety raised as a result of the pronouncement in favour of an intensive policy of transference.' The bishop's committee had, indeed, gone so far as to identify their choice of commissioner, Mr Gibson Jarvie, chairman of Credit for Industry Ltd. Besides this appointment, the remainder of the committee's prescriptions had a familiar ring: the building of a Severn bridge, afforestation, rate relief for local authorities, the relocation to South Wales of a whole or part of the Woolwich arsenal and grants to new companies. Not surprisingly, given the composition of the committee, there was also a call for rail freight relief for South Wales goods.

A rather more original demand emanated from the bishop himself. He pressed Whitehall to support the distribution of surplus food stuffs at especially discounted rates to the unemployed. Drawing attention to the experimental scheme run by the potato marketing board in the north east, the bishop argued for an extended programme covering nutritious foodstuffs such as milk, eggs, fish, bacon and meat 'all of which are either lacking or unduly limited in the dietary of the unemployed'. The cost of any such subsidised foodstuffs should be borne by the new Welsh commissioner's budget.[1]

The committee's proposals received short shrift in Whitehall despite a succession of meetings between its members and Sir Malcolm Stewart, Sir Thomas Phillips, (permanent secretary at the Ministry of Labour) and eventually with the minister, Ernest Brown. Preparatory briefing by officials for the encounter had scathingly disparaged the committee's 'conceptions'. Mr Hubert Wolfe, one of the ministry's more idiosyncratic officials confessed their replies were bound to be disappointing for the very good reason that the bishop's committee's main proposals were fundamentally 'unsound'. There were 'the best reasons in the world for refusing to listen to any such scheme as the appointment of a Welsh commissioner'. Such an appointment would introduce 'a new disturbing element' in the government's 'experiment for the special areas'. It would not only create 'grave extravagance but seriously interfere with the work done by Mr Stewart and 'probably by repercussions react unfavourably upon the Scottish commissioner'. The very notion of giving a Welsh commission £2 million 'to spend as he chose' was 'fantastic'. It also implied assistance by such a commission to private enterprise, 'a conception' expressly ruled out by the Chancellor from the outset.[2]

The meeting between the bishop's committee and Ernest Brown ended in considerable acrimony. Brown, who had succeeded Stanley before the general election, could not have been a greater contrast to his predecessor. A prominent non-conformist with a booming baptist voice, Ernest Brown had begun his parliamentary career as a Liberal member for Leith. He had followed Sir John Simon (later Viscount Simon), in 1931, as a Liberal national candidate, holding junior ministerial posts in health and mines before going to the Ministry of Labour. Brown, most unfortunately, inherited the odium of the UAB benefits regime which made him an obvious target for protest groups.

The Minister's antagonist on the committee personified the tradition of the South Wales coalfield. D.R. Llewellyn, the eldest son of an Aberdare colliery manager, had begun his career as a mining surveyor, later qualifying as an engineer. His technical skills and business acumen brought him chairmanships of local anthracite companies before his partnership with Seymour Berry led to larger acquisitions. The consolidations and amalgamations of the late twenties and early thirties, involving GKN and Powell Duffryn, enhanced Llewellyn's influence and status. He was a natural choice for the bishop's committee.

At the ministerial confrontation, Sir David denounced Stewart's first report as 'feeble'. 'There had been better essays at the Eisteddfod'. Brown was stung into an unfortunate rejoinder. 'There is a great deal said in South Wales that we would not consider gospel'. Llewellyn exploded: 'Is that a reflection upon my nationality? You ought to be grateful to South Wales for returning four national members to the government who have not done anything for them. Other people like Sheffield whom you spoon-fed returned socialists. Don't you say a word against South Wales'.[3]

The fruitless nature of these exchanges did not deter the deputations. A few months later it was the turn of the all party Welsh parliamentary party to depute to the Prime Minister. A private and confidential memorandum submitted by Reginald Clarry, Conservative MP for Newport, on behalf of the all party group covered once again familiar territory. Painting a depressing 'deplorable' picture of unemployment, accentuated by the recent closure of Penarth Docks, another indicator of declining prospects, the group demanded 'the exceptional treatment' promised by Chamberlain in 1934. The Welsh members shared with the bishop's committee the criticism of the commission for special areas' powers and performance. 'The machinery so far set up had produced little if any improvement and certainly had not come up to expectations!' 'Something of a vicious circle' had developed. Complaints on proposals submitted to the government were being referred to the commissioner who only pointed out that he had no power to deal with them and as 'a consequence referred it back to the place from which it originated'. The commission 'had money to spend but no power to spend it!'

Given the all party nature of the group, it surprisingly recommended 'new machinery' - 'a corporation' empowered to raise money with government guarantees to develop hydrogenation, low temperature carbonisation, calcium carbon ferrous chrome plants 'whose products would reduce or eliminate imports and also burn coal'. While commending the recently created special areas reconstruction association (S.A.R.A.), the MPs considered the circumstances demanded a more comprehensive treatment. Foreign firms, for example, should be allowed to set up only in special areas. The Welsh parliamentary party's other central demand involved the appointment of an employment planning authority, charged with the task of expediting the group's proposals, an authority including representatives of local authorities, government departments, as well as industrial and financial interests. The administration of the authority should be placed in the hands of a 'capable energetic' director, full time and well paid. The parliamentary party's employment planning authority foreshadowed the post war Welsh development council.

The Treasury undertook the task of co-ordinating, for Downing Street, Whitehall's responses. They, wearily, rehearsed a familiar line: the government's willingness 'to experiment' with trading estates, land settlement, and the newly created S.A.R.A. The government had been willing to offer a large grant to build the Severn Bridge only to come up against opposition from, among others, Newport Borough Council! South Wales was 'constantly borne in mind' in the munitions relocation programme, though sadly Wales could benefit little from other government contracts because there were few general engineering firms. The Treasury reserved its greatest scorn for the idea of 'a corporation' underpinned by guarantees. It was 'unthinkable' that government should subsidise factories run at a loss. Officials tartly noticed the absence of any reference to 'transference', 'possibly because so much of South Wales was hostile to it'. The Welsh parliamentary party's programme said 'nothing of the need for action and initiative on the part of South Wales itself. It openly assumes that it is for government to come and do everything'. [4]

Discussion between South Wales and Whitehall had reached something of an impasse. The area's demands had crystallised around government action to promote large new technology plants, which would consume the surplus coal, public sector projects and the relocation of armaments production. The government of Chamberlain and Baldwin was just not in the game of public investment in private industry. While prepared to negotiate useful coal trade deals to improve exports, ministers clung to the belief that transference of surplus miners would prove a more viable solution than any artificial scheme to consume surplus coal. Yet there surfaced within the Treasury in early 1936 a tentative recognition that something more might have to be done. An unusually frank internal minute written to accompany the briefing for the Welsh Parliamentary Party acknowledged that:

> 'the general reply to Mr Lloyd George (and other MPs) to the
> effect that the government rely on their general trade policy
> to bring about a steady and growing improvement in
> employment as against his grandiose remedies is a
> little difficult to apply to South Wales, for though there
> has been an improvement in trade there is no
> substantive improvement in the unemployment figures ...'.

One sensible pragmatic remedy to assist coal consumption did lie at hand; a remedy pressed by Lord Weir, one of the semi-detached industrial advisers to Whitehall. The Weir family had made their fortune manufacturing boilers, heaters and pumps for shipping. William Weir had stalked Whitehall's corridors for more than a decade. His reports in 1925 on electricity supply, astonishingly recommending in practice nationalisation of supply and the construction of a national grid, had led to the establishment of the Central Electricity Board. Weir turned to electricity bulk supply for succour to the distressed coalfields. Consulted by the government's official adviser, Sir Horace Wilson, Weir scorned the potential for hydrogenation. 'That was neither justifiable on political or economic grounds'. He graphically described to officials the alternative. Recalling a recent flight over the Thames new power stations at Barking and Dagenham, Weir argued that the country should not increase its 'vulnerability to air attack'. 'Cheaply produced electricity could be generated in large new power stations totalling 2,000MW capacity, fed by South Wales coal and sold into the midlands and southern industrial markets'.

The CEB peremptorily dismissed Weir's proposal. Distrusting the radical trade union tradition in South Wales, which it was considered would endanger supplies to England, the Board also cast doubt on the cheapness of South Wales electricity. It conducted a brief investigation into the costs of locating electricity supplies from South Wales to prove its unviability. The government, initially, threatened the Board with the withholding of authorisation of a south east England power station if it did not consider South Wales, but quickly gave way. Surprisingly, few in South Wales pursued the case for a power station programme which later became the salvation of the South Wales coal field.[5]

'The Situation in Merthyr Tydfil'

One man and one town got further than either the episcopal or the parliamentary deputations. On 2nd September 1936, the cabinet agenda included an item, 'the situation in Merthyr Tydfil'. It had been partly triggered by the remarkable personal intervention of Alderman Frank Treharne James. Alderman James was a rare, if not unique creature - a government supporter from Merthyr Tydfil and, as such, his letter caught the attention of the Minister of Health, Sir Kingsley Wood. Writing as a member of the Corporation for over 30 years, James came to the defence of his beleaguered county borough, seeking to correct the scathing and unflattering Whitehall opinion of its administration. Merthyr County Borough's finances and administration had been the subject of successive probes and enquiries since the late 1920s. Holding the unenviable record of the highest rate in the land, the borough had been pleading with officials and ministers for relief from the burgeoning burden of public assistance for the unemployed. More than half the rate had to be devoted to unemployment relief. The Portal report had confidentially advised ministers that Merthyr could no longer sustain the status of county borough. Faced with that recommendation, they had, in 1935, appointed a royal commission which duly found the authority incapable of sustaining county borough services.

The government's supporter Alderman James, however, sought to persuade ministers that they should address the underlying cause of Merthyr's malaise - 'the overwhelming unemployment factor'. James' prescription, 'the definite and absolute steps' the government had to take, proved unwelcome and uncomfortable to officials. A government sponsored re-opening of the Dowlais iron works and the relocation of an armaments factory to the town met the usual scepticism. The commission for the special areas considered a publicly financed ironworks unthinkable. In its place the commission could only come up with three small sewerage schemes, open air swimming pools and possibly a £70,000 surface water drainage scheme. [6]

Kingsley Wood, however, remained uneasy about the bland official reply that the Merthyr Tydfil situation would be kept 'under close review'. He minuted the permanent secretary, Sir George Crystal, suggesting that the ministers of health and labour should prepare a memorandum for cabinet to underline the ways in which Merthyr was 'an exceptional case distinguishable from other areas'. The various drafts circulating through Whitehall sought to fulfil that remit. They charted Merthyr's industrial collapse. 16,000 miners had only recently mined some 3 million tons from 34 pits. Now in 1936 there were only 4,250 in nine pits (three employing less than ten) coaling only 1.5 million tons. While officials identified other individual communities with higher rates of unemployment, Merthyr's exceptional situation lay not in the extremity of any one aspect of deprivation but in the composite deprivation of the community.

The final draft cabinet memorandum stressed the state of health of the borough's population. A definite physical deterioration among the population could be detected - with the percentage of under or badly nourished children having recently risen from 16.5% to 23%. Dr Stevens, the local medical officer of health, was quoted as saying that 'as a general rule meat is only purchased in any quantities at weekends' and 'we have seldom seen fresh milk in the households visited'. The cabinet on 2nd September first confirmed that ministers had no intention of depriving Merthyr of its county borough status by a merger with Glamorgan county, as recommended by the royal commission. Such a merger would have required a subsidy and some form of central control over Merthyr's affairs. The joint health and labour memorandum stressed the abnormally high level of unemployment, the physical and psychological effects for which bad local administration could not be wholly held responsible.

'A seriously disquieting situation should be met
by the establishment of a government factory under
the rearmament programme. Apart from the number
of people employed, it would have a marked and
immediate effect upon the morale of the
population of whom a large number were giving up
hope and becoming all the more bitter as they saw
themselves destitute in the midst of returning and
increasing prosperity in the country generally'.[7]

The subsequent cabinet discussion reflected the jaundiced official assessments of Merthyr's role and reliability in any rearmament programme. Sir Thomas Inskip, Minister for Co-ordination of Defence, warned the cabinet against 'any false hopes in this particular area which for various reasons was unsuitable for undertakings such as explosives or filling factories'. The British Oxygen company had refused to set up a factory in Merthyr on the grounds that cheap power was essential. The Secretary of State for War reported a similar response 'which had been in all respects very discouraging, though a glimmer of hope was held out that a duplicate to the ICI Billingham ammonia plant might be considered'. The cabinet lamely concluded that service ministers should look further and sympathetically upon the suggestion from the Minister of Health and Labour.[8]

'God bless the revolution ...'

The county borough could not have known of such secret cabinet discussions. Yet Merthyr's plight was certainly reaching a wider and increasingly sympathetic audience. Outside Whitehall, the town was becoming something of a national social cause celebre, attracting in the process some unlikely allies. A curious ginger group within the Conservative party, the Imperial policy group, espoused Merthyr's cause. Coal and iron had provided the sinews of the empire. Neglect or destruction of this capacity threatened to undermine imperial power. An honourable society should acknowledge the debt the nation owed to great traditional industrial communities.
A high profile visit to Merthyr in September 1936, by the group which included MPs Lennox Boyd (Bedfordshire), Victor Raikes (South East Essex) and A K Wise (Southwark), forthrightly denounced 'any government or political party which complacently ignore thousands of the finest workmen, left to stand at street corners day in day out'.

90

'It is no consolation to a man who has all the ambition,
courage and energy to hear that elderly cabinet ministers
are studying memorandum ... and are working out 21 reasons
why no recommendations ever made can be carried'.

proclaimed the group's secretary, Sir Kenneth de Courcy.

The group pledged to carry Merthyr's cause to Westminster, organising a month later a mayoral deputation to meet some fifty government back benchers. The mayor even addressed a gathering at the Dorchester while the Imperial policy group took the cause of the distressed area to the Conservative party conference in Scarborough. Sympathy and demands for action came from all quarters. When three hundred clergy gathered at Caxton Hall they heard Bishop Casey of Bloomfontein renounce his support and trust in the Conservative party.

'I am losing or have lost my faith ... If the government
does not provide a solution in South Wales,
then, when the bloody revolution comes from South Wales
I shall say 'God bless the revolution', for it will be the most righteous
thing that had ever happened'.

The Bishop of London, too, pledged to be Merthyr's 'loud speaker' in the House of Lords.[9]

'Our mysterious lady known as Sara ...'

Even before the crisis in the autumn of 1936, Chamberlain had made one further concession to the growing distressed areas' lobby - the establishment of the Special Areas Reconstruction Association (S.A.R.A). The genesis of the new organisation lay in the 1934 Portal report. Portal had emphasised the financial lacuna of favourable credit arrangements for companies locating in South Wales. He had called for a trust company formed by four or five industrialists working without remuneration but employing a full time managing director. The company should create local boards in each of the special areas offering favourable credit for new specialised industries. The interdepartmental official committee and the chief industrial adviser, Sir Horace Wilson, had initially poured cold water over the idea. He had consulted a Mr Gibson Jarvie, whose Credit for Industry Ltd had already attempted to offer such facilities to existing companies. Sir Horace reported that fundamentally the problem did not lie with credit facilities, but with far too many 'unsound' schemes.

Sir Malcolm Stewart's first report had made the case for such facilities, arguing that something more than Credit for Industry was required. That organisation lent essentially to existing companies against the security of their assets. Such facilities could not apply to new firms setting up in the distressed areas. Ministers, consequently, felt the need to respond. In early October 1935, Board of Trade officials had drafted a scheme by which the government would guarantee 25% of any losses incurred on loans given to develop distressed areas. Treasury officials and, especially, deputy secretary Hopkins remained sceptical. 'As a general rule where losses are made they would be total losses rather than the 25% and therefore a government offer to guarantee 25% would be unattractive except to philanthropists'. The idea was 'pretty horrible though it may be unavoidable'. Chamberlain, however, acknowledged some further step of an experimental character was unavoidable and recommended to ministerial colleagues, in October 1935, that he should consult the Governor of the Bank of England on the best way to implement such a scheme.[10]

The Bank of England had become inextricably involved in the post first world war process of industrial rationalisation. Banking commitment to armaments companies such as Armstrong Whitworth, the Lancashire cotton industry, ship building and steel had led to a collection of industrial securities which, in 1929, the Bank's Governor Montague Norman, gathered into one Trust, Security Management Trust (S.M.T.). A year later Norman supported the newly formed Bankers Industrial Development Corporation (B.I.D.C.), charged with the task of promoting company amalgamations and reconstruction. Norman also acknowledged the growing need for medium term credit to finance industrial re-equipment for smaller companies. He encouraged a new finance company United Dominion Trust (UDT) and its forceful head, Mr Gibson Jarvie. The Bank backed Jarvie's Credit for Industry Ltd to offer capital to companies which could not raise it through public issues.[11]

Norman shared Treasury officials' apprehensions over another venture capital company being mooted by Chamberlain. Such an organisation would only encourage unviable, unsound schemes which would have to be rejected and would consequently, fail to satisfy political expectation. Norman, nevertheless, grudgingly accepted the political necessity and preferred that the Bank shaped and limited the nature of such an operation, rather than allow political pressure to force ministers into even more offensive direct state interference in industrial and commercial activity. Norman put his own private secretary, Mr E.D.F. Skinner, in charge of developing the Bank's policy. Mr Skinner became a major influence in the birth of what became known as S.A.R.A, the Special Areas Reconstruction Association.

Having obtained, in October 1935, an approval from the committee of the treasury, the Bank's main executive body, Norman and Skinner, turned to Gibson Jarvie of UDT and Credit for Industry to flesh out proposals to put to officials and ministers. Jarvie's first suggestions, however, fuelled suspicion in the Bank that the putative company had been designed as much to drum up trade for UDT as any for companies in the distressed areas. Skinner noted that Jarvie had excluded other city competitors and minuted at one stage: 'probably the lot will fall into his mouth if he doesn't open it too wide at first'. Skinner, consequently, sought alternative advice from one of Jarvie's rivals, Edmund de Stein, of Mercantile, who offered a radically different structure for the company. Painstakingly, the Bank cajoled this rival pair into working up a compromise proposal to be put to Whitehall: S.A.R.A. would be subscribed to the tune of £1 million. They hoped to persuade what they called 'the outer fringe of the city' (trust houses, finance houses, big industrial and commercial undertakings) to subscribe £900,000 of preference capital while the Bank and its immediate friends would subscribe £100,000 ordinary capital. A small central board of directors, advised by area boards in the special areas, would approve loans of £5 - £10,000. The Treasury had to cover £25,000 in administrative costs.[12]

The early weeks of 1936 were spent in exhaustive haggling between the Bank and Treasury. The Treasury jibbed at picking up such a large administrative cost, explained by Skinner and co as inevitable in assessing the viability of the likely flood of small applications. Until the last moment the Treasury hoped the government would have, at least, priority in ultimately reclaiming such costs. Skinner was provoked to observe that the department was like 'Oliver Twist', always wanting more. Both Bank and Treasury officials remained deeply sceptical of the practical necessity and efficacy of the new organisation. Treasury officials found the Governor 'very depressed' that the new concern would do little or no business. Although offering to go back to Chamberlain, they reiterated that the Chancellor had been very 'thoroughly into the point' and had concluded that it remained desirable to proceed. Chamberlain had, indeed, made up his mind. While admitting that he was 'not sanguine of success' and that he would be 'surprised if a good part of any money lent is not lost', Chamberlain argued that it had always been his idea to try experiments in the special areas, and 'this one seems to me well worth trying'![13]

The Treasury and the Bank frantically endeavoured to conclude the necessary financing and legislative arrangements to establish S.A.R.A. before any leak revealed the character of their 'mysterious lady, Sara'. A leak would raise questions and hopes when the money to launch the scheme had not been obtained. An increasingly exasperated Governor pressed Chamberlain to give him a firm legislative timetable to put to potential subscribers. Government whips, however, offered little prospect of legislating before the Easter recess, thus forcing ministers to stall on the mounting parliamentary demands. An anodyne form of words was drafted, enabling the Minister of Labour, Ernest Brown to handle questions in the Commons' censure motion (3rd March 1936) and for the paymaster general to reply to Portal in the Lords (12 March). Procrastinating ministerial statements only served to alienate an exasperated commissioner Stewart and add to his deteriorating relationship with Whitehall. Stewart sensed that he was being frozen out of the discussions. He was. Treasury officials felt it might be disastrous 'just at this moment to turn Mr Stewart loose on the Bank'. Chamberlain refused to meet him, deputing Sir Horace Wilson to smooth ruffled feathers. Security over S.A.R.A survived for the Chancellor to announce its birth in his 1936 April budget statement. Chamberlain was at pains to explain to the Commons the experimental nature of the scheme, which did not profess to be the total solution. Interest rates on the loans would be kept as low as possible, but they would have to be fixed 'slightly above the rates available to good borrowers'. A short bill establishing the Special Areas Reconstruction Association was rushed through all its stages in May 1936 and attracted the usual opposition criticism of government policy. Mr Jones, Caerphilly, voiced the general sentiment of South Wales members. S.A.R.A would only offer funds to small businesses while South Wales needed industries on a bigger scale.[14]

The Bank and Whitehall hurriedly sought to raise the cash and appoint central and area boards. The Treasury and the Bank initially attempted to avoid appointing 'a Portal'. Portal had, however, made himself virtually indispensable and was duly appointed. Drawing upon his local knowledge of the South Wales establishment, he quickly recruited an area board, chaired by Mr A.T James K. C. and including Edmund Hahn, D. Morgan Rees and Mr Aeron Thomas, all of whom had been prominent members of the Bishop of Llandaf's committee.

The Bank's Governor, Montague Norman, also moved with alacrity to raise the £1 million. He felt it necessary, nevertheless, to give a chilling warning to Chamberlain that he would have to enter a 'reservation'. 'Explosions abroad or change at home might make it necessary to relieve people from their undertakings', though few approached could refuse a personal appeal from the Governor of the Bank. Insurance companies, the major retailers, Marks and Spencer, Woolworth, ICI, British Matches all felt it politic to accept, while the civically conscientious commissioner, Stewart, volunteered £15,000 from Associated Portland Cement and £10,000 from the family's London Brick Company. By the time of the first board meeting insurance companies had subscribed nearly £300,000, retail companies, £264,000 and industry £200,000. 'Only Scotland' had disappointed the Governor.

Thus, within six months, the first government guaranteed regional financial assistance scheme had been established. A government devoted to free market solutions had been driven to take a further faltering interventionist step. Chamberlain continued to take comfort from the notion that it was just another experiment which carried with it no implications for general economic and industrial policy. In the case of S.A.R.A, he could also claim that it was essentially a private, city and banking operation, though underpinned by government guarantees. Yet S.A.R.A had been born amid deep scepticism within Treasury and Bank of England circles. Their fears that S.A.R.A would fail to satisfy the clamour proved prescient. Within months, the fledgling association was besieged by critics and upstaged by the much more dramatic demands of commissioner Stewart.[15]

Stewart's Last Stand

The tensions between Stewart and Whitehall had been present from the first days in office. The Treasury had feared that the commission would seek to introduce a British style version of Roosevelt's New Deal. Officials also held Stewart in contempt and did little to disguise it from Chamberlain. Contempt was combined with growing alarm at the commissioner's burgeoning budget. In preparing the commissions estimates for 1936/7, officials had begged the Chancellor to intervene personally. The commission's commitments on public works had reached much larger proportions than originally intended. Out of a total anticipated £9 million, more than £5 million involved public works. Could not the Chancellor persuade him 'to go slow upon some of the schemes in the main 'palliatives' of little direct economic value, until his longer ranges schemes (trading estates, housing and land settlement, finance for small industries) were underway?' They suggested 'the jam that could be administered to sugar the bitter pill' of cutting back on public works; congratulations on the work already accomplished, the commitment of the government to second his efforts on the Severn Bridge, and the backing for a new forestry programme. Sir Warren Fisher and Treasury officials hoped the Chancellor would apply 'a dose of flattery and encourage Stewart to regard himself as a colleague of the government.'[16]

Matters were made worse by Stewart's poor relations with Ernest Brown, Minister of Labour. Ministers and officials had constantly underestimated their man. Stewart worried less about his relations with Whitehall than the growing chorus of public criticism about his own performance. Many of the deputations to Whitehall and Westminster had focused on the powerless character of the commission and had recommended alternative initiatives and machinery to address the needs of South Wales. He, therefore, felt obliged to demand a change of policy. Borrowing Chamberlain's phrase, he called, in this third and final report, for a major new 'second experiment' to assist the distressed areas.

Stewart's recommendations were certainly not for the faint hearted within the Treasury. He called for relief from income taxes, though not exceeding £500 p.a., relief from local rates, the local authorities being reimbursed by the exchequer grants or long term loans and a lower rate of interest for incoming companies which brought new technical processes to the distressed areas. Such inducements ought to operate for seven years and to be combined with statutory controls over industrial developments in greater London.[17]

Stewart's report provoked apoplexy at the Treasury and, particularly, within the Inland Revenue. Scornful dismissive observations scorched the minute sheets and memoranda that passed between Revenue and Treasury. Income tax concessions would produce a capricious form of relief that would do nothing effective to achieve its objectives. Mr Forbes, head of the Inland Revenue, submitted a forceful denunciation of the whole idea which would 'query the income tax pitch'. Forbes added that if the Treasury found his memorandum 'long', 'I can only say it would be much larger if we were to explain all the objections that could be advanced'. Income tax exemptions were worthless, for virtually no new company expected profit and therefore, income tax liability. Temporary relief from rates would be prima facie of little value as they were an insignificant fraction of costs, though they might turn some people's thoughts towards the special areas. A memorandum from Sir Richard Hopkins to Chamberlain rehearsed the case against all subsidies.

Inducements such as a wages subsidy, or exemptions from employers' contributions for health and unemployment insurance would distort decisions. The simpler solution would be outright gift of some percentage of requisite capital on any new project. Any kind of subsidy was, however, open to the fundamental objection 'that if offered on a minor scale they would be mere eyewash, and if offered on a grand scale sufficient to bring a substantial quantity of new business into the areas, against the economic facts'. Subsidies would attract other difficulties: destroy transference policy, alarm the employers' federations and undermine S.A.R.A. 'Such subsidies would also bring in doubtful promoters ready to sell pups with a Government cachet to the investing public'.

Sir Richard Hopkins' memorandum to the Chancellor distilled every conceivable argument deployed in the 1930s against regional subsidies; but, on this occasion, he found a Chancellor more preoccupied by immediate political pressures than policy principles . Stewart had announced his resignation on personal health grounds. This had not inhibited opposition efforts to embarrass the government over his resignation. Chamberlain fully realised that once the Stewart report and its unwelcome recommendations were made public the chorus calling for action would become deafening.[18] He also had one other problem to cope with –a proposed visit to South Wales by the King.

'Something Must Be Done'

King Edward VIII's visit to South Wales on 18/19 November, 1936 has passed into valley folklore. 'Something must be done' a phrase the King was reputed to have uttered at the derelict Dowlais works, to a Blaenavon shop assistant, and at Rhymney on his departure, captured the headlines. Unpublished palace memoranda recording meetings between the King's secretary, Major Hardinge, and Whitehall throw light upon the timing and purpose of the visit, offering a glimpse of the tensions that clearly existed between Whitehall and the Palace. Ministers had been peeved by the timing of the visit, coinciding as it did with the hunger marches. Hardinge had felt it necessary to defend such insensitive timing. In one memorandum he noted:

> 'With reference to the criticism of the dates chosen for the
> King's visit to the South Wales Special Area
> I told Sir John Simon [Home Secretary] when he came
> to the Council at Balmoral on 26th of September that
> The King was contemplating a visit in November. Sir John
> referred to the question of the Hunger Marches, and
> I asked if the date ought to be postponed. His answer was "No".'

At a meeting on 7th October with Ernest Brown, he spelt out the King's 'anxiety and desire to help in any way in the possible cleaning up of the problem of the special areas'.

> 'The King looked upon these areas as the one black spot
> in the country, and that it would give His Majesty the greatest
> gratification if the Coronation Celebrations next year
> could be made to coincide with a real improvement of
> the lot of these unfortunate people, whose share in the
> general recovery has as yet been so very limited.'

Brown explained to Hardinge how his department had been preoccupied with redrafting the unemployment benefit regulations after the debacle in February 1935. Now that the revised regulations were 'more or less out of the way', he would use 'all the best brains of his department to see if there were any way in which His Majesty could be associated with a solution of this difficult problem during the coming year' The King insisted upon being accompanied also by the Minister of Health, Kingsley Wood, and sought a confidential briefing from Lord Portal.

Portal's memorandum contained thinly disguised criticism of government policy. The King would be shown various social centres and services which in the main looked after the unemployed. Portal especially commended the job clubs which the unemployed ran for themselves; but the question which had not been addressed was 'procuring of permanent work'. That had only been dealt with by migration of younger men to other prosperous parts of England. Portal recommended to the King that government should give ten year contracts to firms willing to produce in the Special Areas. Most of the major industries were organised into trade federations which had benefited from the introduction of tariffs. An appeal should be made to these federations suggesting that they should place a factory in the distressed areas, linked to government contracts. South Wales was, also, 'admirably suited, from a strategic point of view for Armaments Factories'. Portal commended the King to obtain a first hand report from George Hall, member for Aberdare, 'a man above all others I can recommend to tell His Majesty the conditions of South Wales.'

The Palace followed up Portal's advice, for surviving within the royal papers is a note from the South Wales Trade and Expansion committee of which George Hall was a leading member. The committee had been campaigning for specific measures to revive coal exports, including royalty relief, import duties on foreign coking coal and a new trading agreement with Canada to displace Russian anthracite (250,000 tons per annum).[19]

'A Detour to Dowlais'

The King also concerned himself with the itinerary and arrangements of his tour. On 8th October, Ernest Brown had submitted a programme of visits to instructional and physical training centres and one employment exchange. The Minister assumed the King would want to visit 'a certain number of working class homes'. The Palace accepted this recommendation, but pointedly added 'not only the good ones!?' News of the visit prompted a host of pleading from numerous valley communities that the King should call, and none more strongly than from Merthyr Tydfil and Dowlais.

The fear that the royal visit might by-pass Merthyr Tydfil and Dowlais prompted two mayoral letters from the county borough and a stream of letters from the Dowlais chamber of commerce, the local British legion, the Imperial policy group and even from a government member of parliament, Ivor Guest. Guest, invoking his own family's long connection with Dowlais, quoted from a constituent's letter:

> 'King George and Queen Mary visited the Dowlais
> works in 1912. They saw the works in all its glory and
> Dowlais at its best. What a different scene will today meet
> the eye of their son King Edward VIII. Dowlais, where the
> first iron rail and the first steel rail were made, where
> Trevethick built and ran the first steam engine. Soldiers
> in the Great War from Dowlais, in the east were conveyed
> over the desert to face the Turks in trucks built at Dowlais,
> drawn by locomotives made at Dowlais. What a history the
> town has got, and now it appears to be left stranded
> and forgotten...'.

The King had, himself, noticed that the draft programme had not included Merthyr Tydfil though, as his private secretary noted, 'possibly it may be intended that he drive through it en route somewhere else'. In the end, the royal visit centred upon Merthyr Tydfil and even after the formal itinerary had been printed, 'a detour to Dowlais' was neatly penned into the programme.

The royal tour was shrouded in controversy. Not all the local members of parliament agreed to be present. Aneurin Bevan's refusal attracted the criticism of Rhymney's ladies, while Mr Mainwaring, member for Rhondda East, ostentatiously condemned the tour in the Commons and, especially the participation of the Minister of Labour, the author of the notorious 1935 unemployment benefit regulations. Hardinge observed in a letter to the Ministry of Labour's PS 'Mr Mainwaring evidently does not want to see us next week, but I hope he is in the minority!' The Tillery lodge had promised the Minister of Labour a 'lively reception', while local reports filtering back to the palace claimed that communists were influencing teachers at the local schools 'to tell the children to dress in their worst clothes, the idea being to present to the King the pitiful state of the youngsters suffering from the means test.'

Enormous crowds greeted the King. The last minute visit to Dowlais captured the greatest press and media interest. As the *Times* correspondent described:

> 'the visit to Dowlais was a last minute addition to the programme, and in many respects it was the most impressive. At the top of the hill where the now silent steelworks are located, a large crowd watched the King alight from his car. For a moment he stood on the road hat in hand, looking at the towering furnaces whose fires had been drawn long ago. Then as he passed into the yard a group of men on a mound of debris started to sing a Welsh hymn ... Then looking around at the people who were standing around in groups overlooking the works, he is stated to have said, 'these people were brought here by these works. Some kind of employment must be found for them ...'.

The tour generated phenomenal press and film coverage, universally sympathetic to the plight of South Wales, and both explicitly, and implicitly, critical of the government. British film goers were subjected to a hectoring commentary, accompanying the graphically filmed royal tour.

> 'The King saw for himself the disillusionment and suffering from the long workless years. Social services are not enough. These men want work. New industries must be brought to the stricken areas of South Wales. The visit has brought new found hope that some solutions will be found'.[20]

'These are frankly unorthodox'

The prospect of the royal visit brought additional pressures upon ministers and, especially upon the Chancellor of the Exchequer. The King's intervention had complicated an already difficult scenario. Commissioner Stewart's resignation and his third report would, of themselves, have forced the government's hand. Publication of the report and its unpalatable recommendations would highlight the government's inadequate response to the plight of the distressed areas. The demand that something more should be done would intensify. Worse, public agitation got to the normally supine cabinet. Collectively ministers had scarcely debated distressed areas policy. Stewart's third report had not been submitted to cabinet or the cabinet committee. No formal cabinet record reports any discussion of the King's visit to South Wales, though undoubtedly ministers would have exchanged informal views. The dissenting voices at the cabinet meeting at 14th October appears to have come as a surprise to Chamberlain.

Ministers initially addressed the issues of the hunger marches descending upon London. Clearly fearing the gathering sympathy for the marchers, the cabinet decided to brief selected journalists to put their own gloss on events 'exposing the origins, motives and uselessness of the hunger marches'. To deter recruitment to the marches, it was to be made publicly clear that unemployment benefit was not payable to the marching unemployed. Ministers decided to refuse to meet marchers except, possibly, for a few accompanied by local MPs. The draft cabinet statement emphasized the constitutional character of British government policy making, accountable only to parliament. 'Processions cannot claim to have any constitutional influence on policy'

However, to Chamberlain's dismay, Kingsley Wood, Minister of Health, seizing the opportunity of an agenda item on 'The Physical Condition of the People', warned colleagues of new evidence of the physical deterioration especially of children in the distressed areas. Supported by the President of the Board of Education, who similarly warned of 'some unpleasant facts' emerging from annual school medical reports, Kingsley Wood pleaded with the cabinet 'to consider whether something could not be done to bring hope and life, for example, in Merthyr Tydfil.' Could not something be done to create jobs with the armaments factories? Kingsley Wood's plea prompted the Prime Minister to express the view that the impression that no one cared would be 'fertile soil for communism'.

Sir Thomas Inskip, the newly appointed Minister for Co-ordination of Production, was forced to defend the failure of defence departments to steer rearmament projects into South Wales. If rearmament programmes were 'to be advanced at maximum speed' then the government could not afford to relocate production in South Wales. Inskip and Chamberlain pleaded with the cabinet not 'to take premature decisions' and adopt 'completely uneconomic ideas at short notice'.

Chamberlain may have headed off rash cabinet commitments but pressure upon him personally remained. Brown, the Minister of Labour, had obtained the ear of the Prime Minister. As Chamberlain reported to

Treasury officials, Brown had claimed to Baldwin that 'the position in South Wales was almost dangerous'. In turn, Baldwin had pressed his Chancellor about a coal to oil project for South Wales. Alas, Whitehall departments had unanimously concluded that such a project was commercially unviable, as were any proposals to site a calcium carbide plant in South Wales. Bleakly they advised Chamberlain that they 'could not find anything useful to say about Merthyr Tydfil'. Commissioner Stewart had been considering a land clearance scheme in Dowlais 'but he does not say what industries are likely to go there which will assist Merthyr's unemployed miners'.

The stream of negative advice that poured into the Chancellor's office condemning the Stewart report and its unacceptable jobs incentives and dismissing a role for South Wales in the rearmament programme had, however, become politically untenable. Confronted with a parliamentary debate on the distressed areas, most unfortunately falling on the eve of the King's visit to South Wales, Chamberlain overrode all official advice. A hand-written minute attached to a submission from deputy secretary, Sir Richard Hopkins, encapsulated Chamberlain's highly personal approach, a profound scepticism that anything could really be done by government but now tempered by a belated recognition that existing policy was politically unsustainable:

> 'I think it is possible to destroy very effectively any proposal for attracting new industries into special areas. But politically speaking this is not a wholly satisfactory method as it leaves things as before. On the other hand the Commissioner has made certain proposals and politically it might be helpful to say "these are frankly unorthodox but we are ready to try them in these areas". If they failed, as I think they would, we should have done little harm but we should have met the reproach that we neither accepted others' suggestions nor produced any of our own ...
>
> In view of the provisional conclusions arrived at in the memorandum, I suggest the commissioner's actual proposals be very carefully examined and reported on. Not so much with a view to whether they are likely to be effective for the purposes the commissioner has in mind as to whether they are likely to be harmful in the consequences as to be dangerous...'

Having dismissed departmental objections, Chamberlain rose during the course of the all night debate (17th November) and, as the King travelled to South Wales, announced the government's acceptance in principle of Stewart's recommendation. He had taken the extraordinary precaution of rushing across a copy of his speech to the Palace, presumably in the hope that the government's policy would be seen in a more favourable light. In the Commons, Chamberlain confessed that 'no appreciable improvement in South Wales could be detected and indeed if one took the special case of Merthyr, things were actually worse'. He, therefore, accepted that 'further experiments should be tried.'. Such experiments were entirely in line and accord with government policy. Ruefully admitting that the new proposals would not have 'a very warm reception from the Treasury and, if applied to the country as a whole, he would himself be inclined to resist them,' Chamberlain clung to the temporary, experimental nature of the exercise. His statement, at least, proved sufficient to buy off a potential government back bench revolt. Viscount Woolmer, nevertheless, starkly threatened that, if the measures 'did not match the need' there would be a revolt, because the suffering of the depressed areas 'threatened the pride of the nation'.[21]

'After South Wales You Can't Let Him Down'

Ministers had viewed the King's tour with considerable apprehension. Yet, in the wake of that visit, they faced a potentially more alarming scenario, confrontation with the King over his wish to marry an American divorcee. We now know that Baldwin had held his first crisis meeting with the King on the eve of the South Wales visit at which the Prime Minister had frankly advised that public opinion would not accept Mrs Simpson. The King had seemingly accepted this, though chiding Baldwin's speaking 'as if he were a gallup poll.'

But, buoyed by the warmth of his reception in South Wales, Edward was now tempted to challenge the government's position. Baldwin reported to the cabinet that the King now felt that he would have the sympathy and support of a large number of people. While the King acknowledged that Mrs Simpson would not be acceptable as queen, a morganatic marriage might be, if the government was willing to introduce the necessary legislation.

Ministers had reason to be concerned. There were signs of an emerging King's party promoted by the press magnates Rothmere and Beaverbrook. A mischievous Daily Mail leader (23rd November), 'The King Edward Touch' starkly contrasted the King's obvious empathy with the unemployed and the government's apparent indifference.

'The lot of the humblest people had always been
his nearest anxiety and continual preoccupation
and the people of South Wales realised that here was a man
who cares supremely for their well being. The contrast to the
way in which national questions are customarily
approached can escape nobody. There is consultation;
committees are appointed and conferences take
place in the solemn apartments
of Whitehall but few go boldly forth to see
for themselves ...'.

Baldwin and the cabinet, however, held their nerve, supported by Attlee and the official opposition and a host of prime ministers from the Dominions. The *Telegraph* and the *Times* sonorously warned of the constitutional dangers of pitting King against government. 'Grave damage will be done if the King's visit to South Wales is seen as a rebuke to the government'. Some of those, such as Churchill, who had been tempted to back the King found that they had misjudged the mood of both the Commons and the public. Whatever an immediate impression he had made upon the desperate unemployed of the valleys, they shared the general national sentiment which was disgusted by the prospect of an American divorcee as queen. The very same ladies of Rhymney who had chided Aneurin Bevan for refusing to meet the King now congratulated their M.P. for his foresight and moral stance! News of the abdication did bring onto the London streets loyalists bearing cards calling for support:

'After South Wales you can't let him down.
Come to the Palace and cheer the King ...'.

But the pleas went unheeded. Whatever hopes the valleys had harboured of royal intervention, it had become plainly evident that their future lay not with the Palace, but within the Palace of Westminster, where Chamberlain had already committed the government to 'a second experiment' in the distressed areas.[22]

1936: 'Something must be Done'

'Don't you say a word against South Wales'

1. Correspondence relating to the Bishop of Llandaf's committee LAB 18/38.

2. For the role of Mr Humphrey Wolfe in the Ministry of Labour, R.Lowe, *Adjusting to democracy*, 68-69.

3. Minutes of the deputation, LAB 18/38.

4. Papers relating to the Welsh Parliamentary Party's deputation, T172/1850.

5. Weir's observations and recommendations T172/1850A; The CEB's dismissal of a South Wales power station, L Hannah: *Electricity before Nationalisation, A Study of the Development of the Electricity supply Industry in Britain to 1948, 139.* CEB Minutes, 18 December 1936.

'The situation in Merthyr Tydfil'

6. Alderman James' letter and departmental consideration HLG 30/53. The unpublished draft Portal report BT55/14. The various enquiries into Merthyr county borough HLG 30/20, HLG 12/15; the appointment of a royal commission and consideration of its recommendations, HLG 53/181.

7. Draft cabinet memorandum and cabinet consideration , HLG 30/48, HLG 30/53, CP 229, CAB 24, 264 (28-8-1936), CAB 56(36).

8. CAB 56(36).

'God bless the revolution'

9. Activities of the Imperial Policy Group, and the various representations made by Merthyr county borough council were extensively reported in the local news paper; the Merthyr Express
Sept 1936.

'Our mysterious lady known as Sara'

10. Early discussions on the new credit arrangements; BT 55/14, AST 7/31 T175/90, CAB 27/577, T161/83/S39260/1, T161/930/S414848/1.

11. Bank of England records (B.O.E) SMT 2/16,17.

12. B.O.E. records, SMT 2/17/18.

13. Bank of England/Treasury exchanges, T161/930/S414848/1.

14. T161/930/S414888/1; Debates on the bill, HC 19,22, 26 April 1937.

15. The organisation of S.A.R.A and Portal's role, B.O.E., SMT 2/18,22;T161/7791/S4961.

'Stewart's last stand'

16. Treasury/Stewart relationships T161/930/S4369536.

17. Stewart's third report, Third report of the Commissioners for the Special Areas (England and Wales) Cmnd 5303.

18. Treasury and Inland Revenue objections, T172/1828 CAB 27/578 CAB 8/208

'Something Must Be Done'

19. I have kindly received the gracious permission of Her Majesty The Queen to quote the following references from the Royal Archives: Memorandum by Major Hardinge, 15.10.1936, RA/PS/G VI/PS01182/012: Memorandum by Major Hardinge, 7.10.1936, RA/PS/GVIPS01182/006: undated memorandum by Lord Portal, RA/PS/GVI/PS01182/024: memorandum by George Hall MP, November 1936, RA/PS/GVI/PS01182/132

'A detour to Dowlais'

20. Letter from T.S. Chegwidden (PS to Ernest Brown) to Major Hardinge 8.10.1936; letter from Major Hardinge to T.S. Chegwidden, 9.10.1936, RAPSGVI/PS01182/009
The mayoral and other letters. RA/GVI PS1182
Letter from Ivor Guest MP to Major Hardinge 10.11.1936, RA/PS/GVI/PS01182/091
Letter from Major Hardinge to TS Chegwidden 9.10.1936, RA/PS/GVI/PS01182/009
Aneurin Bevan's position and correspondence with the Rhymney ladies, Michael Foot, *Aneurin Bevan, Vol 1, 241-243 (Paladin 1975)*
Letter from Major Hardinge to TS Chegwidden RA/PS/GVI/PS01182/019
Anonymous note dated 10.11.1936 sent to Major Hardinge by Evan Williams on 13.11.1936, RA/PS/GVI/PS01182/022

'These are frankly unorthodox.'

21. Detailed exchanges between Chamberlain and the Treasury T172/1827, 1828 Chamberlain's speech to the Commons HC, 17 Nov 1936

'After South Wales you can't let him down'

22. Cabinet, royal and the Chamberlain papers relating to the abdication remain unavailable. Published accounts of the crisis: Brian Inglis, *Abdication*, (Hodder and Stoughton 1966); other accounts of the crisis can be found in P Ziegler, *King Edward VIII*, (Collins 1990), Frances Donaldson, *Edward VIII*, (Weidenfeld and Nicolson, 1974), Michael Bloch, *the Reign and Abdication of Edward VIII* (Bantam press 1990).

The Royal Visit; IS IT THE DAWN

BUCKINGHAM PALACE

9th. October, 1936.

Dear Chegwidden,

Many thanks for your letter of October 8th.

The places which Mr. Brown suggests that The King should visit in the special area of South Wales have been approved by His Majesty, although it is realised that time may not admit of his visiting them all.

I think that the next thing to be done is for you to draw up an itinerary, and I can now give you some indication of the timings which His Majesty has in contemplation.

The King proposes to travel by night on November 17th. to the most distant part of the area, and will be ready to start out on his tour at 10 a.m., on November 18th. His Majesty will be prepared to go on until about 5 p.m., by which time it will probably be too dark to do anything more. He will spend the night in the train which, if necessary, can be moved to some place convenient for the next day's tour.

Memorandum by the King's private secretary, Major Hardinge

ii

The King will be ready to start a little earlier, say 9.30 a.m., on November 19th., and finish by about 4 p.m., which would enable him to get back to London in time for dinner.

I am in communication with Mr. Potter of the Great Western Railway regarding the train, and it might be desirable for whoever is drawing up the itinerary to communicate with him also.

I ought to add that The King would certainly like to visit at least one Employment Exchange and some working-class houses, not only the good ones !

His Majesty also drew attention to the fact that no mention was made of Merthyr Tydfil, though possibly it may be intended that he should drive through it en route somewhere else.

I shall be glad to see you as soon as you are in a position to bring an itinerary and a map.

Yours sincerely,

T.S. Chegwidden Esq.,
    Ministry of Labour,
        Montagu House,
            Whitehall, S.W.1.

Visit of H.M. The King to South Wales

Programme for Wednesday, 18th November, 1936

Llantwit Major Station.		Leave train at 10 a.m.
Boverton.	Co-operative Farm (Welsh Land Settlement Society).	Arrive 10.10 a.m. Depart 10.40 a.m.
Dinas, Rhondda.	Voluntary Scheme. Ex - Service and St. John Ambulance Rally.	Arrive 11.35 a.m. Depart 12.5 p.m.
Pontypridd.	Physical Training Class.	Arrive 12.20 p.m. Depart 12.35 p.m.
Pentrebach.	Intermediate Training Centre.	Arrive 1 p.m.
	Luncheon Interval.	Depart 1.55 p.m.
Merthyr.	Maternity and Child Welfare Centre.	Arrive 2.10 p.m. Depart 2.20 p.m.
	Employment Exchange.	Arrive 2.25 p.m. Depart 2.40 p.m.
	Home Training Centre (Women).	Arrive 2.45 p.m. Depart 3.0 p.m.
Aberdare.	Halt in Victoria Square	Arrive 3.20 p.m. Depart 3.30 p.m.
Penrhiwceiber.	Quarter Acre Group Holding.	Arrive 3.50 p.m. Depart 4.5 p.m.
Mountain Ash.	Pavilion. Gathering of Social Service Workers.	Arrive 4.15 p.m. Depart 4.55 p.m.

detour to DOWLAIS

Join train at Mountain Ash (Cardiff Road) Station 5 p.m.

I

A

(34549)

dinner in train at Usk . 8 p.m .

'A detour to Dowlais the King's programme

iv

The King with Captain Geoffrey Crawshay, Mr Ernest Brown
and Mr Bean inspecting land tractors and lorries at Boverton

The King greeted by large crowds at Dinas, Rhondda

The King greeted by large crowds in Merthyr

The King mixes cement at Pentrebach Training Centre

The King;s visit to the Merthyr Employment Exchange

The King stands amid the dereliction of the Dowlais works

5

1937: A SECOND EXPERIMENT

Chamberlain had been compelled to embrace the commissioner's unpalatable proposals, Stewart's 'second experiment'. His parliamentary statement on 17th November had been made without the approval of the cabinet or any discussion in the cabinet committee for the distressed areas, an indication of the haste forced upon the Chancellor by parliamentary pressure and the royal intervention. The interdepartmental official committee, which had previously sifted through the commissioners' reports, was now left to translate political decisions into legislative and administrative action. Officials barely disguised their contempt and scepticism for Stewart's flawed and ill considered recommendations. It, also, has to be said that Stewart's report did beg a host of questions and threw up new arguments over the respective roles of the special areas commission and Whitehall departments.

The newly appointed commissioner, Sir George Gillett, spelled out the range of new inducements. He argued, in a letter to the Minister of Labour (23rd December), that the practical immediate need of the special areas had to be the clearance of the unsightly, derelict industrial sites and the partial or total remission of rent on land and buildings. The trading estate companies should be asked to act as agents to the commissioner, purchase sites and erect factories. He had already submitted a number of possible locations, including the Dowlais site in Merthyr Tydfil. These infrastructure improvements, he argued, had to be combined with training subsidies to companies, long term loans at low interest, apart from Stewart's recommendation of remission of income tax and rate relief. Gillett strongly urged that the new inducements should not be automatic. The commissioner should have the power to vary the inducements according to the undesirability of the area or possibly according to the type of industry. If all the inducements were automatic, most firms would simply go the trading estates and avoid the worst 'spots' of south west Durham and Merthyr Tydfil. The ultimate decision, after seeking advice from Lord Portal and other colleagues, had to rest with the commissioner himself. Gillett admitted that it would indeed 'be an extremely difficult piece of administration' and 'I shall be open to all sorts of pressure, political or otherwise but I don't see who else is to bear the responsibilities as since all subsidies would paid out of the special areas fund.'[1]

While Whitehall accepted the principle of 'variable inducements', the Ministry of Labour felt the necessity to attempt to establish specific criteria to govern such variations. In doing so, officials attempted to construct, for the first time, a graduation of special areas' status. The ministry devised five categories:

Class 1 - places where the automatic inducements of income tax and rate relief would alone suffice: in South Wales, Resolven.

Class 2 - places already fairly suitable for industrial development but for a small additional inducement could be justified to bring them into reasonable competition with class 1: in South Wales, Clydach, Cymmer, Neath, Pontyclun, Ebbw Vale, Bargoed, Ogmore Valley, Port Talbot, Tonyrefail, Pontypool, the coastal belt between Cardiff and Newport and between Port Talbot and Barry.

Class 3 - places less suitable than class 2 and requiring a higher degree of inducement: in South Wales, Treforest Trading Estate, Pembroke dock, Aberdare, Aberkenfig, Bridgend, Caerphilly, Mountain Ash, Pontycymmer, Porth, Taffs Well, Treorchy, Abergavenny, Abertillery, Blackwood, Blaenavon, Pontnewydd, Risca and Tredegar.

Class 4 - places which at present have no natural attraction for fresh industries but in which it is thought that new industries might be developed with a reasonable chance of continuing success if they can be given maximum inducements for the first seven years: in South Wales, Brynmawr, Merthyr, Ferndale, Tonypandy, Pontlottyn, Pontypridd, Blaenau and Maesteg.

Class 5 - included no hope areas in South Wales, the Upper Vale of Neath and certain small towns (e.g. Nantyglo) to be regarded as 'dormitory areas'.

Just the attempt to devise a more sophisticated special areas' scheme convinced officials themselves of its impossibility and the administrative and political nightmare of introducing such a scheme. The eventual interdepartmental official report submitted to ministers disregarded such a complex system in favour of commissioner's discretion, the exception to the rule being the new cheap loan scheme which had to remain with the Treasury.[2]

Officials had, however, to make sense of Stewart's other central recommendations: the remission of income tax, the lifting of the public assistance burden from local authorities and the provision of cheap credit. They, ruefully, observed to ministers that, hitherto, it had been 'axiomatic' that no inducements should be offered to private enterprise. The Inland

Revenue was now faced with the most objectionable of all inducements - relief of income tax. The Revenue fondly hoped that the Chancellor would retreat from such a promise. Officials sought to minimise its value. The lowering or waiving of any tax on profits could not, in itself, do anything to turn a loss into profit. Relief on profits of £500 would be worth £120, 'a sum equal to the wages of one worker for a year'. During the parliamentary stages of the special areas' amendment bill, Whitehall, forlornly, hoped that Chamberlain would relent and accept government back bench amendments to delete altogether the new tax provision.

Treasury and Housing and Local Government officials had greater success in beating off the second objectionable demand in Stewart's report, the equalising of the public assistance rate throughout the country. A sub committee within Whitehall had been appointed to advise on the complex issues of local government finance. The committee, predictably, found that rates levels were not only the normal symptoms of acute industrial depression but also of 'lax standards of local administration' which acted as a greater deterrence to industry. High rates were not exclusive to the special areas but could be found in rather more prosperous areas such as Hull. Equalling of public assistance was open to grave objection in principle and presented 'insuperable administrative difficulties and stood little chance of acceptance by other local authorities.'

Officials drew ministers' attention to the fact that expenditure already falling on public funds borne by the exchequer accounted for 57 to 69% of counties' expenditure in the special areas and 39.9 to 58% in the county boroughs. The introduction of national unemployment assistance and the new proposed block grant was worth 2s and 5s in the pound to Merthyr Tydfil (£7.10s in all), 4s 1d to Monmouthshire and 2s 9d to Glamorgan. If ministers felt that they had to respond to the distressed areas' pleas, then any exchequer assistance should be confined only to relieving the burden of certain costly schemes of water supply and sewerage in Merthyr Tydfil and in certain urban districts of Glamorgan and Monmouthshire. [3]

The cabinet gave short shrift to any further concessions to local authorities. At their meetings of the 11th and 23rd February 1937, only the Minister of Labour pleaded for assistance and the 'only place about which he felt strongly was the county borough of Merthyr Tydfil'. The depression in the town, he told colleagues 'was in a class by itself'. While Chamberlain accepted the burden upon Merthyr Tydfil 'with high water and sewerage rates due to expensive schemes carried out in better times', he argued, successfully, that the cabinet should take no decisions until after the implementation of the block grants bill. The Ministry of Health backed the Treasury forcefully. The new bill offered Merthyr 5s in the pound relief. If total relief was offered, it would be nothing more than a 'blank cheque encouraging the extravagance exemplified by the county borough's administration.'

The officials' committee had taken a rather more sympathetic view of one other plight facing local authorities, the difficulties of financing services relating to health and physical well being of school children, maternity and child welfare facilities. Health and Education ministers had expressed concern to colleagues about children's welfare and nutrition in the area of highest unemployment. Hastily denying that special assistance was being advocated 'on grounds of rate relief', officials tentatively concluded that the importance of nutrition and physical welfare should not suffer because of the financial circumstances of local authorities. It was, nevertheless, 'appreciated that the subvention by the commissioners of a revenue service (as distinguished from capital expenditure) would mean a specific extension of their powers, and attracted objections of principle' from the Treasury. The Treasury was, indeed, hostile to any such extension and Chamberlain successfully talked colleagues out of pursuing this recommendation.[4]

'A Sister to SARA'

The Treasury faced an even greater headache in drafting the new special areas' bill with the introduction of a new Treasury loan scheme, which Stewart had recommended and Chamberlain had endorsed. Such a scheme threatened the Bank of England's newly established Special Areas Reconstruction Association. S.A.R.A. already faced competition from one other newly established private trust financed by the motor magnate, Lord Nuffield. This £2 million trust, launched in December 1936, was not bound by the market constraints placed upon S.A.R.A.. It had been devised by Nuffield to be dispersed quickly, with few demands for security, offering capital in the form of 5% redeemable preference shares or even, in some cases, ordinary shares. The fund ultimately expended half of its funds in share rather than loan capital.[5]

This attractive alternative would have been challenging enough without another competitor, in the form of a Treasury loan scheme, and mounting public and parliamentary criticism of S.A.R.A.'s own performance. That performance had been impeded by personality clashes within the board, differences of interest rates policy and tensions between the central board and its area advisory committees.

Personality clashes revolved around the board's chairman, Lord Portal, and the 'bullying' Mr Gibson Jarvie. The Bank of England's representative, Skinner, explained the differences to the Governor:

'The skeleton which has poked his head
out of the cupboard will, I think, be there all the time.
We will find, on the one side,
(which I think I can mitigate) a deep desire, for the
Chairman to be rid of Jarvie, while the others, as
they get to know him, will be willing to put up with
him. Jarvie unless we tone him down, will sooner or
later threaten to resign but will not in fact do so
because he does not want to offend you - "the only
master he recognises", as Lord Portal put it'.

At Skinner's request, Montague Norman successfully applied 'a little oil' to mollify the angry Mr Jarvie. Differences of personality later reflected differences of views over interest rates. The board, Skinner informed Norman in a secret memo, was 'spiritually' divided between P and H (Portal and Hodges) plus Gibb, the managing director, who wanted his own way, and 'those whom they describe as bankers on the other'. The 'non bankers' had forced a concession on the maximum interest rate 'right on the eve' of a key parliamentary vote in February 1937.

Another internal wrangle surfaced publicly - the role and relationship of the area committees to the main board. Clearly, the frustrations felt by the local boards, at the sharp end of the many refusals to lend by the main board, had strained relationships. Both the North East and the South Wales boards conveyed their increasing dissatisfaction, prompting Skinner at the Bank and Portal as chairman to seek to clarify the local board's role. Portal proposed a dinner at the Savoy to provide 'the lubricating medium'. Skinner's preparatory notes for the Governor reveal the Bank's concern that the local boards had become too much involved in the intricacies of lending money, 'a business of which they generally speaking have no experience.' Local boards should conduct the procuring and initial vetting of applications for loans, based upon what was thought to be locally desirable industrially. The local board should offer a recommendation on grounds of the suitability, integrity, experience and competence of the applicant but it had to be the central board's decision as to whether the loan was 'a reasonable hazard, remembering that as trustees for the funds of the share holders and a responsibility to the tax-payers, they had to ensure the mandate laid down in the articles was strictly observed'.

Portal's Savoy dinner was not an unqualified success. Certainly the South Wales chairman, Aeron Thomas, went away still dissatisfied as subsequent draft letters to him from both Skinner and Portal infer. They found it necessary to remind Aeron Thomas that local boards could not make commitments which the London board were 'expressively debarred from fulfilling'. They, painstakingly, explained to a disgruntled Mr Thomas that the act definitely precluded them from offering specially low interest rates to attract business. Skinner reminded Thomas that the government only guaranteed 'a certain portion of the capital losses' and 'the interest on the capital was not guaranteed at all'. If S.A.R.A called upon its capital it would, itself, have to earn interest on it. One of Portal's letters to the South Wales chairman was ultimately converted into a public defence of S.A.R.A. through the letter columns of *The Times*. Portal, patiently, sought to underline S.A.R.A.'s limitations and the need 'to take proper care that the loans it makes will be of permanent value'.

Portal's and ministers' efforts did little to assuage the rising chorus of criticism. In the submission to Whitehall upon the amendments to the Special Area Act, the North East development board disparaged S.A.R.A.'s performance. The security asked for by the Association was very large in relation to any loan. The insistence that the applicant should himself invest an amount equivalent to a high percentage of the loan granted ruled out most applications. The North East memorandum concluded that the policy could not be said to be 'sufficiently unconventional or flexible'.[6]

The chorus of complaints washed over ministers during a debate in February 1937. Protracted delays in handling claims, the large numbers of refusals, the rate of interest, excessive demands by the Association for both security and insurance from applicants helped to make life uncomfortable for junior Treasury ministers replying to the debate. It was not made any easier by the fact that the internal dissensions within S.A.R.A. and the local boards fed the debate. S.A.R.A., in the eyes of W.H. Mainwaring, MP for Rhondda East, had been transformed from Whitehall's 'mysterious lady' to an 'old maid', probably 'infertile'. Mainwaring wanted to know how many 'little Isaacs' were going to be born in South Wales. He knew only of one that had been at 5% interest instead of the newly announced 4% or 4.2%. He added, ominously, that it was 'a notorious fact that the South Wales board were prepared to resign and even finish with it because of the utter futility of it...'. 'The board in South Wales was in revolt ... and spoke even more vehemently than any member of parliament of their lack of powers. Would the government's new proposed Treasury loan scheme, 'SARA's sister' be 'any less barren?'

The birth of 'a sister to SARA .' was also proving to be a laborious process for both Bank and Treasury. The Governor and Bank officials had been dismayed by Chamberlain's decision to set up another loan scheme. At an uncomfortable meeting between the Bank and Treasury officials, the Governor attempted to persuade Whitehall just to give the new £2 million to the Nuffield trustees. New money on Nuffield lines but separately administered from S.A.R.A. would damage S.A.R.A. seriously. The little company would get worse terms from S.A.R.A. than the Treasury or Nuffield, which would 'expose the S.A.R.A. board to severe and unfair criticism'. Treasury officials remained keenly aware of the political imperatives. It was agreed that it would be politically undesirable to wind up S.A.R.A. after so short a life. Sir Richard Hopkins had minuted on the dilemma facing the Treasury and the Bank:

> 'A small man goes to the Nuffield trustees, and who says "no
> you only want capital on commercial terms ..." He then goes
> to S.A.R.A. who says "we cannot lend to you, you are not a
> safe borrower". He then has a question asked in Parliament'.

The ubiquitous Lord Portal came to the rescue to exert an extraordinary influence over both the policy and its implementation. S.A.R.A., the Nuffield Trust and the Treasury loan scheme, could be operated in a co-ordinated fashion - the co-ordinator being Portal himself. As he explained to Treasury officials, an applicant company could, for example, receive £10,000, from Nuffield at 2.2%, £5,000 at 4% from S.A.R.A. plus, if need be, a larger low interest loan from the Treasury. Lord Portal, chairman of S.A.R.A., an advisor to both the Treasury loan scheme and to commissioner Sir George Gillett, as well as a Nuffield Trustee, could ensure the complementary nature of each offer from the respective funds to any applicant. It meant that up to £250,000 could be offered on special terms.[7]

There remained one other major issue for ministers and officials to resolve - whether to extend the special areas' boundaries. Since the passing of the 1934 act, a disparate range of representations had been made to amend the schedules defining the areas' boundaries. Informed economists' opinion had pressed for the incorporation of the more prosperous growth areas adjacent to distressed areas; Professor Marquand and others in South Wales had made the case for including the Cardiff/Newport coastal area. Elsewhere, Lancashire members had argued rather differently. Not wishing to be stigmatised as a depressed area, they had argued for separate financial inducements to develop trading estates. The government's chief adviser, Sir Horace Wilson, diligently courted the politically sensitive northern members and became an advocate of this particular kind of concession.

Changes to the special areas preoccupied the cabinet committee for the whole of its meeting on 26th January 1937. Fearful that the parliamentary floodgates would be opened, ministers gingerly reviewed four options put to them by officials. Chamberlain, in fact, shaped and determined the committee's conclusion. Claiming that he had 'always thought it erroneous to regard unemployment as a temporary problem which would go away when trade and industry revived or as one capable solution by mere palliatives', the Chancellor believed that the ultimate responsibilities for those areas with persistent unemployment would lie with the unemployment assistance board. The commission should never be regarded as 'permanent machinery'. The committee should reject any option suggesting that degree of permanence. He suggested a limited variation. The government might take powers to set up one or two public utilities (on the lines of the trading estates companies) to operate outside the areas - in effect the Lancashire option. Ministers accepted Chamberlain's strong steer to confine any alteration to such limits, even recommending that the financial resolution accompanying the bill be so tightly drawn as to rule out amendments on the areas. The decision to do so later caused a furious procedural wrangle in the House.[8]

'Blue' and 'Pink' Plans

A short nine clause bill emerged from these tortuous discussions, lifting the restriction upon the commissioner to offer inducements to private industry, and empowering him to make contributions by way of rent, income tax or rates for five years. Clause four lifted restrictions on making grants towards local authority expenses for the repair and maintenance of streets, 'as being those wholly or mainly required for purposes other than those of through traffic', and for drainage schemes. Clause five provided for financial assistance to 'site' companies on the recommendation of an advisory committee through offering capital or a loan not exceeding a third of the share capital of that company.

The bill was subjected to a much greater parliamentary assault than its predecessor. By the spring of 1937, the socially draining experience of long term unemployment had made untenable any general government case that improvement in trade would somehow resolve the difficulties in the special areas. The bill itself was an admission of the fact. The experience of the first half of the decade had also concentrated oppositions' minds and fuelled debate outside the Commons which had gone beyond Lloyd George's new deal. Professor Marquand had published, in late 1936, a second survey of South Wales which, unlike its predecessor in 1931/2, offered a prescription, in fact, two prescriptions - a 'blue' and a 'pink' plan. The 'blue plan' reviewed the option that Marquand felt fitted within the parameters of the National government's policy thinking. The blue plan, he argued, could address the surplus of 60,000 workers by a limited miners' retirement scheme, the raising of the school leaving age to 15, an extensive land settlement and an afforestation programme, the targeting of new and not so new industries, the manufacture of rolling shutters, hosiery, glazed cement, sheets and tiles, steel tube furniture and dairy equipment, all to be promoted by a Minister without portfolio responsible for the special areas. [9]

Marquand's 'pink plan' reviewing the Labour Party's proposals had, however, been overtaken by the time of its publication. Having hitherto declined to find 'palliatives' to reform the unreformable capitalist systems, the Labour party now adopted Hugh Dalton's more pragmatic view. At the national executive in November 1936 the party had decided to establish a policy commission led by Dalton. He had toured the distressed areas during early 1937, including South Wales and, at the end of January, published an interim report 'Labour and the Distressed Areas; a Programme of Immediate Action', followed by five regional reports (the South Wales report was published in May). It quoted a *Times* leader of 19th January which warned the government against 'the view which lingers in some quarters that these areas should be considered as economic cemeteries, the character of which may be made more pleasant by planting a few flowers, straightening a few tombstones and employing a sexton or two, but cannot be radically changed. The condition of the special areas was a challenge to the efficiency of the government and of the democratic system'. The population, the Labour party document claimed, were the innocent victims of an unplanned capitalism which in these areas, had collapsed in ruins - wasted by an 'economic earthquake'.

The party advocated 'a vigorous and authoritative minister of cabinet rank' to be put in charge. The device of special commissioners 'doomed to run to and fro with little more authority than errand boys between governmental departments in Whitehall, was not enough'. The Labour party proposed:

'a special exchequer grant to reduce local
authority's rates and lift the crushing burden
of public assistance.

power to the Minister for the Special Areas
to require all new industries or factories
or substantial extensions on existing and
industrial concerns to be established in
special areas, unless they can prove to
his satisfaction that there was conclusive
overwhelming case for going elsewhere.

Further support for non profit making
trading estates, to include a number of smaller
estates in areas of greatest depression.

improved communications, road and rail,
afforestation and powers for the Minister to
encourage tourism.'

The party condemned as 'stark lunacy' the concentration of new factories
in greater London from a security and defence point of view, and called
upon the government to transfer work into the areas not transfer workers
out.[10]

The Special Areas amendment bill

The new competition in policy ideas fuelled the parliamentary debates on
the Special Areas amendment bill. Angered by the drafting of the money
resolution so tightly to prevent any amendments, Dalton, Bevan and co
fought a ferocious but unsuccessful parliamentary battle to delay the bill
and extract concessions. Bevan, supporting an amendment to appoint a
Minister for the Special Areas, condemned the commissioner as little more
than a 'decoy' for the Treasury bench. He deeply resented having the
humiliation of having to go to a non elected, irresponsible person to put
before him the grievances of his constituents.

From Carmarthenshire and west Wales, Jim Griffiths and Daniel Hopkins
doubted, with justification, that grants to new 'site companies' could or
would apply to communities such as Garnant, Glanammon, and
Brynamman, outside the special areas but suffering every bit as much from
chronic levels of high unemployment arising from tin plate closures. Jim
Griffiths drew the striking contrast between government subsidies for
sugar-beet (some £50 million over the previous 12 years and £3 million a

117

year alone for the county of Norfolk) and the modest £11 million or so for the special areas.

The bill drew muted criticism from a government Welsh member, Sir Reginald Clarry (Newport). He emphasised the omissions from the bill and especially any provision for promoting oil to coal processes. The nation was spending millions in imported oil whereas neither an ideal indigenous source of fuel, coal, nor men ready to work it were being fully utilised. For 'the mercies' in the bill Mr Clarry was grateful but a great deal more needed doing and he warned against any 'feeling of complacency'. Another critic, Harold Macmillan, sardonically accepted 'gratefully' and 'gracefully' what they had been given 'for we are not likely to get more at present', but not without some tart observations upon the role of the commission and the character of the new commissioner, Sir George Gillett. The commissioner had 'a position in our constitution which was 'neither fish, fowl, or fresh herring'. The government had appointed the new commissioner, 'a greatly respected and rather elderly gentleman with not much expertise of industry but considerably more of banking'. Macmillan held no doubts that the commissioner would 'be still tamer' in the hands of the Government than the last one. 'After all he was a member of the National labour party and they are well known to be the tamest among the tamest of God's creatures'.

The government had, however, done just enough to buy off any further back bench revolt. Chamberlain, during ministerial discussions, had been particularly anxious to present the bill within the context of the overall government effort and achievement for the distressed areas. He had not wanted the positive news stories to be 'dribbled out' and had persuaded cabinet colleagues to publish with the bill a statement trumpeting such achievement. Brown, the Minister of Labour, had claimed on 9th March that South Wales would benefit from government projects worth £1.5 million, including a gun powder factory and a mines' depot. In a lengthy personal apologia, Chamberlain rejected the caricaturing of the attitude of the Chancellor of the Exchequer as 'a man who from the beginning had taken up a pessimistic and cynical position.' Claiming that there had been no man or minister who had worked harder or longer to solve the problem of the special areas, Chamberlain rehearsed his oft repeated refrain that there was no single remedy. There were five ways - help to revive the staple industries, induce new industries, land settlement, transference, improvement of local social conditions - to which a sixth should be added, the armaments programme. Updating recent figures, Chamberlain told the House that £35 million of government contracts had gone into the special areas. Rearmament was beginning to revive steel and iron. In South Wales and Monmouthshire, production of pig iron had gone from 491,700 to 741,000 tons, steel ingots and castings from 1,846,000 tons to 2,404,000. A series of coal trade agreements with Argentina, Uruguay, arrangements with Holland, France and Italy had helped to stabilise the industry. The coal for cattle agreement between Britain and Ireland had been particularly valuable to South Wales. Ministers claimed that between November 1934 and January 1937, unemployment had fallen by 26%. In South Wales numbers had fallen from 157,174 to 125,175 (20.4%). While admitting some of the reduction had been achieved by transference, the insured population had fallen over the previous two years by only 20,000 compared with a fall of nearly 120.000 in the number of unemployed.[11]

With the passing of the Special Areas Act, the government could claim that they had empowered the commissioner to clear sites, erect factories, promote trading estates and offer remission of rent, rates and income tax to any company. Such companies could also enjoy cheap credit and support from one or other of three sources, the Nuffield Trust, S.A.R.A. and the Treasury. Finally, the government had committed itself to create full-time jobs in the distressed areas through its rearmament programme. While Chamberlain confided to his diary that some of the measures were 'thin', the Special Areas' amendment act represented a significant shift in attitude and policy from those of 1931/2, though the fundamental question remained: would these measures be sufficient to match the scale of the unemployment and distress already borne for more than a decade in Britain's traditional coalfield communities?

1937: 'A Second Experiment'

1. Sir George Gillett's memorandum and correspondence; LAB 8/205

2. Reports on State provided inducements to attract industry, 1936-7, LAB 8/205

3. Treasury memoranda and bills papers, T161/777/S41642, S41674, S41716; T161/779/27237,T161/779/S41961/01: Other new bill papers, HLG 30/45.

4. Cabinet committee memoranda and minutes, CAB 27/577,578; discussion on supporting local government finance, HLG 30/45.

'A Sister to SARA.'

5. For the work of the Nuffield Trust; Nuffield Trust papers, Nuffield College, Oxford.

6. B.O.E records on S.A.R.A, SMT 2/16-29; Criticisms of S.A.R.A, HLG 30/45.

7. Treasury/B.O.E discussions T172/1828.

8. Cabinet committee discussions and memoranda, CAB27/577,578,579. Other cabinet committee discussions on the bill, CAB 26/21 (Home Affairs HAC.4), 22.2 1937.

'Blue and Pink Plans'

9. Professor Marquand's plan for South Wales: *Second Industrial Survey of South Wales*, 3 vols, (Cardiff, 1937).

10. Labour Party's policy commission report Labour and the Distressed Areas: A programme of Immediate Action; for the work of the commission, Hugh Dalton, *Fateful Years, 1931-1940*, 120 - 128 (F. Muller Ltd, London).

The Special Areas amendment bill

11. HC debates on the bill, 2nd reading 6 April, committee stage, 19,22 April, Report stage 22 April, Third reading, 26 April, 1937.

6

1937/8: 'HOPE DAWNS ON DOWLAIS'

The activities that flowed from the shifts in government policy and the introduction of the Special Areas amendment act have more than a modest claim to a place in the industrial and social history of South Wales. The derelict land reclamation programme at Dowlais was the first publicly financed project of its kind. Treforest trading estate also broke new ground and became the South Wales home for the majority of the first wave of inward investors and entrepreneurs of the century. The arrival of new companies transformed local economic and social life: Polikoff at Ynyswen, Rhondda, Porth Textiles, Kayser Bondor, Dowlais, Leiners, Treforest, Pilkingtons and Weston Biscuits in Monmouthshire became an integral part of industrial social life, turning pit villages into manufacturing communities. There could be no more a vivid illustration of both the success and limitation of the policy than that of Dowlais and Merthyr Tydfil. Dowlais had personified the destitution of the distressed areas. The King had stood among the rubble of a once proud iron centre. Those images had been transmitted by word and film to a huge audience. Whitehall received a first hand report through Captain Crawshay, the district commissioner for the special areas, of the meeting with the local chamber of trade: in one Dowlais street 31 shops lay empty or in disrepair. The decline in purchasing power and escalating debts corroded the remains of normal commercial life. If renewal was to mean anything, it had to accept the challenge of Dowlais.

The decision to undertake the reclamation programme of the abandoned Goatmill Road works had been made, in principle, before the King's visit, albeit accompanied by familiar officials' and experts' scepticism as to the value of doing so. Consultants reported that the site had little or no industrial value, 'there being neither a shortage of flat land or demands for factory sites'. But both they and Crawshay accepted that refusal to clear 'would be tantamount to saying that Merthyr had no chance of industrial revival'. Crawshay had, initially, envisaged a clearance scheme at the other derelict Merthyr iron works, Cyfarthfa; but a chance meeting with Hollings, managing director, Guest Keen & Baldwin (GKB), paved the way for action at the Goatmill road site. The commission approved the decision in principle in May, putting the best possible gloss upon Dowlais' potential. The Dowlais site offered 'easy accessibility and an ample labour supply already housed nearby'.

Work did not effectively begin until early 1937 after the formal Treasury approval for a 100% grant of £25,000 to level the site. A few weeks later, the *Western Mail* reported: 'Hope dawns at Dowlais. Stagnation has given way to feverish activity; but more important than all, the long suffering Dowlais community is acquiring new hope for the regeneration of their once famous village'. 'Feverish activity' created local political cross currents. In a society destitute by unemployment, the prospect of jobs exposed tensions and envy. Impossible queues gathered for the most menial of jobs. The potential of 200 jobs on site clearance instantly created local divisions. Under pressure and influence from the National Union of Unemployed Working Men (NUUWM), it was agreed that a work sharing scheme should be introduced through a nine week working rota arrangement. Initially welcomed locally, the work sharing scheme proved costly, disruptive and divisive. Having, at last, got a job, many of the longer term unemployed resented being dumped back on the dole at the end of the nine weeks. 'It was only natural', district commissioner Crawshay explained, 'that men who after a long period of idleness had tasted a spell of employment should resent being displaced by others'.

The local commissioner's headaches in Dowlais were not confined to the work sharing scheme. Crawshay had trouble, too, with Guest, Keen and Baldwin. An immense amount of derelict machinery, buildings and chimney stacks littered the site. Guest, Keen and Baldwin sought to remove all valuable scrap and plant capable of being recycled at their new Cardiff works. The company's attitude rekindled long standing enmities between the community and the company. As Crawshay reported in June 1936 to Tribe, secretary at the London commission's office, 'a great deal of ill feeling exists between the people and Guest, Keen and Baldwin.' Tribe experienced some of the company's obstructive behaviour. The site itself was surrounded by six great reservoirs capable of holding 1/2 to 2 million gallons, which had served the Guest works in its heyday. Tribe considered them considerable assets for the future development of the site, though inspections deemed them 'unsafe' - 'a catastrophe waiting to happen' Guest, Keen and Baldwin disputed the perceived dangers but responded by proposing their total demolition and removal. Eventually, the commission itself agreed to acquire and restore the reservoirs.

Having committed so much public money to the Dowlais scheme, Whitehall and the commission were determined that the site did not fall into the hands of the Merthyr county borough. New industries would, they felt, be attracted more by a private entrepreneurial image than that of a radical and socialist council. The management of the site was transferred to the South Wales Estate company. Despite local political cross currents, company greed and obstruction, and the difficult technical task of clearing a part of one of the oldest iron works, the commission could, in early 1938, plan a grand opening of the site by commissioner Gillett, accompanied by

Mr Oscar Guest, chairman of Hall Telephones, the first company to occupy a factory on the site.

Bizarrely, the decision by Hall Telephones had risen out of a parliamentary altercation between Guest, as member of parliament for north Camberwell, and George Hall, member for Aberdare, during the debates on the Special Areas bill. Guest had spoken dismissively of Dowlais' suitability; far better, he claimed, that activity should be concentrated on the new trading estates. Hall had responded by challenging Guest as to whether he had visited a town so well known to his ancestors. Guest admitted later that the subsequent conversation between the two members had prompted him to propose Dowlais to the company's board. At the opening of the factory in March 1938, he confessed that 'it was very much up to the Guest family to do what they could for Dowlais': 'for a long period of years Merthyr and Dowlais did a great deal for the Guest family'. One hundred and fifty jobs at Hall Telephones may have been a very poor substitute for the loss of 3,000 when the Dowlais works had closed in 1930, but it was a beginning. The Western Mail and the South Wales' News, reporting the opening ceremony, 'as the people of Dowlais flooded spontaneously' onto the 30 acre cleared site, compared the occasion 'to the first glimpse the children of Israel had of the promised land'.[1]

'The Promised Land'

The Western Mail's allusions to the promised land proved inadvertently apposite; for one of the most remarkable features of pre second world war inward entrepreneurs to South Wales was their Jewish origin. No fewer than 48 of the 78 companies to establish themselves at Treforest were Jewish. The arrival of so many Jewish entrepreneurs was less fortuitous than, at first, it might have seemed. Whitehall made conscious efforts to cajole and steer Jewish professional and business refugees into the distressed areas. The earlier wave of Jewish immigrants from Russia and Eastern Europe, between 1880 and 1914, (an estimated 120,000) had tended to be destitute, and remained a community apart, inciting strong populist anti-semitic sentiments. The government had been compelled, in 1902, to establish a royal commission review of aliens legislation, leading to the 1905 Aliens act. The prospect of another major influx worried Whitehall and excited press and parliamentary comment. Refugees inventing and creating jobs in distressed areas offered a viable defence. As one cabinet paper stated: 'It would be in the public interest to try to secure for the country prominent Jews who were being expelled from Germany'. 'Not only would they obtain for the country the advantage of their knowledge and experience but could also create a very favourable impression world wide.'

Entry qualifications remained stiff; refugees required visas and sponsors depositing £50 to £105 as guarantees. Work permits were denied except for those areas of scarce labour (domestic servants and agricultural workers) and for those who sought to establish new businesses. The Ministry of Labour wanted to go further. Invoking commissioner Stewart's second report, recommending that 'persuasion' should be exercised on refugee industrialists, ministry officials argued that 'the earliest opportunity should be taken of raising doubts whether permission to enter will be given if the foreigner proposes to establish his factory in London or the home counties'. Accepting that it would be impossible to refuse entry on such grounds, the ministry believed that 'if the general policy' became known 'foreigners will be induced to act accordingly without pressure or persuasion'. To make sure that they got the message, applicants were confronted with a lengthy questionnaire and a letter containing the Commons resolution, 12 March 1936:

> 'that HM government endeavour to discourage the undue
> concentration of modern industries in the southern
> counties ... and to establish them in the older industrial areas.'

More positively, the Home Office encouraged the commission for the special areas to promote the opportunities offered by the Treasury loan scheme, the Nuffield Trust and the Special Areas Reconstruction Association. The British Embassy, Berlin, nevertheless, reported resistance from applicants to go to the distressed areas, though 'one or two might find their way to the Cardiff district!' The Ministry of Labour, the Board of Trade, with a degree of collusion from the Home Office, sought to route Jewish entrepreneurs from the consuls of Berlin and North Bohemia into the new network of committees determining the loan schemes. [2]

Decisions on loans granted by either S.A.R.A, Nuffield Trust or the Treasury were made by a very small group. The system set up in the wake of the 1937 Special Areas act endowed one person with extraordinary influence. Lord Portal presided over, or participated in, all the loans discussions. He trawled his business and commercial contacts for applicants and, having found them, frequently 'bounced' his colleagues into prompt and positive responses. S.A.R.A, first in the field, bore the brunt of the initial applications. Surviving records reveal that by the early weeks of 1937 the board had drafted a format for dealing with applications, requiring details of the company, background, capital structure, loan requirement and, occasionally, a business plan and market forecasts. Local South Wales' applications carried a recommendation from the area board. A 'green' form application to board members signified a negative recommendation. Submissions were frequently extremely sketchy. The board was left to make subjective judgements, though, occasionally, members appointed a person to survey the project. At their request, a Mr Maxted viewed the state of the Pwllgwaun brickworks. He found the buildings derelict but the kilns practically new and capable, with modest investment, of an annual production of 4.5 million bricks. He doubted whether £1,000 was sufficient working capital but recommended the board to grant a loan. Loans from S.A.R.A, with their normal limit of £10,000, inevitably attracted the smallest of applicants. Mrs Mary Jones, 112 Llewellyn Street, Pentre sought £250 over five years to expand her 'factory' at the rear of her sweet shop, making wooden electric blocks for switches and ceiling roses and employing six people. A local surveyor found inadequate security for a loan larger than £150. Rather more substantially, RR Paton Garth Works, Taffs Wells, sought a £10,000 loan to acquire a machine tool business from a Wolverhampton company. The business had become available because that company had secured large government contracts for the aircraft industry. Paton's associate company, British Conway Shovels, manufactured tunnel and heading machinery unique to the country and under an American patent. The board's investigations revealed Paton's 'good connections' with leading local colliery and engineering companies. Paton become one of Treforest's earliest tenants.

At least these were local companies which could be subject to thorough assessment and analysis. A large number of the refugee applications offered a different challenge to S.A.R.A. Information about the companies or individuals for profit assessment was often hearsay. The board turned away a number of refugee applications. Mr Max Lang, a German Jew, who had received permission from the Home Office to remain in Britain until March 1938, sought to manufacture a patent type of dry powder fire extinguisher. Ironically, the board was informed that such extinguishers were in wide circulation within German offices including 'the barracks of the Stormtruppe'. Despite such a recommendation, members felt, upon the available evidence, unable to grant Mr Lang his £2,000 loan.

They turned down Mr Haechtal, a shoe manufacturer from Leipzig. His German factory had been taken over without compensation. The Board of Trade advised against any loan. The market for shoes was already adequately served; it was, therefore, 'inadvisable to start up a shoe factory even in a special area'. Others did not receive such outright rejections. The inventive spirit of a Swiss Austrian company, Associated Chemical and Electrical Works, seeking £3,000 to manufacture their new gelatine bottle cap, was not summarily dismissed. Nor was Mr Arthur Vogal, a manufacturer of lacquered paper bound for suit cases and shoe stiffeners.

He applied for £2,500 over 5 years to establish production in South Wales which, until a few months previously, had been made at his Esslinger factory, Germany. Like so many, this Jewish family business had been forced to sell up under Nazi persecution.

L P Koppell's London Metal company also succeeded in reaching the Treforest trading estate. Koppell acquired London Metal in 1938 as a company vehicle for the manufacture of a new kind of aluminium covered fastener patented by a Czech company, Hans Diffmayer. The Board of Trade found hostility to assistance for such production from none other than the mighty ICI whose lightening fasteners had, it was claimed, made it unnecessary to create any 'new capacity'. The Board of Trade, however, considered that there was something to be said for small concerns, especially those with products of original design. Potential conflict between the giant ICI and Mr Koppell was averted when the latter agreed royalty payments to ICI Lightening Fasteners. To establish production at Treforest, Koppell invited to South Wales a handful of the skilled Czech engineers. By early 1939, forty nine Jewish companies had commenced production, primarily in clothing, textiles, footwear and furniture.[3]

Not all Jewish inward investment to South Wales was of recent refugee origin (an estimated 80,000, German and 55,000, Austrian refugees entered Britain between 1933 and 1939), Nor were they just S.A.R.A supported. More established families, such as the Leiners, were in a position to drive tough bargains. Arnold Leiner first made contact with Lord Portal in December 1937, seeking, very much on his own terms, a loan from the Nuffield trust. He wrote to explain that he was contemplating a chemical company to produce gelatine. On his valuation, land at Treforest was little more than £100 an acre rather than the £2,000 assumed by the estates company. He sought £7,500 free of interest for two years and 5% thereafter and expected to be relieved entirely from the national defence contribution. He was looking to employ 50 - 75 unskilled people but anticipated doubling the size of the plant. He further explained to Portal his reason for such a pre-emptory set of demands. An operation at Treforest would carry the additional transport burdens of shipping his raw materials through Liverpool or London, as Cardiff could not handle them. Leiner got almost all his way, compromising modestly upon his demand for relief from the national defence contribution. Originally manufacturing glue gelatine in 32,000 sq ft, the company and its factory expanded to some 150,000 sq ft for employing 250 men, producing high grade technical gelatine for photographic material in bank note manufacture. Leiners became synonymous with Treforest trading estate for more than a generation.[4]

Buttons and Silk Stockings

The new Jewish inward investors primarily clustered around Treforest trading estate, but not exclusively so. Some found new homes and companies within the valleys and did so, as in the case of the Adler family, after exercising ingenuity and fortitude to leave Nazi terror stricken central Europe. Welsh Products' (the Merthyr button factory as it became known locally) origins lay in the small Czech town of Tachau and the village of Galtenhof close to the German border. The company had grown impressively through exports of its mother of pearl buttons to Marks and Spencer. Rudolph Adler had already once been a prisoner of war, in Russia during the first world war. He had never made any secret of his revulsion of Nazi doctrines and the family believed their name to be on Gestapo files. Carefully and surreptitiously, through the contact of the British Consul in Northern Bohemia (an agent for a Gloucestershire company), the family laid its plans to remove machinery and equipment. The British Consul fortunately was an 'Evans', familiar with the government's special area policy and, consequently, guided Rudolph Adler in 1938 both to S.A.R.A and to the lord mayor of Cardiff, He, in turn, introduced the Adlers to Merthyr's town clerk and its member of parliament. In August 1938 a new company, Welsh Products, was incorporated and work began on a 7,800 sq ft factory, financed by the commission for the special areas, designed by Alexander Gibbs and adjacent to the newly built Hall Telephones. S.A.R.A offered a £1,500 loan. The company was planning a further expansion when war broke out. The skills and machinery for wood and plastic button making were ingeniously adapted to make altimeter protection caps for mosquito fighters at the neighbouring Lucas war production factory, Rotax. The company was to prosper in post war Merthyr and at the time of its closure, some fifty years after the arrival of the Adlers, it was the oldest surviving Merthyr pre-war company.[5]

The cases coming before the Treasury committee and Nuffield trustees became increasingly complex and speculative, raising issues of policy which required clearance from the Chancellor. The size and character of these loans applications pushed Whitehall policy to its limits. In early 1938 Isaac Sieff, of Marks and Spencer approached the Treasury to consider the application of their major silk stocking supplier, Kurnet, a Czech company residing in Warmsdoff, a few miles from the German border. The Kunerts, who supplied some £400,000 stock to Marks and Spencer wished to flee from the approaching nazification of the border areas; and it was Marks and Spencer's company policy to refuse to buy from any nazified area. Kunert and Sieff had explored the possibilities of relocation into Dowlais, Merthyr Tydfil where the commission for the special areas would erect a factory, adjacent to Hall Telephones, capable, ultimately, of employing 2,000. Agreement had been reached with the hosiery union to pay union rates of pay, while Sieff had committed Marks and Spencer to purchase the whole stock.

The proposition, involving eventually £600,000 capital and a massive £340,000 from the Treasury, presented policy problems for the department. Deputy secretary, Sir Richard Hopkins, advised permanent secretary, Sir Warren Fisher, and Chamberlain that it would break a general Whitehall rule not to lend to a company where more than a half the equity of the business lay in foreign hands. Kunert's case would also be the first time that financial facilities on such a considerable scale would have been made available for 'foreigners flying from nazification'. Hopkins, nevertheless, endorsed the scheme as 'sound' and not competitive with any existing British concern. He could not see any quarter from which criticism was 'likely to flow'. Hopkins' lengthy minutes drew from the hitherto ultra conservative Sir Warren a remarkable and simple endorsement; 'this sounds desirable' - far cry, indeed from Fisher's belief, only four years previously, that 'nothing new or heroic' could be done for Dowlais other than 'transference'.

The Nazi invasion of Czechoslovakia sadly overtook the tortuous negotiations with Kunerts. The Treasury picked up unsubstantiated rumours that the Kunerts were clandestine Nazi sympathisers. An apologetic Sieff, however, returned to the Treasury with an alternative for Dowlais. A British supplier of silk stockings, Full Fashioned Hosiery company from Baldock, Hertfordshire, producing under the name of Bondor were prepared to pick up the project if equally, if not more generous, inducements were on offer. The Treasury, the Nuffield trust, S.A.R.A and the commission for the areas began a second round of negotiating with Baldocks' managing director, Mr Goodenday. Goodenday ruthlessly sought to extract even greater concessions than the 100% rent and rate relief for two years in the factory, the five years' tax remission and at least another £20,000 on the initial £160,000 loan from the Treasury and Nuffield. At one stage, Goodenday attempted to transfer production, with the inducements, to a Newport site, in view of the 'difficult freight arrangements' to Dowlais. Portal firmly reminded the company that the offer was only available at Dowlais. A senior Treasury official, Sir Thomas Padmore, conceded that, because of the advisory committee's strong support for the scheme, there was 'no question of a calling a halt on account of the excessive use of the agreed concessions', despite the fact that the first stages of development 'earmarked' £150,000 out of the Treasury £2 million loan scheme. Linking with the leading US silk stocking company, Julius Kayser, Baldocks established at Dowlais, a company and a household name for more than a generation.[7]

Portal's connections, influence and manipulative skills brought one further investment into the most distressed of the distressed areas, Merthyr Tydfil. His initial connection with a putative company, British Sewing Machine (BSM) and its chairman, Sir Reginald Graham, may have been made via Sir Charles Hambro, a fellow G.W.R. director. At the Treasury advisory committee in February 1937, the special areas commission secretary, Tribe, reported that Portal had a company in mind, if a factory could be provided. A month later, the committee agreed to clear the 60 acre site at Merthyr's other great, but derelict, iron works, Cyfarthfa, if Portal received a genuine undertaking from the Company. That was successfully obtained and, indeed, was steered through the S.A.R.A board, though not without some anger and the alienation of a number of board members, including the Bank's governors' representative, Mr E D Skinner. Mr Skinner wrote sharply to S.A.R.A's secretary that he could not recall the board having agreed such exceptional terms to, what in any case, was an extraordinarily large loan for S.A.R.A. 'I do not remember being told that the loan was to be redeemable in 15 years after the first five'. Secretary Roney sheepishly confessed that he had not drawn direct attention to these exceptional terms and, in his defence, Roney reminded Skinner that the discussion had been 'somewhat abruptly closed by the chairman, Lord Portal, as he, in common with the majority of the board, was keen that this particular participation should be taken by S.A.R.A'. The loan required Treasury consent, but again, as Roney discovered, Treasury officials were not predisposed to cavil. The S.A.R.A board found, in a frank discussion with Treasury officials, that they shared the Bank of England's concern at the 'propriety of doing this class of business'; 'but the powers that be are keen just now on swelling the volume of business done by S.A.R.A'. The Treasury would, therefore, turn a blind eye to the most questionable feature of the transaction, namely the redemption dates.

The new British Sewing Machine company, therefore, got its £25,000 loan along with £75,000 from the Nuffield trust and a 30 acre factory site. They were accompanied by the usual remission of rents and rates and potential income tax relief to produce sewing machines under a Czech Minerva patent, creating an estimated 368 jobs. Delays in negotiating the patents, not made any easier by the fact that the Minerva people 'talked nothing but Czechoslovakian', and problems of site clearance and factory building prevented production starting before 1939. Looming war demands led to an agreement with Rotax, a subsidiary of Lucas, in April 1939 to take over all but a small segregated part of the factory earmarked for sewing machine manufacture. BSM was never to make a machine in Merthyr Tydfil.[8]

The Dowlais and Cyfarthfa sites had been financed directly by the commission for the special areas, but managed and operated by the Treforest South Wales' Estates company. The company had taken responsibility for relocating a small and impecunious business, Worldwin pistons, from Cyfarthfa to Treforest to enable the construction of BSM 140,000 sq ft factory. The commission and the estate company continued to collaborate on the development of other 'single sites', which brought into the Rhondda two companies which became fixtures in the local industrial scene for two generations.[9]

Flex Fasteners and Porth Textiles, a joint venture in a subdivided factory, and Polikoffs, Treorchy, carried Jewish investment into the heart of the Rhondda mining communities. Flex Fasteners were the products of the Nuremburg works of Mr Richard Benedict and co-director Mr Bernsteil whose machine tool company helped to make possible a new coloured fastener. Benedict's original intention had been to emigrate to America but Michael Sieff of Marks and Spencer had suggested setting up in Britain. Both Marks and Spencer and Woolworth supported the company's application to S.A.R.A. Marks and Spencer confirmed that if goods produced by Benedict in Britain were up to their German standards, there would be a ready market in fastener supplies for blouses, skirts and leather goods, currently being imported from France. Despite company losses in Spain, as a result of the civil war, the S.A.R.A board enthusiastically backed Benedict and Bernstiel for their £10,000 loan and the prospect of 150 jobs (120 for women). Through the commission for the special areas, they found their way to a factory site, 17,000 sq ft at Porth (Dinas) Rhondda.[10]

Polikoff's arrival in Treorchy, Rhondda, came through a rather different route. Like the Lieners, the Polikoffs were from an earlier period of migration. As Alfred Polikoff explained, in a long rambling letter to Lord Portal in August 1937, his company had been trading and producing ladies clothing before the first world war and during the war, had made great coats and tunics for Kitchener's army. A workforce of five hundred, had risen, he claimed to 3,000 to produce among other things, 300,000 demob suits. Polikoff had made a rather untimely investment in Frankfurt in 1923, a business which had been sold in 1929. He had opened another factory in 1932 in Dublin employing 700. Polikoff now came forward with the idea of creating some 3,000 jobs for young girls, shipping some 250 girls each few months to London for training. He considered it essential that a canteen be set up because these young children of the

Rhondda valley were 'so badly underfed and clothed' that they would require 'heart to work'. Not suprisingly, this incoahate scheme first presented to the South Wales' estates company, initially attracted little support, until contact was made with Portal. By the autumn of 1937, Portal had introduced the Polikoff proposal both to the Treasury and the Nuffield trustees. The Treasury offered a £40,000 debenture loan despite the fact that enquiries cast doubt on Polikoff's 'not very comfortable' financial position. 'The Polikoff's didn't know what a profit was'.

The company struggled to put up their £25,000, being rebuffed by Woolfsons' Great Universal Store company to whom Polikoff had turned. Neither Portal nor the Nuffield trustees were to be deterred from pushing through a scheme offering hundreds of jobs. The trustees agreed an extra £10,000 share capital to their initial £25,000 to ensure that the company would not miss the 1939 spring season shows. The factory site also proved problematic and increasingly costly. The company's first choice, a 20 acre site, had been turned down by it owner, the Ocean Colliery company, which claimed that they had plans to develop an oil from coal plant. Polikoff was, fortunately, attracted to the neighbouring Ynyswen 16.25 acre site which, despite its two levels, was capable of housing 240,000 sq ft factory space. The commission grimly bore the escalating site subsidence costs, offered the usual rent and rate and tax relief, to witness some three hundred girls beginning work in March 1938. The company rapidly, but precariously, expanded at such a pace that by mid 1939 concern was growing that they would 'run out of girls'. They began the task of persuading boys to take to machinery automatically associated with women's employment. An analysis of the work force, in July 1939, revealed some 700 came from a two mile radius of the factory; 120 within four miles, 77 within 6 and 36 within 8 miles. Polikoff's Ynyswen factory transformed the local employment and industrial scene, to become one of the Rhondda's largest employers.[11]

The commissioner's sites had brought new industries to Dowlais and the Rhondda. They also accommodated other new comers in Monmouthshire. At Llantarnam, on an 8 acre site in a factory of 76,000 sq ft, the Canadian Biscuit company owncd by Garfield Weston was personally opened in November 1938 by Lord Nuffield, whose acquaintance with Weston probably accounted for this investment. With the support of £33,000 by the Nuffield trustees, an estimated 425 jobs were anticipated. The Nuffield trust also contributed to the second development at Cwmbran by a Wolverhampton based company, Saunders Valves. Their fluid control valve with a special form of diaphragm was to be made by a newly formed Cwmbran Engineering company, capitalised at £50,000, with contribution from Nuffield of £25,000 in 5% non cumulative redeemable preference shares. The company, also, successfully obtained a £30,000 treasury loan to deliver its distinctive valves, products and castings to the Admiralty, War office, colonies and the government of India. Within six months, the company had returned to the Treasury, complaining of a shortage of working capital as a result of the heavy expenses of transferring from Wolverhampton to Cwmbran. The company had wanted to maintain some production at Wolverhampton, but, given the reduced asset value of the parent works, were finding it very difficult to borrow further from the banks, as the Nuffield trust and the Treasury had pressed it to do. Following discussion with the Nuffield trust and the Treasury advisory committee, the trustees agreed to guarantee the company's bank overdraft while Portal and Campbell endorsed an additional treasury loan of £5,000 for a fixed term of five years at 4%. Thus, another company of some stature had successfully rooted itself in South Wales to become a significant part of the post war local Monmouthshire manufacturing scene.[12]

A third did so with the greatest reluctance. The mighty Pilkington Glass company had absolutely no intention of establishing a presence in South Wales, until it got wind of a possible new comer to glass production who was seeking the support of both S.A.R.A and the Nuffield trustees. The threat came from a German, Dr Eckhert, who was contemplating setting up two works, on the Tyne and in South Wales, with a combined capacity of 4.2 million sq ft per annum. Pilkingtons discovered that the new company had, already, the backing of Lord Portal and the issuing house, on behalf of the new company, was to be Messrs Herbitt Wragge, whose directors included a Mr Campbell, one of the Nuffield trustees. Disparagingly, Pilkingtons' executives alleged that Eckhert 'spent his time trying to obtain slight alterations to other people's patents and processes and palming them on unsuspecting firms'. Eckhert had already been instrumental in arranging for a sheet glass plant to be instigated in India.

Pilkington felt sufficiently concerned to mobilise an immediate lobby through the National Union of General and Municipal Workers and their local M.P. and to make direct representations to a senior Board of Trade official, during which the company claimed that it could expand to meet the entire British market. Pilkington's real concerns surfaced at a subsequent board meeting. Eckhert's scheme would enjoy a 'distinct colour of government backing owing to the fact that S.A.R.A had, with the consent of the Treasury, agreed to subscribe up to £60,000 debenture stock. The establishment of independent factories would result in a considerable reduction in prices that would bring about the termination of the industry's plate and sheet agreements. 'The price war would be very costly'.

The Pilkington board, therefore, concluded that, as the government was 'so far committed', the only reason for which they could be expected to withdraw support from Eckhert would be the decision of P.B to establish a works themselves in South Wales. To spike Eckhert's plan, Pilkingtons had been forced into an instant commitment to invest in South Wales. The board 'generally agreed' that the distressed areas of South Wales were not such as the company would have chosen and it was felt, that the best result that could be hoped for was to break even. Reluctantly, but unanimously, the board agreed to seek a £100,000 financial support package from agencies and further concessions or advantages from local authorities. Pilkington's alternative proposal successfully led to S.A.R.A's withdrawal of support from the Eckhert scheme and an offer of a loan at 3.5%. The company preferred a site at Pontypool, rather than at Merthyr Tydfil. Production first began in September 1938 and survived until 1975.[13]

'Working Against The Ring'

If, numerically, foreign entrepreneurs accounted for the largest number of new pre war South Wales' companies, an important core of British companies followed Pilkington and Cwmbran Engineering/Saunders Valves into the distressed areas. They tended to be owned or managed by mercurial individuals, industrial outsiders, often at loggerheads with the industrial establishment, the 'victims' of the powerful corporate industry federations or associations. Aberdare Cables represented just such a case. The company created by Mr Usher, from the parent, Industrial Combustion, to produce low tension electric cables had been excluded from 'the ring', the cable makers association. Indeed, that association had introduced a discriminatory pricing policy, offering discounts to electricity companies if they bought exclusively from members of 'the ring'. Largely as a result of G.W.R director, Lord Portal's, 'persuasion', Usher and Aberdare cables had set up on G.W.R land in Aberdare in early 1937. Ironically, the company had proceeded with the erection of the works too quickly and, consequently, had been debarred from the new loan facilities of the 1937 act. Now, a year later, Mr Usher approached the Treasury via Portal for a £20,000 loan to expand, explaining the heavy charges upon the company of training unemployed miners. The Treasury recognised that the company had 'a grievance following the misunderstandings' of the previous year, but felt it necessary to consult the Board of Trade. As Mr Usher was working against the ring, Board of Trade officials were asked whether 'in view of their knowledge of that ring any loan to an outsider such as Aberdare cables would be particularly hazardous. Trade officials acknowledged that the cable makers had not liked the intruder, and had introduced a discriminatory pricing policy, which had been the subject of vigorous objection by Aberdare's local member of parliament, Mr George Hall. Pressed, however, by Portal, who argued that the company had got over the worst of the opposition, the Treasury granted a £20,000 five loan at 4.2%. Aberdare cables grew impressively. The Nuffield trust, three years later were to turn to the company to bail out the ailing Whitehead Switchgear.[14]

Portal and G.W.R land figured in the arrival of another midlands company and another mercurial chairman/managing director, Mr Cranshaw of Welsh Metals Ltd. Cranshaw's parent company Ludlow Bros, Birmingham, had been in hollowware production for half a century. News had reached him that the Nuffield trustees were contemplating assistance to start up a new hollow-ware company. Cranshaw warned that the making and production of hollow-ware had been much overdone. Seven companies had recently been put into liquidation; but if the trustees insisted, he would consider setting up a branch of his own company in South Wales. The trustees assured Cranshaw that they would refrain from backing any new undertaking if Ludlows committed themselves to the area. Portal had got news of this possibility for the newly named Welsh Metals company were promptly steered to surplus G.W.R land at Caerphilly. Cranshaw later complained that he had found himself 'in the hands of the G.W.R on a 5.5 acre site at £80 per acre'. S.A.R.A offered £10,000 and Nuffields £45,000 while Ludlows promised a £10,000 contribution in the form of transferred machinery from Birmingham, with the intention of making pails, dust bins, small tanks and aluminium ware.

From the earliest days, Nuffield trustees found Mr Cranshaw an extremely difficult and unreliable partner. His highly individualistic style of doing business was mirrored in his home made draft press release which Nuffield trustees were anxious not to endorse. 'The Croakers', Mr Cranshaw claimed, 'have already advised Mr Cranshaw that he would find nothing but trouble in South Wales'. He had been told that 'the work people will always be on strike' but he found that Welsh people were not dull; they were inherently willing 'to put a good foot forward' and soon Mr Cranshaw hoped to 'look down from the hills on a hive of industry'. The trustees, sadly, found Mr Cranshaw willing to produce in his hive almost anything but that originally promised. Sensing lucrative war time contracts, he sought loans and guarantees to produce sheet metal and aircraft machine tools and shells. An increasingly exasperated Nuffield trust bemoaned the fact that Mr Cranshaw held only a small financial stake in Caerphilly, a concern solely constituted by means of borrowed capital and had not even fulfilled his original obligation to transfer machinery from Ludlows to the Welsh Metal company. Both the Treasury and the Nuffield trustees attempted to divert his request for support to the air ministry. Cranshaw pressed his case for a tool making plant which would also attract back to South Wales skilled tool makers from the midlands. Portal tentatively backed him. 'As I understand it the authorities greatly need this sort of production'. The irrepressible Cranshaw claimed, correctly as it turned out, that the War Office wanted to put in a plant for shell manufacturing which would employ 135 people on three shifts. A weary Treasury official feared Cranshaw was 'holding us to ransom'. If he obtained the £20,000 in loans or guarantees, he thought 'Mr Cranshaw needs to be told very plainly that it is the end'. 'I fancy he has the notion that he can go on asking for money indefinitely'. Shell making, tool making, latrine pails poured off the Caerphilly production lines, while the unpredictable Mr Cranshaw's Welsh Metals continued to draw criticism from within Whitehall and, even more so, from an irate local member of parliament, Ness Edwards. Incidents at the factory, which led to the dismissal of the works manager for drunkenness, may have been exaggerated in their reporting to Whitehall.[15]

Treasury and Nuffield trustees had found the experience of inducing to, and the financing of Welsh Metals in South Wales a particularly peculiar one. The other joint midlands/South Wales venture also proved to be vexatious. A local Pontypridd engineering company, Brown Lennox, had seemingly found an ideal partner in the Wolverhampton concern, Hingleys and Taylor. Their new joint company, South Wales' Forgemasters, was established to produce forgings and cable gear and especially, a new kind of chain, 'Tayco' used by the Admiralty, Mercantile Marine and the liners, including the new Queen Mary. A five acre site at Taffs Wells was acquired for that production. Hingleys' chairman, Mr Cyril Lloyd had approached the Nuffield trustees and the Treasury to find £30,000 out of the £40,000 needed to set up the company to employ a 100 people initially but rising to 250. The trustees jibbed at the 'disproportionate' contribution expected of them and passed the papers to the Treasury. Treasury officials were no more enamoured by the prospect of such an insecure loan of that size and generosity, but were reluctant to refuse, for Mr Lloyd had a powerful supporter at court, fellow G.W.R director, Lord Portal. Portal persuaded the advisory committee to support the project in principle. 'The best security lay in the character of the applicants'. Lloyd held his ground, refusing to offer greater security and claiming that he could locate the new production facilities in Staffordshire without assistance where 'all this class of work was at present manufactured and where a suitable supply of experienced labour remained'. Under this kind of industrial blackmail and Treasury fears of alienating Portal, who had 'always been keen' and would 'rather resent a refusal by the Treasury to people who are personally known to him', a compromise was reached by which Lloyd put up an additional £3,000 in equity. The Treasury were left with £17,000 and S.A.R.A £10,000.[16]

One other case illustrated the extraordinary transformation that had taken place within Whitehall industrial policy since the passing of the 1937 act. Only a year or so earlier, the notion of the Treasury and Board of Trade offering a huge loan to buy coal mines would have induced apoplexy. It had, of course, been a consistent South Wales demand for a decade that government should assist and promote coal sales. Owners and miners had pinned their faith in the alternative utilisation of coal through hydrogenation and calcium carbide plants. The government had remained unconvinced, preferring to promote coal exports through a series of international coal agreements with Scandinavia, as well as the coal for Irish cattle deal. The dramatic collapse in South Wales' coal export markets had not, however, been arrested. Commissioner Stewart's first report in 1934 had called for 'the application of scientific methods whereby coal's latent production could be extracted'. Ideas of coal gas driven vehicles made little progress.

More promisingly, there remained the growing market for smokeless fuel and, in the spring of 1937, yet another mercurial character, Colonel Bristow of Low Temperature Carbonisation (LTC), proposed setting up a new South Wales Coalite company, capitalised at £6000,000, which required two large contributions of £162,000 from the Treasury and Nuffield trustees. The trustees' money financed the initial purchase of the Meiros Colliery company mines, of Wern Tarw, Pencoed, employing a thousand miners. Production from the mines would serve a newly built coal distillation plant, its foundation stone being laid by the Earl of Dunraven in December 1937.

Bristow claimed to the Treasury and trustees considerable experience and success in operating such a plant at LTC's works in Barugh and Bolsover. Such experience, sadly, did not ensure the early success of South Wales Coalite. The estimated costs of purchasing and modernising the collieries rose from £133,000 to £226,000. Labour troubles, difficulties in the 'pentre seams' and a slump in the coal market contributed to significant losses. When he bothered to reply to agitated enquiries from Nuffield trustees and Sir Alexander Faulkner, permanent secretary at the Mines department, Bristow, complained bitterly of the growing problem of keeping miners and skilled foremen who were being attracted to the new munitions factory at Bridgend. A mining specialist, Mr Harley, sent by Faulkner and the Nuffield trustees to investigate, found the problems to be managerial. In fairness, neither the local management nor the unpredictable Colonel Bristow could be blamed for the company's most serious problem in March 1940, the diversion of some 3.400 tons of coal a week from the coal plant to the Port Talbot steel works. Sir Alexander Faulkner had to admit sheepishly to the Treasury and trustees that, at the outbreak of war, all Wern Tarw's 4,500 to 5,000 tons weekly production would be required by the steel company, leaving the new coal distillation plant on little more than a care and maintenance basis.[17]

Another large Treasury loan brought to South Wales one of the most remarkable of the pre war inward investors - the Swiss Aluminium company, despite powerful Treasury objections. Senior Treasury official, J Barlowe, harboured 'the gravest doubts' about the project and its promoter, a Mr Philip Hill. In a lengthy letter to Lord Portal (26 May 1938), Barlow advised that Mr Hill was not viewed with favour within the financial world. He hinted darkly that the Governor of the Bank could elaborate further. As for the project itself, the Services' requirements were served by existing stocks and the British Aluminium company's expansion plans. That company had been pressed by the government to expand without government assistance, and, therefore, could hold a 'considerable grievance' if a new arrival now attracted support. Anyway, Barlowe doubted the necessity of making a loan to the Swiss company. Given the company's fundamental requirement for anthracite it would have to seek a South Wales location. Finally, the suggested £400,000 Treasury loan in a total capitalisation of £700,000 broke 'the Portal rule' in limiting public financial support to foreign controlled companies.

Portal, initially, accepted as 'conclusive' the Treasury case that any assistance would appear discriminatory against the British Aluminium company. Quickly, officials had to confess that their original advice on this point had been misleading. It appeared that, in 1936, the Chancellor had intimated to the company that government assistance would have been forthcoming. When, however, a Canadian company had threatened to double their production of 30,000 tons a year, British Aluminium had promptly agreed to go ahead with their expansion, without a loan, upon a simple guarantee of a 15,000 ton order from government departments.

At a subsequent meeting, Mr Hill, on behalf of Swiss Aluminium and a Mr Devereux of High Duty Alloy Ltd., a major purchaser of aluminium, also successfully persuaded Board of Trade officials that departmental assessments of future requirements under estimated the growing demand, and would put the country at the mercy of a cartel. The Germans had expanded their capacity from 40,000 tons to 200,000 tons. The Swiss Aluminium scheme would produce at £65 to £70 a ton compared to the cartel's price of £100 to £105. Bauxite supplies would be assured from the Swiss suppliers in the South of France, Yugoslavia, Australia and

British Guyana. Their new plant would consume 180,000 tons of coal a year. The Treasury eventually relented, though successfully capped any loan at £200,000.

That did not end the wrangling over the project. News of such a potential 'catch' reached the ears of the Ammanford urban district council and the area's local MP, Mr James Griffiths. James Griffiths had been bitterly disappointed that the Amman valley had originally been excluded from the special areas. He and the local councils had endeavoured to attract 'a site company' which, under the terms of the 1937 act, could have attracted state aid to establish an industrial trading estate. Their efforts had failed. Now the news of an aluminium company requiring anthracite coal, their community's richest reserve, prompted, in June 1937, urgent representation to Ernest Brown, Minister of Labour. James Griffiths spelt out the disastrous tinplate and colliery closures that had befallen Ammanford and Garnant. Richard Thomas had also bought a number of plants for their quotas and then closed them. A string of collieries had been shut down, leaving a dangerous dependence upon the remaining collieries of Amalgamated Anthracite Ltd. The company had been endeavouring to entice the Swiss Aluminium company westwards, but suffered from the area's exclusion from special area status, despite higher unemployment levels. Such representations, which foreshadowed the post war politics of development area status, taxed officials. As one ruefully observed; 'this sort of thing will continue as long as we have various inducements available in particular areas. This kind criticism is bound to occur'. Officials subsequently drafted a diplomatic reply, reaffirming that it had been the company's decision to locate at Rheola in the Neath Valley, which would allow them to draw labour from some of the very highest unemployed districts of Merthyr and Aberdare. Eventually, the company and the project that emerged from protracted haggling between the promoters and Whitehall became a combine of all three aluminium producers, Swiss, British and Canadian. The Treasury's £200,000 loan was secured against the building and machinery of the new plant, costing some £627,000.[18]

Behind the scenes, one man, Lord Portal, a Nuffield trustee, S.A.R.A's chairman, a member of the Treasury advisory committee, had cajoled and persuaded a doubting and reluctant Whitehall to finance an increasing number of maverick developments. There was one revealing exception. British Coated Board Mill was the first company to enter the new Treforest trading estate and the only major new comer not to be sponsored by Nuffield, S.A.R.A or the Treasury. The company, led by another individualist and outsider, a Mr Harrison, had acquired the Ely Paper Mills in Cardiff some eight months before their application for treasury support in the early months of 1937. Mr Harrison and his company had incurred the wrath of the papermaking cartel. The secretary of the papermaking association, Mr McCarthy, sought to poison relations between the company and Whitehall. At a meeting with Tribe, secretary to the special areas commission, he dismissed the new company as 'having little prospect of success'. Importers would not supply wood pulp. No machinery from Germany would be available for at least three years. The great Wills company of Bristol were already providing the specialist paper envisaged by British Coated Board Mills.

On this occasion, the new company could expect no help from Portal, a director of the rival Wiggins Teape company. He excused himself from Treasury committee meetings, though not before querying how the new company could have made a commitment to the South Wales' trading estates corporation to take a major factory prior to any approval of financial support. Indeed, British Coated Board Mills' only ally proved to be the trading estate company's chairman. Vainly, Mr Bruce pleaded with Whitehall that occupation of such a very large factory would offer the estate 'a wonderful start'. 'Were the scheme to fail it would have the most damaging effect'. Without the usual enthusiastic commitment of Lord Portal, the new company and the trading estate were no real match for the powerful vested interests of the paper making ring and, an all too eagerly sceptical, Whitehall. A fateful meeting between the president of the papermaking association, Sir Arthur Reid MP, and Mr Campbell, a Nuffield trustee, further damaged the company's application. Reid, disingenuously, argued that he was only seeking to save the government and Whitehall the embarrassment of being involved with a scheme and a person inevitably heading for a 'smash'. Harrison had built up a 'vast and unstable network of companics.' Such disparaging assessments were fed into the Treasury advisory committee where Sir Frederick Marquis washed his hands of the company. It was of 'no concern to the committee that through anothcr channel of the South Wales' Estates company, the country will have spent a vast amount of money in the building of a factory that no one will operate'. Echoing such sentiments, Thomas Padmore at the Treasury argued that the trading estate had made a mistake; but it was 'bad policy to attempt to rescue them by expending more government money'. Despite Whitehall's rejection, British Coated Board survived to set up one of the flagship companies behind one of the impressive factory facades to be built at Treforest. In a public statement in November 1937, Mr Harrison was clearly alluding to the suspected influence of Portal and Campbell and the papermaking cartel when he called for a reform of the Treasury loan scheme. It should be in the hands only of permanent Treasury officials. The company had clearly been a victim of the industrial politics growing around the new special areas investment incentives, though upon the evidence of a number of case studies Mr Harrison would have fared little better at the hands of the Treasury mandarins.

Contemporaries ridiculed the character and nature of the jobs created under the Special Areas Act. Analysis of the range of products made by the new companies illustrates the point. They represented the skills and experience of the Jewish refugee community more than those of the indigenous South Wales population. It was not difficult to ridicule the making of wristwatch straps, toys and suitcase liners as suitable substitutes for coal, ironmaking and engineering. Presenting, in February 1938 to a cabinet committee, the first year's experience of operating the Special Areas Act, Lord Portal claimed an estimated job creation of more than 5,000 from more than forty new companies. His memorandum demonstrated the interesting internet working of the three agencies: Nuffield, S.A.R.A and the Treasury. Nuffield Trust money had made the most immediate impact. Deliberately designed to be dispersed speedily, the Trust funds had taken the greatest risk in a series of offers of equity capital. Commitments in the first year had exceeded £600,000 and, at the outbreak of war, had reached more than £1 million.[20]

Nuffield trustees occasionally interpreted their terms of reference in a way that was impossible for both S.A.R.A or the Treasury undertaking rescue operations of existing enterprises. Their investment, for example, in the Abercrave collieries saved at least one corner of the South Wales' coalfield. A much more problematic challenge arose in attempts to save the Blaenavon works, Monmouthshire. The works had been suffering severely from the lack of new technology in the making of solid wheels for railway wagons. The company's cash-flow and margins had made it virtually impossible to finance the capital expenditure required. Approaches to the trustees were made easier by the fact that the Blaenavon work's solicitor, Mr Roney happened also to be a Nuffield Trustee. The trustees initially offered, in 1936, £100,000 interest free for two years to install a solid wheel plant along with a wheel furnace and axle plant. The trust offered a further £50,000 in the autumn of 1937 for the installation of two modern open hearth furnaces. The new investment allowed the works just about to survive pre war competition for the rail wagon business. [21]

Nuffield trustees combined with the Treasury to make a most significant investment in South Wales' Coalite plant, Cwmbran Engineering and Polikoffs. Equity involvement drew trustees into operational and even board room politics. They bitterly reacted to the seemingly devious practices of the Polikoffs and the greed of British Sewing Machines' directors. The latter never built a sewing machine, but continued to draw salaries for the modest effort of renting their Merthyr factory for wartime production to a Lucas company subsidiary, Rotax.

S.A.R.A had been subjected to a continuing chorus of criticism from almost the first days of its existence. Perhaps that had been inevitable, given the multitudes of small company applications that had poured into the board and the high rejection rate. S.A.R.A, had, nevertheless, played a key role in supporting and clinching a number of investments introduced by the Nuffield trustees and, especially, the contentious £25,000 towards British Sewing Machines. S.A.R.A money (£40,000) had been crucial in bringing to South Wales one of the most prestigious new companies - Pilkingtons.

The third player, since 1937, had been the Treasury. At the outbreak of war, Treasury loans exceeding £1 million had supported a dozen companies that had come to South Wales. In these cases, they represented the largest individual commitment made by pre war government agencies - £162,500, to South Wales' Coalite, £200,000 to Swiss Aluminium, and £220,000 for the manufacture of silk stockings by Kayser Bondor, Dowlais. The very notion, even five years earlier, that Treasury mandarins, Sir Richard Hopkins and Sir Warren Fisher, would have been minuting each other on the merits of investing state money in silk stocking manufacturing would have been unimaginable. Sir Warren had in 1935, dismissed Portal's report on South Wales as 'nothing new, nothing heroic'. Senior officials were now sucked into a new form of industrial administrative decision making, passing judgement on the financial viability of new and often risky ventures frequently on the basis of flimsy draft accounts and business projections. They tended to rely upon the small coterie of semi-detached industrial advisers and, especially, upon the ubiquitous Lord Portal. As we have seen in a number of case studies, Treasury doubts were disregarded as the political imperative to produce results grew. Chamberlain and officials may have continued to take comfort from the fact that the whole exercise had always meant to be a time limited experiment; but when, in 1939, ministers faced the decision to allow the powers to expire, they felt it politically impossible to do so.

The experiment in regional industrial incentives began the process of changing the Whitehall culture from the 1920s and early 30s total rejection of any form of 'inducement' into the active regional assistance, which became the norm of post second world war politics. It is impossible to make an accurate numerical assessment of the impact of the new policy. Portal attempted it in his memoranda to ministers, but, essentially, relied upon impressions, linked to highly speculative job creation estimates. He, rightly, drew attention, not only to the regenerating capacity of the new industrial trading estates, but also to the effectiveness of the smaller site development, such as Dowlais, which brought into very local communities of highest unemployment, new factories, companies and hope. Yet, many of these factories never produced the products originally planned for them. Hall Telephones and British Sewing Machines rapidly made way for production of a very different kind. Events beyond the boundaries of the special areas were to dictate their development and future. Virtually the whole of the Treforest trading estate was requisitioned for war production. New royal ordnance factories - involving millions of square feet and far greater than any size contemplated under special areas legislation were erected in locations hitherto dismissed (by officials) as industrial wastelands. South Wales had pleaded with Whitehall, for more than five years, to relocate strategically vulnerable military production only to be met by scepticism and prejudice. Now, South Wales, its people and its resources were needed for the survival of the state.

1937/8: 'Hope Dawns on Dowlais'

1. Details of the Dowlais reclamation programme: BT 104/5-9.

'The Promised Land'

2. For an authoritative account of Jewish investment, Anthony Glaser's essay *in The Jews of South Wales*, ed Ursala Q. Henriques, Cardiff U.W.P. 1993, see also see BT104/49.

3. For S.A.R.A.'s minutes and deliberations, BOE records, SMT 2/16-29.

4. Leiner's applications, Nuffield College Box No 60b, BT 177/1077.

'Buttons and Silk Stockings'

5. Welsh Products, a personal interview with the Adler family, Nuffield box nos 68-70.

6. For an account of the Nuffield Trust: PWS Andrews and Elizabeth Brunner, *The Life of Lord Nuffield*, (Blackwells Oxford); Nuffield Trust records can be found at Nuffield College Oxford catalogued under various company box numbers.

7. Kunerts/Kayser Bondor, T187/49, Nuffield Box nos 68-71.

8. British Sewing machines , BT104/47, BT 177/1106 B.O.E. SMT 2/29, Nuffield Box nos 17a, 46a.

9. For a fine general account of the Treforest Trading Estate, G Percival, *The Government's Industrial Estates in Wales, 1936-1975*, (Welsh Development Agency 1978).

10. Flex Fastners, B.O.E, SMT 2/29.

11. Polikoffs, T187/33, BT 177/110, Nuffield box no 37A.

12. Saunders Valves, T187/46, BT 177/1057, Nuffield box no 29.

13. Pilkington Glass Company records P.B. 258, 139.

14. Aberdare Cables, T182/66.

15. Welsh Metals, T187/63 Nuffield box no 55A. B.O.E. SMT 2/29.

16. South Wales Forgemasters/Brown Lennox, T187/38.

17. South Wales Coalite, T187/70/10. Nuffield box no 49B.

18. Swiss Aluminium, T187/55.

19. British Coated Board Mill, T187/13, BT 177/984.

20. Portal's report to the cabinet committee, CAB 27/579.

21. Blaenavon Works, Dr JP Evans, unpublished MA thesis, *'The Decline and Fall of the Blaenavon Iron Works'*, (Cardiff 1991.)

The Welsh Products factory, Goatmill Road, Dowlais

Kayser Bondor

Great Outbreak of Prosperity in the Depressed Areas.

7

1939:'A BIG GESTURE'

'A large and growing family ...'

The War Office and service chiefs disliked South Wales. They found a myriad of reasons why the area was unsuitable as a location for any new armaments programme. South Wales was strategically vulnerable, presented considerable transportation difficulties, lacked appropriate engineering skills, and had gained a reputation of containing an unreliable work force. This last factor underlay much of military's dogged resistance to re-siting existing or diverting new arms production into the area. They, more than most, shared a widely held prejudice that represented the South Wales work force as radical and strike prone, which would jeopardise essential production. Yet the possibility of utilising armaments expenditure to address the frightening levels of unemployment in the distressed areas had gained early support from unusual allies, Chancellor Chamberlain and the Treasury. It, also, became a central demand of local authorities in the distressed areas, vocally supported by the commission for the special areas. Some of the most bitter arguments within Whitehall arose from the conflicting requirements of the military and the Treasury and Ministry of Labour seeking to use the rearmament programme as a solution to mass unemployment in the distressed areas . Treasury deputy secretary, Sir Richard Hopkins, bitterly observed to Chamberlain in a minute (November 1936).

> ' ... Once we had hoped that, at any rate, the new government
> factories, a large and growing family, could be located
> in distressed areas. We have been disabused of these
> fanciful ideas. We are defeated by the war cries of the
> Defence Department. It is maddening that when
> a golden opportunity so unexpectedly came into
> the government's hand, it had to be largely sacrificed for
> the swift preparation of imminent war.'[1]

The earliest clash occurred in 1934 when official attention focussed upon the strategic vulnerability of the three operating ordnance factories at the Woolwich arsenal, the Waltham Abbey gun powder works and Enfield's small arms production. An unpublicised interdepartmental committee chaired by a junior War Office Minister, Douglas Hacking, had been given the remit to review alternative locations. Word, however, got out that ministers were planning the dispersal of the Woolwich arsenal and, indeed, that it was to be set up in South Wales. Such rumours prompted an immediate appeal from the mayor of Merthyr Tydfil, extolling the strategic virtues of Dowlais, 'protected by surrounding hills with the finest water supplies and 5,000 skilled and semi-skilled men'. Discomforted by the publicity and anxious not even to admit the existence of the Hacking committee, officials stonewalled in replies to both Welsh and Scottish local authorities. Hacking was personally scathing about South Wales' suitability. Something of a prisoner of his service chief's unbending belief that only a few parts of Britain could be declared invulnerable from air attack, Hacking dismissed the whole of South Wales as 'unsafe'. Its closeness to the Severn estuary with its easily identifiable topography made it particularly vulnerable. Transport facilities were insufficient, 'having regard to the fact that the heavy shells and empty cases would be mainly manufactured in the Midlands'.

The committee's first report reflected the extreme position of the service chiefs and marginalised the views of the government's industrial adviser, Lord Weir. It confirmed the Woolwich arsenal and the Waltham Abbey gunpowder works were vulnerable and went further in identifying one other major production complex at risk, ICI's Billingham plant on the North East coast. The committee bizarrely alighted upon Oswestry as their favoured relocation of the Woolwich arsenal, tamely claiming that the proposed ordnance factory could draw upon the labour from the colliery districts of St Martin's, Chirk, Ruabon and Wrexham. The nearby Queensferry first world war explosives war factory was the committee's first choice for the Waltham Abbey gunpowder production. As an alternative they suggested Gretna, Scotland, on the site of a former wartime cordite factory.[2]

Rearmament became one of the battlegrounds of distressed areas policy. The growing clamour from the coal field areas gained the support of the commissioner for the special areas, Sir Malcolm Stewart. In February 1935, he pleaded with the War Office Minister, Hailsham, to offer a 'big gesture' to the distressed areas:

> 'I am doing my very best to get new companies to go into
> the special areas - but if the government steered production
> such as the Woolwich arsenal the whole outlook would change.
> The pessimism which had been growing for years could be
> transferred into a feeling of optimism and determination'.

These external demands gradually found their way into the labyrinthine committee structure which made up the Whitehall decision making process, a series of interdepartmental committees, and sub-committees of the august Committee for Imperial Defence (C.I.D.). It was at such a committee meeting in April 1935 that the case for South Wales was first heard. The Hacking committee's recommendations for Oswestry and Queensferry received a hostile ministerial reaction, led by the Chancellor of the Exchequer whose department was expected to approve the £7 million cost of relocation. Why could not the serious situation in South Wales be taken into account and how had the chiefs of staff totally excluded the area from consideration? Their reply that they had taken 'a long term view of the next 50 to 100 years' drew a scornful response from Chamberlain about such crystal ball gazing. While the committee endorsed the Hacking report's conclusion in principle, including the necessity to consider the ICI Billingham plant, it rejected the specific Oswestry and Queensferry recommendations on relocation, and agreed a further review in which the needs of the distressed areas should be taken fully into account.

The Imperial Defence Committee's acknowledgement that rearmament should be directly linked to the needs of the distressed areas was a modest first victory. It reflected, primarily, the government's and, especially, Chamberlain's fear that unemployment would influence a forthcoming general election during which he hoped skilfully to link jobs to rearmament. But such a shift in policy brought no immediate relief or joy to South Wales. The review ordered by the C.I.D in August 1935 cast grave doubts upon suitable South Wales sites for the dispersed Woolwich arsenal. Emphasising the significance of good rail communications, the War office sought the advice of the general manager of G.W.R. Only one site at Bridgend qualified and even that site was a long way from sources of shell supplies in the midlands and north. Secondly 'the Tuskar rocks' at the mouth of the river Ogwr offered enemy bombers 'a very definitive landmark' as they 'followed the course of the river Severn'. The joint Hacking/War Office review found a much better alternative in Chorley, Lancashire.

Officials confessed that Chorley, unlike Bridgend, did not fall within a distressed area; but a larger depressed population lived within easy reach of Chorley than at Bridgend. Bridgend's insured working population combined with those of Maesteg, Ogmore and Port Talbot of 22,100 within 12 miles and Pontypridd/Porth's 22,000 within 15 miles compared unfavourably with Chorley's employment hinterland of a quarter of a million. The review, however, had to admit to the Bridgend areas having much higher levels of unemployment of 40 - 50% compared with 25% plus in Chorley. Chorley, on the other hand, offered skilled labour, and a female labour force used to factory work. For one man the choice of Chorley proved particularly embarrassing. The hapless junior War Office Minister, Hacking, lamented the fact that no one would believe that he had not been manipulating the decision in favour of his own constituency - Chorley. 'Any statement that I have not pressed the claim will not be universally accepted. I may have to consider my position in the War Office' (He was, in fact, transferred to the Dominions department in mid 1935). [3]

Chorley was a precursor to the major reconstruction of the north west economy based upon armaments production. Preston, Blackburn, Oldham and Accrington factories were to follow. When, however, the cabinet met in 31st July 1935 to endorse the Chorley choice, ministers clearly remained sensitive to the South Wales situation. They agreed yet another interdepartmental committee, under the chairmanship of Sir Arthur Robinson, charged with the task of discovering 'the possibility and desirability to establishing some part of the filling factory at some site in South Wales'. The Robinson committee revisited the Bridgend argument and, on this occasion, found a role for a third filling factory (after Chorley and the long-standing Hereford ordnance factory) to make minor components, fazes, pyrotechnics, primers and the filling of cartridges. The committee considered two sites, a 900 acre site embracing Bridgend, Coity and Brackla and 1200 acres south of Llantwit Major. The latter site proved unacceptable to the military, vulnerable to coastal attacks, too close to St Athan' airfield and, anyway, at the heart of Glamorgan Council's smallholders' programme. Although not finally approved by the Committee for Imperial Defence, Ramsay Macdonald was able to trailer the decision in a parliamentary debate on the distressed areas on 2nd March 1936. The new £2.5 million ordnance factory would create 500 jobs in peacetime (of which 190 would be skilled drafted into the are) but, more than 20,000 during the war.[4]

'The plain truth ...'

The decision to build at Bridgend had been political. It did little to resolve the more intense political demand from the most depressed of the distressed areas, Merthyr and Dowlais. On the contrary, it added to their frustrations, made worse by the fact that not inconsiderable objections were raised by the country land owning folk in the Bridgend area to such a large development there, when it would have been triumphantly welcomed in the valleys. Within Whitehall, during the summer of 1936 there had, nevertheless, been a growing acknowledgement of the exceptional suffering and distress felt in Merthyr and Dowlais leading to the cabinet paper and discussion in September 1936. Ministry of Labour officials looked to the rearmament programme to assist local regeneration, only to find continuing hostility and scepticism to any such proposal. When they turned to Sir Arthur Robinson, who had successfully steered the Bridgend project through the C.I.D., he offered unpalatable, brutal advice.

> 'the plain truth to my mind is that if you want to ameliorate the
> evil conditions which have happened in the population of Merthyr
> your policy will have to be directed to one object, removing
> that population as quickly as you can and where it can
> find industrial occupation. Money spent this way will be well spent.'

Nor could the valleys expect much support from the newly appointed Minister for Co-ordination of Defence, Sir Thomas Inskip. This post had been hastily created to head off a vociferous parliamentary demand for a full scale defence reorganisation and the establishment of an integrated ministry of defence. Inskip proved to be no enthusiast for deploying armaments factories in the distressed area; he became another voice of caution around the cabinet table. One official Treasury minute summarised the position and attitudes in the autumn of 1936.

> 'South Wales has been kept constantly in mind in dealing
> with the defence programme. Whenever there has been
> any proposal for a new factory, the claims of South Wales
> have been specifically named and South Wales is getting a
> new explosives factory at Bridgend , a new aircraft
> depot, a petrol depot at Pembroke Dock and Milford Haven.
> The difficulty about Merthyr Tydfil is geographical:
> everything has to be hauled uphill and down again. Sir Horace Wilson
> has some hope of getting a commercial firm to go there. I do not
> see what more the Cabinet can do but it will not harm
> if they again impress on the Services the necessity of
> bearing South Wales in general, and Merthyr in particular,
> in mind'.

A filling factory at Bridgend, and another ordnance factory at Glascoed, Monmouthshire, a flying boat station at Fishguard and a mines depot at Milford Haven hardly constituted a sufficient political response to the valleys' demands. Nor was the one other significant prize achieved in 1936/7. The Robinson committee found one other 'gesture' to make to south West Wales. Having assessed additional explosives requirements the committee proposed, and ministers accepted, the location of a TNT production plant at the disused Pembrey ordnance site. Pembrey had produced gunpowder and dynamite as early as 1881. A First World War state financed factory to accommodate Nobel's explosive company had temporarily boosted employment, but had closed in the 1920s save for the central administration block, used as a convalescent rehabilitation centre for the children of unemployed miners. Service officers found Pembrey a strategically sound operation. The dunes offered protection and the expansive 200 hectare site stood close to communities of very high unemployment. [5]

Bridgend and Pembrey represented significant political gestures to the demands of South Wales, though the areas continued to be dogged by the reputation of poor skills and industrial relations. It, certainly, compared unfavourably with the rival north west. The Bristol Aeroplane Company snubbed South Wales in opting for Accrington as the site for a shadow engine factory. Ford of Dagenham chose to expand hugely an aero engine plant at Trafford Park. A Treasury official found it necessary, gently, to remind Prime Minister Chamberlain that ministerial speeches should not draw undue attention to Lancashire. Lancashire was not a special area and government members 'might be accused of favouring the area' where 'their supporters are in a majority at the expense of South Wales where political opponents are strong.' Sensitivities within Whitehall reflected the increasingly politicised character of the debate upon rearmament and the location of armaments' production. Universal parliamentary outrage greeted a cabinet decision in early 1937 to locate an airframe factory in Berkshire. The cabinet had been told that the key company, Rootes, had rejected any suggestion of going to South Wales 'on account of the fear of labour trouble.' Parliamentary pressure compelled an instant re-think. Chamberlain told the House that, in view of the wider considerations, the Secretary of State for Air was 'prepared to waive his preference for White Waltham site and, in co-operation with Rootes, was taking immediate steps to find a suitable site in Lancashire.

The government ran into similar trouble when it backed the Caledonian bill which would have paved the way for a major calcium carbide plant to be erected by B.O.C. in the Scottish Highlands. Despite evidence submitted to the Commons testifying to the essential requirement of cheap water and energy, Scottish and Welsh miner members blocked the bill, arguing that any such plant ought to utilise large supplies of coal. Chamberlain as Chancellor, had again taken in cabinet a critical view of the highland proposal, insisting that, as public money had to be spent, B.O.C. had to commit itself to South Wales. Under the imminent threat of war a carbide plant was eventually located at Kenfig, Port Talbot. [6]

Shadow factories

The succession of announcements on armaments relocation gave cold comfort to the distressed valleys coalfield. Merthyr had made a bid for the calcium carbine plant. Hopes, too, of a major hydrogenation plant that would consume millions of tons of surplus coal were dashed with the publication of an official report (The Falmouth Committee's) which exposed the unviable nature of any large scale coal to oil scheme. Distressed areas did, however, receive some satisfaction from the government's other rearmament strategy, the construction of agency and shadow plants. The government's three industrial advisers, Sir James Lithgow, Sir Arthur Balfour and Lord Weir had, as early as 1933, recommended a policy of shadow munitions capacity which would duplicate or supplement existing production. The committee for imperial defence had accepted, in 1934, the principle of shadow agency factories paid for by the state, but built and managed by the major specialist companies. An obvious and significant player had to be ICI. As early as August 1935, service chiefs had identified one such complex vulnerable to air attack. Subsequently, a sub-committee, the Billingham committee, chaired by ICI's John Rogers, began deliberating on alternative sites for ICI's ammonia and ammonia nitrate production. It concluded, at the first meeting, that possibly four new small ammonia plants might be required. The committee had already been made aware of the need 'to take into consideration' requirements of distressed areas in South Wales and Scotland. At a further meeting, 24 November 1936, a glimpse of hope for Merthyr emerged. One of the ammonia plants 'could be usefully sited in Merthyr Tydfil'.

Conflicting advice to the committee, changing assessments and some pressure from ICI itself to extend the Billingham plant rather than build new shadow factories delayed any decision. ICI had put forward a proposal to retain at Billingham production of at least 525 tons a week even during war time. Secondly, Fisons had proposed the construction of an ammonia plant at Scunthorpe for another 250 tons a week. ICI hated the idea of going to Merthyr. The company, in April/May 1938, investigated the optional sites, concluding that not one was good enough 'for a commercial plant'. They identified Dowlais as the one with the least serious drawbacks. At least, on this occasion, ultra cautious service chiefs stood on the side of South Wales. Dismissing any confidence in Billingham production surviving air attacks, they pressed for the development of shadow ammonia factories. At a meeting of the full committee for imperial defence (24th February 1938) the permanent secretary at the Ministry of Labour, Sir Thomas Phillips, backed the case for locating a second plant at Merthyr. (The committee had already accepted a factory for Mossend, Scotland). Phillips told the committee that 'because there had been strong representation which had been received by the Minister on behalf of Prime Minister Chamberlain, the Minister of Labour would want the second plant to go to Merthyr'.

Even better news followed. First, at the Billingham sub-committee on 30th March a higher assessment of need (700 tons a week) meant a larger plant at an estimated cost of £1.2 million. The full committee confirmed the decision in April, and Ernest Brown, Minister of Labour, announced the decision to the Commons. Secondly, the frantic acceleration of the armaments factory programme added a further dimension to the ICI's Dowlais development. In January 1939, the Billingham committee identified an urgent new requirement for methanol production for explosives. The War Office gave rapid approval for the incorporation of a methanol plant within the Dowlais complex capable of producing 2,250 tons a week at a construction cost of £460,000. Prophetically, final clearance for the scheme was given on 31st August 1939.

The building of the plant at Dowlais proved a herculean task. As the ICI company records reveal, the company came up against several difficulties in providing essential services such as rail, transport, electric power and water supply. An existing embankment facilitated railway access but inadequate space for sidings compelled them to agree with G.K. Baldwin to use their lines. Electricity supply was brought from the Upper Boat generating station at Treforest. ICI engineers had to fight hard for a stand by supply, especially as 'supply lines running over mountain tops were exposed to damage by storms'. The million gallons of water a day became the subject of lengthy negotiations with the Borough Council. Foundation work was completed by the end of February 1939 and, with the assistance of key skilled workers transferred from Billingham, 80% of the plant had been installed by the outbreak of war in September 1939. Ammonia at Dowlais was first made on 13 January 1940.

For Merthyr, the coming of ICI represented salvation. Construction jobs at the ammonia plant rose from 16 in September 1938 to 710 in September 1939, while in the additional methanol works construction jobs peaked in June 1940 at 290. Operating labour for both rose from 155 in March 1940 to more than 500 for the peak war years. As much as the jobs, the coming of ICI symbolised the borough's right to survive rather than be 'evacuated'. Ironically, the reason for the relocation of the ICI plant never materialised. The German bombers never successfully destroyed the Billingham plant.

ICI and the shadow agency programme led to one further significant development in south west Wales. In 1936 the War Office had requested ICI to furnish estimates for two new ammonia nitrate plants. One had been designated for the company's Huddersfield plant, but the second, it was agreed in August 1938, could be sited at Pembrey, adjacent to the TNT plant, reinforcing the role of the area in munitions production.

It had been an uphill struggle for South Wales to be recognised within the pre-war rearmament programme. During the course of that struggle, the area found some unusual allies in the Treasury and the Chancellor. 1936 had been a turning point in Chamberlain's approach to the distress of the South Wales coalfield. He had grudgingly realised that general improvements in trade and the economy would not, of itself, address the suffering of the worst distressed areas. Having accepted the need to embark upon a rearmament programme he and Treasury officials sought to harness rising defence expenditure to employment in the coalfield areas. Tension and conflict in this policy area was fuelled by interdepartmental and service chiefs' disagreements. Their deeply held scepticism about the suitability of South Wales as a location for armament production had been eventually overridden by political considerations and imperatives. Such inhibitions, regularly expressed within Whitehall and at cabinet and committee meetings between 1936 and 1939, were to be swept aside by the declaration of war, when, suddenly, the resources of South Wales, the people and their supposed limited skills became vital for survival. [7]

1938/39: 'A Big Gesture'

'A large and growing family'

1. The best general account of the Treasury view of rearmament, GC Peden, *British Rearmanent and the Treasury 1932-1939*, (British Academy Press, 1979). Sir Richard Hopkins and Chamberlain minutes, T172/1827, 1828.

2. Various memoranda, minutes and committee meetings on the Woolwich Arsenal, WO33/1366, WO185/126, CAB 2/65; The Hacking report, Committee of Imperial Defence (CID), 208A, 22 March 1935, CAB316, CID 208A.

3. Stewart's call for 'a big gesture' WO185/125/126; other relevant papers CAB316, CID 210A, 211A; the report on Bridgend, CAB 102, 65.

4. The Robinson committee and report, LAB 25/6, 25/79, CID 223A, 12 Feb, 14 March 1936.

'The plain truth'

5. Sir Arthur Robinson's and Treasury observations and Merthyr's pleas, T175/50; the Pembrey development, CAB 102/165.

6. Cabinet discussions and memoranda on the air frame factory and the Caledonia bill CAB3 (37), 25 Jan 1937, CP62 (37) 17.2.37, CAB42 (37), CP 235 (37), CAB1 (38).

'Shadow factories'

7. The Falmouth report on the hydrogenation, 18 May 1938, Cmnd. 5665; the memoranda and minutes of the Billingham sub committee, CID, Defence Policy Requirements, (DPR) nos 161, 242, CAB 16/168; the establishment of ICI's shadow plants. the coming of ICI to Dowlais, DPR sub committee on Billingham, nos 161, 242, CAB16/168.

ICI Dowlais

i

8

1939 - 1945: SOUTH WALES AND WHITEHALL AT WAR

'Regional devolution has become vital'

The demands that Whitehall direct some part of the rearmament's programme to South Wales, to make 'a big gesture', had, in part, been met by September 1939. Whitehall had, reluctantly, accepted that South Wales should be an integral part of the rearmament programme. Large shadow or agency factories and plants had been approved. The development at Bridgend had been an utterly political decision. The commitment to a naval filling depot at Glascoed had derived more from inter service rivalry. The navy had pressed for a separate dedicated building programme. The War Office and the Minister, Sir Thomas Inskip, had resisted. However, by 1938, it was clear that naval requirements could not be met from Woolwich or the alternative plans at Hereford. Glascoed was agreed after land adjacent to the navy's Fishguard depot was found to be too boggy. Glascoed was built to complement production at Bridgend. Together, they formed the first substantial government commitment to South Wales. Together, they anticipated more than 30,000 jobs.

The exigencies of war brought another major ordnance investment to the most unlikely of places and community. Anyone who might have suggested that the small, isolated mining and iron village of Hirwaun, at the head of the Aberdare valley, should become the site of a new million sq. ft factory, housing more than 10,000 jobs, would have been greeted with ridicule. Significantly, the decision to locate at Hirwaun was made not on strategic geographical grounds but upon the availability of labour. The Hirwaun factories, approved in January 1940, entered production a year later. They became the second largest royal small arms ammunition factories, with an estimated output of 10 million rounds a week. [1]

The war effort forced an administrative revolution upon the traditionally centralised Whitehall, requiring a very different relationship between central government and the area. As Minister for Production, Oliver Lyttleton, put it to the newly formed Welsh Regional Production Board in July 1942. 'Regional devolution in production and administrative matters had become vital'. Between 1940 and 1942, Whitehall itself searched for the appropriate administrative model to co-ordinate war supplies. New departments were created and then merged, co-ordination committees formed and disbanded. From the administrative upheaval there emerged a structure, singularly lacking before the war in South Wales, a regional administrative industrial machine capable of assessing manpower and factory needs and, consequentially, becoming an advocate for the area and its people. A new Welsh administration was born, and was not to be disbanded at the end of the war. Welsh administrative life was never to be the same. A new regional Welsh industrial administrative machine took its place alongside the longer standing Welsh health and education boards.[2]

The various wartime departments of production, supply and labour, the trade and factory and storage control agency all appointed regional controllers and area staff. The central production executive, attempting at Whitehall to co-ordinate supplies, had its regional counterparts. The new Welsh administration drew upon the late thirties' innovators - the South Wales estates company at Treforest and the district commissioner for the special areas. Percy Thomas, the architect of the Treforest estate, became controller of the ministry of production and chairman of the Welsh regional board. Crawshay, district commissioner for the special areas, assumed responsibility for aircraft production. They combined with experienced civil servants, Steel at the Ministry of Supply, Humphrey at the Ministry of Labour and national service, controllers at the factory and storage ministry and at the Board of Trade, to form a Welsh regional executive for wartime production. The executive, in turn, were linked to three representatives from industry and three from the trades unions to form a Welsh regional board. The board was serviced by area advisory panels, West, East and North, composed of representatives from industry and the trades unions.

This new structure completely reshaped relationships within South Wales and between South Wales and Whitehall. It attempted to replace the essential confrontational nature of industrial relations by a consensual process. For the first time, the organised trade union movement was brought into the centre of the decision making process. Regional departmental officials became powerful influences within the area, known and respected. They became the area's voice within Whitehall and, increasingly, represented the informed opinion to which the central administration turned. Micro planning and management of production created a new statistical base. The unfamiliarity and the ignorance of central Whitehall officials so characteristic of 30s decision making, was replaced by informed detailed submissions from regional administrators.

This newly formed regional administration, however, scoured South Wales for existing industrial building and monitored the huge expansion of new ordnance factory space authorised in the first year of the war. The minutes and memoranda record one of the most detailed industrial planning exercises conducted by a British administration. Their initial

156

target had to be the newly constructed factories at Treforest and the commission for the special areas' developments in Merthyr, Dowlais and individual scattered sites further west. A memorandum, in November 1939, identified 75 factories completed or near completion at Treforest, two at Dowlais for Kayser Bondor and Hall Telephones, as well as a proposed adjacent site for an oil plant to be managed by Unilever. A halt was called to all projects not under contract and to all colliery site clearance. The 'rationing' of labour, as much as materials, became an imperative.

Requisitioned

The most ruthless requisitioning of factory space took place at Treforest. The host of small, and mainly Jewish, businesses clustered on the estate lost their premises to priority war production. As foreign aliens, a number of individuals were interned or disallowed access to the estate which had, within twelve months or so, become the home of key Ministry of Aircraft Production (MAP) projects. Some twenty units were requisitioned to accommodate the major arrival in South Wales of BOAC, estimated to employ 1,650. Another 17 factories, of varying sizes, were commandeered for Helliwells, transferred from Walsall airport, while K.L.G., employing an estimated 830, took an entire factory of 132,000 sq. ft. Another significant newcomer, Simmonds Accessories, added to the transformation of jobs and skills on the estate. The contrast could not have been greater. Embroidery, gloves, leather goods, wristwatch straps and chocolates gave way to aircraft parts. A South Wales workforce was exposed, in many cases for the first time, to engineering production skills and experiences.[3]

Such skills and experiences were not confined to the trading estate but reached into the valleys. The dispersal and expansion of a subsidiary of the Lucas company, Rotax, specialising in the manufacture of magnetos for tanks, meant a completely different production line at the newly built Cyfarthfa factory, Merthyr, originally intended for sewing machines. A further extension of Rotax production reached Brynmawr. Rotax created more than 2,500 jobs, introducing for the first time large scale employment opportunities for valleys women. These jobs complemented the enormous Lucas workforce of 10,000 at Cwmbran. Other companies, new and old, expanded. Halls Telephone at Dowlais converted their production to small arms and ammunitions taken over by British Small Arms, (BSA). The Aluminium Company and Welsh Metals, both the creation of previous Treasury and Nuffield largesse, received new capital investments from the ministry of aircraft production; while one of the most traditional of industries and companies, the Blaenavon iron works, enjoyed a similar boost.

The emergencies of war did not totally dispel the instinctive reluctance or scepticism of Whitehall to direct production into the area. A Board of Trade memorandum to the Production Executive in November 1941 rehearsed again the area's limitations. The labour available was 'generally speaking immobile, electricity supplies acute.', 'the gas position bad, road and rail transport services already over burdened.' 'The capacity of South Wales to take increased war production was, therefore, governed by factors other than the supply of suitable premises'. However, clearly under the influence of the new regional controllers, a further secret review in February 1942 painted a rather different picture. The authors of the review admitted that the small number of pre-war factories had only brought limited precision engineering experiences. Generally speaking 'machining capacity was of a somewhat rough nature'. Traditional work in steel and other materials industries had, nevertheless, expanded; several disused ship repairing docks had been reopened and South Wales had coped with its full share of ordnance production. The area had successfully welcomed companies such as BOAC, ICI and Helliwells from strategically vulnerable or blitzed areas. The review, however, noted that expansion had been led by these and other newly established companies. The capacity of native firms had been little used, except in relation to their normal practices of maintaining and servicing heavy industry plant. The supply departments in Whitehall had initially turned a deaf ear to area representatives to utilise existing native companies. Yet several 'native' firms, by the addition of new plant, had been found ready and able to undertake production of guns, shells and bombs. These undertakings, in some cases, had been transformed from 'semi rough maintenance works' into really useful production e.g. New Crown Forgings, Powell Duffryn, Blacnavon works, R.R. Paton and Saunders Valves. The review concluded that further capacity existed to assist an intensified tank production drive.

This secret review also stoutly defended the South Wales' labour force record - 'as good a record of freedom from labour friction as any area'. Where troubles had occurred, managerial incompetence had been found to blame. The trades unions had accepted the policy of 'dilution' of skills, allowing Wales to head the list of regions in the percentage of women employed in engineering and allied trades, though such dilution had been more fiercely contested in traditional industries. On the labour performance the review concluded that, despite the revolutionary change in the type of production and the transference of so many workers from the region, it had been possible to build up, around the nucleus of skilled workers, a skilled, semi-skilled and unskilled force which had, in large measure, met the demands made upon it'. The February 1942 review also sought to reassure Whitehall that a number of the alleged shortages in electricity 'often quoted as an insuperable hindrance to expansion' no longer presented a difficulty.

These reassessments, in part, reflected the growing working co-operation forged within the Welsh regional production board and its areas advisory boards. They did not eliminate tensions or industrial conflict, but provided, for the first time, an institutional channel through which grievances and concerns could be addressed. Collectively, the board grappled with the competing demands for labour. Discussions, for example, at the fifth meeting of the Council, on the 25th July 1942, illustrate the operational nature of its work. Chaired by Percy Thomas and attended by W E Clement, the industrial member, and by W E Hopkins, representing the trades unions, the meeting faced awesome decisions in the redeployment of labour. The regional controller at the Ministry of Labour and national service briefed the board that some 20,000 women would, in all probability, be required to bring the factories in South Wales up to full strength. His initial estimate indicated approximately 1,000 women unemployed and a further 6,700 who had volunteered but whose, 'suitability for employment of this nature' had not yet been verified. Planning was being 'rendered more difficult' by 'wastage represented by leaving their employment without permission,' and the influx of 'Irish women employees at Bridgend had all been transferred or left in other ways'. The controller accepted the widespread criticism regarding the transfer of Welsh women to work in England, and now considered that such transfers should be suspended, especially in the light of the latest assessment of R.O.F. labour requirements. Mr Eugene Cross area labour manager, Ministry of Supply, advised the board that Hirwaun's requirements would probably reach 13,000 by July 1943, making a future total of 30-35 thousand within the South Wales R.O.F.s 85% of the new workers would be women. He informed the board that 2,272 workers at the Bridgend factory resided in the Aberdare and Merthyr valleys. Their transfer to Hirwaun would save 15 buses per shift at a cost of £1,050 per week. Of the 1,135 workers at Bridgend, from the Neath Valley accessible to Hirwaun, only 21 were men. Cross finally felt it necessary to inform the board of the serious accommodation and housing problems generated by the 800/1,000 imported skilled workers into the Hirwaun factory.

These issues remained with the regional administration for the whole war: a constant juggling of labour requirement within South Wales and a continuous debate within Whitehall over the transfer of women into England. In 1943, Whitehall again confronted the Welsh region with the prospect of cutting the Bridgend factory by 3,000 though increasing Glascoed by 500. The extreme political sensitivity of such a decision had been immediately recognised by Whitehall planners. The desperate need to relieve labour shortages in the Midlands had to be set against the 'strong political opposition to moving mobile Welsh girls into English factories'. Officials minuted that the Ministry of Labour were willing to stand up to this provided the Ministry of Supply were prepared to say that cuts at Bridgend were based on production grounds, a claim the supply ministry was reluctant to endorse.

Discussion and debate about 'surplus' labour and 'transference' evoked the most immediate and bitter memories of the inter war years, and, naturally, led to protest, deputations and numerous representations. From West Wales came a consistent appeal to utilise the large number of closed tinplate works for new manufacturing jobs. Of the 83 works, 38 had been closed down to bitter protests locally; 35 of them had been taken over by government for storage purposes, creating very few jobs. Area and regional officials, under pressure, regularly surveyed and re-surveyed these works, and, equally regularly, concluded that the works were generally unsuitable for alternative production.[4]

Arguments over transference of war time 'surplus' labour were most keenly and bitterly felt in the areas of highest inter-war migration, Merthyr and Dowlais. Suggestions that some four hundred women working at the Rotax factory, Cyfarthfa, in 1942/3 should be transferred into England provoked a stream of deputations by the local MP, S O Davies, and the county borough's mayor and councillors to regional staff and even to the junior Minister for War Production, Garro Jones Officials from the regional office toured a series of local buildings, the blast engine house at Dowlais, the Taf Vale brewery, the Merthyr traction company premises and even the market hall to consider their suitability for further war production, though almost invariably reporting back that none were really adequate.

Ministers and officials, however, began to recognise that the increasingly desperate pleas by Merthyr borough's representatives were directed not only to the immediate threat of transfer of war time labour but to the more powerful underlying concern that a post war society would be little different from that which had preceded it. After meeting S O Davies and a Merthyr deputation in June 1942, the Minister, Garro Jones, felt it right to write to his superior, the Lord President of the Council, Sir William Jowitt, and Hugh Dalton at the Board of Trade conveying such concerns. The Minister minuted that he felt the deputation had really come to express 'the deep seated fear that peace for them' would 'herald the arrival of the spectres of the past, unemployment, continued migration and municipal financial troubles!'

'The patience of the people in this town, at any rate, is turning
into real bitterness and that it may very soon become
necessary to give some indication that action will be taken
to prevent their worst fears from being realised'.

In June 1943, the war had not been won, but for the people of the
distressed areas of South Wales, thoughts were already turning to the
winning of the peace. [5]

Reconstruction and the Advisory Council

Public opinion, throughout the war, remained apprehensive and sceptical
about post war employment prospects.   The government's home
intelligence unit, responsible for polling and surveying opinion, found 'a
great majority of workers believed that the war will be followed by
depression and heavy unemployment'.   These fears grew from 1943
onwards when manpower needs began to change. Ministers had felt the
need to respond to such concerns as early as 1941, if for no other reason
than to maintain war morale.   Following a robust debate within
government, a reconstruction problem committee and a supporting
secretariat had been set up at the end of 1940, though it remained largely
ineffectual until its reconstitution in 1943. A new Ministry of Town and
Country Planning was also set up in 1942 to handle the three reports
presented to ministers: the Barlow report on the distribution of population
(1940), the Utthwatt committee's recommendation on compensation and
betterment issues arising from planning, and the Scott report on land
utilisation in rural areas.[6]

The Barlow report held particular relevance for South Wales, the enquiry
having originated from commissioner Stewart's third report calling for the
restriction on development in London.   Barlow had recommended a
'central planning authority to oversee the dispersal of population and
development from the congested areas', a far cry from the common
assumption, only a decade earlier, that transference into the areas of
industrial growth offered the only solution to the distressed areas. The
'Barlow ban' upon development became one of the planks of post war
employment and regional policy.   Ministers also decided in 1941 to
appoint a Scottish reconstruction advisory council curiously composed of
former Secretaries of State for Scotland, a decision which promptly led to a
vociferous Welsh demand for an equivalent committee.

Ministers were, initially, inclined to resist, resting their case on the historically different function of a Scottish Office and the Secretary of State for Scotland. Following a meeting in November 1941 with the all party Welsh Parliamentary Party the minister, Arthur Greenwood, nevertheless conceded the case. Whitehall officials resentfully acknowledged that 'since the Welsh members of the House of Commons are so well organised I suppose we must have one'; though all the suspicions of yet another regional body surfaced. 'It will become a pressure group having as its main object the securing of special treatment and special benefits for Wales'. Officials also faced another dilemma. If the proposed Council's remit was confined to subjects referred to it by ministers 'it will then become morally incumbent upon the Minister to refer something to the Council; and worse 'he would have some responsibility for every recommendation which the Council might make'. 'Unfettered independence, on the other hand, would incite the Council to wander into general policy areas, thus complicating ministerial decision making'. For that reason, officials drafted the council's terms of reference directing its members to matters which lay 'in conformity with the general framework of the studies proceeding under the direction of the Minister without portfolio'. These fine borderline distinctions became the source of periodic tension between the Council and Whitehall.

The knotty problem of the terms of reference paled in significance compared with the unseemly wrangling that broke out over the membership of the advisory council, while only confirming Whitehall's worst views of Welsh parochialism. Many of the problems arose from Whitehall insistence that the Council should not assume a 'representative' character. Officials were also unhappy about a council of 'experts'. Such experts 'would never rest until their own pet subject were brought before the council'. Officials preferred to appoint a Council of nine, individual, distinguished Welsh men and women. Neither Whitehall, or, it seems, the chairman of the Welsh parliamentary party, Sir Henry Morris-Jones, initially considered that the Council had to be chaired by a Welshman. Official favourite was Lord Sankey (of Coal Commission fame), though David Lloyd George canvassed the judge Lord Atkins of Aberdovery. Some thirty names emerged for membership of the Council, creating increasing despair within Whitehall as the pressure to expand it size grew and grew. Appointing became further complicated by a change of minister in February 1942. Sir William Jowitt, clearly less enamoured by the whole idea of a Council, found unattractive a number of the suggestions of his predecessor, Arthur Greenwood. Jowitt wearily negotiated with Welsh members to whittle down the proposed membership from 29 to 15, and sought an alternative chairman, Sir Gerald Bruce, former chairman of the Treforest industrial estate company. Having

162

failed to obtain Bruce's release from his war time duties, Jowitt conceded to the request of Welsh members to appoint the Principal of the University, Cardiff, J F Rees. As Jowitt confessed to Portal, to whom he had turned for support:

'The Welsh members pressed for Principal Rees and I thought
it wise to give way to them to prevent parliamentary attacks
on the composition of the committee. Finally we got down to a
list of 29 people. I then again saw the Welsh members
with Mr Lloyd George and suggested that such a large
committee was completely unwieldy, and asked them to
perform a drastic surgical operation by reducing the list of names
to not more than 15. This they have now done. I can't pretend
that I think the list altogether satisfactory but it was the least
I could do. At any rate I have got their assent. If Welsh
members had been more ready to accept the suggestions I put forward
we should have had a stronger and better body.'

Such exhaustive canvassing, sadly, did not insulate the new advisory council for reconstruction from continuing sniping criticism. Local authorities, including the Cardiff City Council and a number of Valley councils, complained bitterly that they were not represented. The Welsh Industrial Council and especially its chairman, Councillor George Williams, took umbrage at this personal exclusion. The advisory council never really recovered from the unedifying squabble over its membership, an early illustration of the peculiar politics of quango making.[7]

The Challenge of Peace

However much Welsh members and representatives might have quibbled over the new Council, few frankly saw it as the source of post war salvation. They recognised that power resided with ministers and in Whitehall. An ever increasing stream of deputations visited ministers and departments from mid 1943 onwards, as the prospect of peace threatened war time jobs. While the Nuffield college surveys commissioned by Lord Reith at the Ministry of Works and Buildings delivered broad and general assessments of post war employment, Board of Trade officials were beavering away at micro regional assessments of future job requirements, mainly in preparing defensive material for ministers' meetings with deputations. Had these confidential local job assessments been made public, they would have further fuelled the fears of local members of parliament and councils. They made grim reading.

A 1944 review of industrial development prospects conducted by the new ministry of town and country planning, written in very much the language of the new planners, carried a familiar message. Many of the valleys were 'too narrow and too bleak'. 'Where there is no prospect of development that fact should be recognised as soon as possible in order that efforts should not be wasted upon them which be used to better effect elsewhere'. 'The future for these communities might be found on the open ground where the rivers debouch from the hills'. At least in 1944 migration was envisaged as local rather than the mass countrywide transference of a decade earlier.

The planners, also, conceded that, despite earlier prognostications, some communities originally considered beyond the pale - Merthyr and Dowlais for example, had enjoyed 'a successful beginning with the introduction of new industries'. More was needed. Sites existed and 'for psychological reasons alone it would be dangerous to let depression fall on Merthyr again'. It had become 'a by word for the evils from which all South Wales had suffered'. Yet all estimates of post war prospects, in Merthyr and Dowlais, and the likelihood of a mass civil demobilisation from war production pointed to the very return to the evils of pre war mass unemployment. Before the war, employment in Merthyr's iron and steel had fallen from 3,000 to 300, and in coal from 12,710 to 6,643. Officials claimed that some 5,000 jobs had been created: Hall Telephones, 518 rising to 1,212: Kayser Bondor, 432 in 1941 were hoping to employ 1,700: Welsh Products, the Czech firm producing wooden clasps and jewellery, had in June 1940 employed 165 which had now risen to 235.

Measured against the job requirements, these pre war industrial developments were hardly sufficient. Some 4,000 men and 500 women would be demobilised from the services. War time companies, Rotax, would shed more than 1000 - 600 men; Hall Telephones in Merthyr town nearly 500. The closure of ICI at Dowlais would account for another loss of 600 jobs. The total number seeking employment would exceed 6,300 men and 928 women. Officials gloomily concluded that the prospects of the range of new industries, furniture manufacturing, bricks, hats, gloves, motor and air craft parts seemed slight even with the inducements offered by the special areas legislation. Significantly, they advised 'the only sure course' would be the maintenance of war time powers - direction of industry under the location of industry (restriction) orders or similar legislation.

The regeneration of Merthyr and Dowlais required draconian state powers. The same applied to the neighbouring valleys of the Rhondda and Pontypridd, including 'the problem towns' of Mountain Ash in the

Cynon Valley, Treorchy and Tonypandy. The pre war population of 152,000 had witnessed, during the depth of the recession, unemployment rates of 55 to 73%. The Treforest estate had offered hope to the lower part of the valleys, while new companies had reached Porth and Ynyswen. The 'full employment enjoyed during the war' would give way to some 8,000 unemployed representing 16 - 18%. Women might remain in demand and there might even be a shortage of some 1,000 juveniles. Officials however, confessed to themselves that 'these figures were based upon an optimistic assumption of an increase in the coal industry of more than 2,000 and that only some 30% of the women now in industry would remain in employment after the war'.

These crude assumptions lay behind most of the mid war planning forecasts. Officials confessed to themselves that the future of Pontypridd and the Rhondda lay firstly in restoring the large number of small firms that had been displaced from the Treforest Trading Estate. Secondly, it would be crucial to encourage a few of the larger firms currently engaged in war time production to remain. BOAC Engines were employing nearly 2000, Simmonds Accessories another 2,000 men and women. Brown Lennox making chains and boons for the Admiralty, had taken on 1,000 men and boys, working alongside its associate company, South Wales Forge Masters. K.L.G employed 1,000 making sparking plugs, though it was questionable whether the company would continue production after the war without special measures for securing its retention. War time contracts had also allowed two pre-war Rhondda companies, Polikoffs and Flex Fasteners to expand.

This definitive mid war analysis considered the situation for the rest of South Wales, Newport, Cardiff areas and, in the jargon of the new planners, 'the West Central Region' constituted by the towns of Neath, Port Talbot, Bridgend, Maesteg/Cymmer and Aberdare. These communities had, also, shared the suffering from the collapse of coal, pre war unemployment in Maesteg reaching 77%. Neath and Port Talbot had enjoyed a relative recovery from a more diversified industrial base. The new acetone works at Kenfig, the decorated tin box and canister manufacturing in Neath and light engineering in Bridgend provided hope for these post war communities, and, of course, all development had been dwarfed by the massive ordnance Bridgend/Brackla factories.

Tentative projection of post war unemployment of 10,000 to 11,600, some 14 - 18% of the insured population in the region, begged the really big imponderable questions: what would happen to the Bridgend and Hirwaun R.O.F. factories employing a staggering 35,000? The key to the transition from war to peace for the planners' 'west central region' lay in maintaining a portion of the government contracts which had sustained both the ordnance factories and other companies such as Robert Byass & Co at Port Talbot producing light alloys, the South Wales Aluminium company at Rheola, British Industrial Solvents, Kenfig, and the low temperature carbonisation plant at the Wern Tarw collieries. The Metal box company's expansion of its canister production had depended upon light bomb production to sustain a work force of 600.

Despite the imponderables, in many of these 1943 projections of post war employment needs of communities stretching from Llanelli in the west to the Eastern Monmouthshire valleys, the secret planning exercise was a remarkable attempt to focus official and ministerial attention on the employment challenges of moving from war to peace. For South Wales, more than 50,000 of 66,800 employed in war time production faced redundancy: only 21% of war time production was likely to survive. The challenge of peace required new prescriptions and solutions.[8]

A Princess and A Secretary of State for Wales

The Welsh advisory reconstruction council had been appointed, albeit resentfully by ministers, to offer such prescriptions. Sadly, by the time the council came to present, publicly, its findings, it had lost the confidence of most Welsh representatives and had suffered from a contemptuous Whitehall reaction to its deliberations. Chairman Professor Rees had been reduced to complaining regularly that their unpublicised recommendations were not being given 'due consideration'. The Council's interim reports had argued for a Welsh planning authority, a Welsh representation upon the forestry commission, a Severn crossing, a new north/south Wales trunk road, the maintenance of a good proportion of war time production, a pilot plant for synthetic rubber production, cheap electricity, derelict land clearance programmes and the building of advance factories.

The Council's suggestion to embark upon a major review of Welsh local government with the full panoply of public evidence hearings, however, induced apoplexy among Whitehall officials. Such an enquiry would intrude upon internal policy making and the deliberation of the cabinet reconstruction committee. They remained anxious to keep the Council 'on side' by minimal concessions. In July 1943 one official brutally summarised the situation:

> 'There are certain signs that the Advisory Council are
> getting restive under the replies of departments which
> show a tendency to say, "sometime never" instead of
> "this year, next year"...'[9]

Whitehall had another concern. Welsh parliamentary representatives had already discounted the value of the Council, possibly resentful of their exclusion from its work and deliberations. These jealousies and dissatisfactions renewed, in a more concerted form, Welsh demands for the appointment of a Secretary of State for Wales to promote post war regeneration. They may have also been prompted by the original decision to constitute a Scottish Advisory Council, composed of secretaries of state. There had to be a Welsh Secretary of State. In June and July 1943, D R Grenfell and S O Davies pressed Churchill at Prime Minister's question time. Officials feared that possible resignations from the reconstruction council would be further exploited for political purposes. Churchill's response was understandably an impatient one. 'In the present circumstances' it was 'not practicable' to set up a completely new office of state. He was 'well aware of the sentiments cherished by the people of Wales and also of the warm desire to gratify those sentiments which is the instinct of the English and Scottish,' but he preferred 'to be a little backward in the matter'.

These initial parliamentary exchanges only prompted an all party call by the Welsh parliamentary party for a meeting to discuss their unanimous plea for such an appointment. Churchill, steadfastly, refused to receive a proper deputation led by the Conservative, Arthur Evans, accompanied by the father of the House, Lloyd George and members of the Liberal and Labour parties. He did, however, offer emollient sentiments. 'It is no doubt a very fit and proper matter for discussion in a transition period or when peace is restored'. Clutching at this minimal admission, the Welsh Parliamentary party pressed him to refer their demand to a cabinet committee on the machinery of government. Churchill agreed but did little to push forward consideration of the matter. In November 1944, Megan Lloyd George bitterly complained to him of the absence of any progress, only to be met by further prime ministerial stonewalling. The 'far reaching implications' of such a proposal required 'detailed considerations by the many authorities concerned'.

The parliamentary and public exchanges between Welsh MPs and Churchill were fruitless. One very modest proposal and one fascinating suggestion surfaced. Home Secretary, Morrison, suggested to Churchill that the cabinet respond to Welsh demands by offering a full supply day to debate Welsh affairs. Morrison admitted that the proposal might, in fact, 'stimulate the Welsh to ask for more on the ground that there should be a minister who could lead the debate.' The cabinet, nevertheless, agreed to make the offer. They did not, however, pursue another intriguing suggestion which it was felt might be considered a response to Welsh national sentiment, the conferring of the title of Princess of Wales upon the heir to the throne, Elizabeth, on her eighteenth birthday. Lloyd George was reported as 'not really strongly in favour of the "Princess of Wales" as he feels that it is a mistake to ask for too many things at once and he would prefer to press for a Secretary of State for Wales'. The cabinet, in February 1944, chose not to proceed with the matter.[10]

The Distribution of Industry Act

These distractions, frankly, bore little importance and value to the most vital decisions made within Whitehall and the war cabinet in 1944/5 which shaped the post war South Wales society. They were not to be found among the entrails of local Welsh politics or among the symbolic propositions surrounding a Secretary of State or a Princess of Wales. The future of South Wales was hammered out within the context of ground breaking policy making on employment. The 1944 white paper on employment and the 1945 Distribution of Industry bill were the new life lines. The 1945 Distribution of Industry Act, the coalition government's last piece of legislation, has a legitimate claim to be placed alongside the 1944 education act and the subsequent national insurance and health service acts in founding the new post war social order. Its architect, Hugh Dalton, had earlier been responsible for the Labour Party's 1937 report on the distressed areas, during the preparation of which he had toured South Wales. If his constituency experiences in Bishop Auckland and the North East primarily informed him, South Wales was never far behind. His war time diary records the assiduous and painstaking way in which he guided the cabinet committee's deliberations, first in obtaining a definitive statement on the location of industry in the white paper on employment and, then, the Distribution of Industry bill which gave legislative force to the principles of that paper.

In January 1944, Dalton sought agreement from colleagues to make a pre-emptive statement to industrialists that the government would like them to consider, in the national interest, the possibility of putting factories into the distressed areas. The South Wales area was significantly redefined to include Cardiff, Swansea and Newport, a policy change which had been contentiously argued ever since the 1934 Special Areas Act. In seeking such a statement, and within the newly defined areas, Dalton acknowledged the support received from Lord Portal, now a minister, who had 'practical knowledge of the question and has come much nearer to my way of thinking'. This crucial decision to extend the development areas to include Cardiff, Swansea and Newport was, subsequently,

168

incorporated in the Distribution of Industry Act. By March 1944, Dalton had successfully negotiated a key passage into the white paper on full employment, which kept the 'inducements' to industrialists in-tact, committed the government to building factories in advance of need, and bestowed power upon a post war Board of Trade to require 'all industrialists to come and talk to officials about their plans, and to prohibit development in congested areas' – 'a Barlow ban in small and in defined instalments'. The paper envisaged joint ministerial responsibility (Trade, Labour and Town and Country planning) with joint regional staff and boards. Later, such cumbersome tripartite responsibility was abandoned in favour of the Board of Trade as the lead department.[11]

The New Believers

The advance factory building got underway even before the introduction of the legislation. The government announced, in April 1944, a national 18 factories building programme, six of which were to be constructed in South Wales; Blackwood, Merthyr Tydfil, Ystradgynlais, Swansea, Ammanford and Neath. They became the home of a new wave of inward investors and the base for a major expansion of one of Merthyr's pre war captures, Kayser Bondor. Progress was never smooth. The introduction of new industry into the traditional coalmining communities of Treorchy met obstruction from the powerful coal interests of the Ocean colliery company. Dalton's delight that the valve factory, Cos-sors, had chosen Treorchy turned to anger when he discovered the colliery company 'pulling strings within the ministry of aviation and fuel and power' to prevent the development. He fumed at 'the barefaced effort by these unspeakable coal owners who had reduced the whole area to misery and dereliction'. He saw in their lobbying an attempt to prevent alternative employment being found for men, youth and even women of the valley.

> 'They know that, if such an alternative arrived no one will
> go down their damned pits anymore, unless the whole miner's
> life is changed for the better. We shall have this sort of impudence
> in every mining district where we introduce - as I plan to do in a
> great number of areas - new light industries.'

Dalton, with the backing of the local MP, WE Mainwaring (not Dalton admitted one of his natural allies within the Labour party), triumphed over the coal owners 'to the delight of the local people and council'.[12]

The Distribution of Industry Act gave legislative force to the fine words of the white paper on full employment. All industry had to give notice if it intended to build any premises above 10,000 sq. ft. It allowed loans to industrial estates and grants to provide basic facilities such as power, lighting and roads. The Treasury was empowered to make grants and loans on the advice of the development areas Treasury advisory committee (D.A.T.A.C), superseding the pre war S.A.R.A. and the Nuffield fund. The act abolished the commission for the special areas. A schedule to the act defined, in detail, the development area envisaged in the 1944 statement to industrialists. It stretched from Pembroke, Kidwelly and Llanelli in the west to Pontypool and the eastern Monmouthshire valleys. It brought in Ystradgynlais, Vaynor and Penderyn, Brynmawr and Crickhowell and, in conformity with the 1944 statement, embraced Cardiff, Swansea and Newport.

The war time administrative structures of the Ministry of Supply, Factory and Storage Premises, and Board of Trade were rationalised into a fully fledged regional industrial administration, holding almost absolute power over building and development. Regional controllers represented the minister within South Wales, and the regional distribution of industry panel mirrored the national arrangements. A reconstituted South Wales Industrial estates company became the major vehicle for reconstruction and regeneration under the chairmanship of Sir Gerald Bruce, and as joint managing director with Eugene Brunning, a former associate of Lord Woolton. They, in turn, worked closely with the regional controllers and, indeed, national officials such as Sir Philip Warter emerged as major figures in their own right, the representatives of their powerful post war political masters. Warter was to play a seminal part in bringing to South Wales one of the most important post war industrial inward investments, the Hoover company in Merthyr Tydfil.[13]

For the second time, inside a decade, ministers and officials, armed with new legislative powers and administrative instruments faced the challenge of job creation. The powers of the 1945 Distribution of Industry Act and the regional industrial machine were incomparable with the first timid Special Areas Acts of 1934/1937 and the national and district commissioners. So, too, was the environment within which they worked. War had been a watershed in terms of the accepted and acceptable role of government. Whereas in 1918 there had been a consensus, even an eagerness to demobilise war time powers, in 1945 those powers were deemed essential to combat the evil of unemployment to prevent as one junior official observed in 1943, 'a depression falling on Merthyr again, a by word for all evils from which all South Wales had suffered!'. A new generation of public servants had been baptised in state power. They were the new believers.

1939-45: South Wales at War

'Regional Devolution has become vital'

1. Bridgend and Glascoed in the cabinet historical record series: CAB 102/625: Hirwaun, CAB 102/673,629,633,LAB 8/256.

2. Regional administration and devolution, BT 168/1.

Requisitioned

3. The Treforest estate's war production, G. Percival, *The Government's Industrial Estates*. Departmental records, LAB 8/272, BD41/32.

4. Board of Trade production executive assessments Nov. 1941, BT 168/2; the review of South Wales production, Feb. 1942, BT 168/1, Welsh regional production board minutes and memoranda, 27 July 1942 and others, BT 168/29.

5. The Merthyr deputations and ministerial exchanges, June 1942, BT 168/29.

Reconstruction and the Advisory Council

6. Public opinion assessments during the war, Paul Addison: *The Road to 1945 British Politics and the Second World War*, London, (Cape, 1975).

7. Reconstruction Problems and the Reconstruction Committee CAB 87/1-9; Minutes upon the terms and membership of the Welsh Reconstruction Advisory Council, CAB 117/254, 255, Prem 4/36/9, BT 64/3559.

The Challenge of Peace

8. The 1943 reviews of jobs and post war industrial prospects, BT 64/3392, BT68/3239; other surveys, CAB 124/440, CAB 117/157-174.

9. The council's reports and interim recommendations, CAB 24/319; CAB117/257.

10. The proposals for a Princess of Wales and a Secretary of State, Prem 4/36/9, CAB 117/256.

The Distribution of Industry Act

11. The evolution of the bill and Dalton's role, H Dalton, *Second world war diary 1940-1945 ed. Pimlott*, pps 406, 451, 540, 456, 596, 600, 602, 618, 641-2, 645, 667, 684, 700, 717, 769, 794.

The New Believers

12. For the Ocean Colliery Company's obstruction, Dalton's second world war diary, 731.

13. The account of reconstructing the Welsh Industrial Estate's Corporation, G. Percival, *The Government's Industrial Estates in Wales*, 1936-1975,(Welsh Development Agency 1978).

9

1945 – 1951: Something Will be Done

War had recast the whole relationship between South Wales and Whitehall. The parliamentary deputations kept on coming to see ministers and officials. The exchanges could still be bitter, but they were of a very different kind. They were now concerned not whether government would influence industry to come to South Wales but how and when. The deputations and meetings were characterised by impatience and irritation over the pace of factory building, shortage of materials and the balance of male to female jobs being created. They remained, however, within mutual parameters of policy. Officials believed in the policy of regional industrial development, and of direction. They enjoyed nearly total power over the materials and resources for development. Almost every building resource was rationed; space and materials had to be jealously husbanded and made to count in the task of reconstruction. They had inherited and now had to convert (for peace time purposes) the largest ever government owned industrial real estate.

Cripps And Warter

Having inherited such sweeping powers, officials, backed by ministers, were prepared to exercise them. In the series of case studies considered below, officials conducted something of a poker game with companies. Companies sought to maximise assistance from the state in the knowledge that government needed to deliver to traditional South Wales mining communities. Officials knew that they held the power to withhold building permission, controlled the precious scarce materials of steel and bricks and had property to lease. The fact that such powers resided in regional and central administration also altered the process of parliamentary representation. Mr Hopkin Morris member, for Camarthen, understandably raised a constitutional eyebrow when the Welsh Parliamentary Party was met not by Sir Stafford Cripps but by his official chief lieutenant, Sir Philip Warter. Officials' role in the detailed decision making of industrial relocation inevitably drew the politicians into a dialogue with regional and national civil servants. Warter played an extraordinary personal role on behalf of his Minister, Cripps. Described by Dalton, president of the Board of Trade in the coalition government, as a young energetic business man, Warter had been recruited from his family's wharfing company, to become controller of the Factory, Storage and Premises department. He became an indispensable part of Dalton's team preparing for the post war conversion of war time space and location policy. He played a role in attracting the huge ICI development to

Teeside and, subsequently, the coming of Hoover to Merthyr Tydfil. Warter left Whitehall in 1947 to become president of Associated British Picture Corporation, and chairman of Thames Television. He was at the centre of much of the negotiations which brought key companies into the heart of the coalfield. He is one of the little known heroes of post war South Wales' regeneration, playing the role in a very different Whitehall environment that Portal had played in the late 30s. Regional policy redefined official and political roles. Persuasion replaced protest.[1]

The new partnership of Whitehall, trade unions and local industry - the war time trinity - survived into post war planning arrangements. The regional and central industry boards enshrined partnership. The South Wales and Monmouthshire estates company also re-emerged as the main engine to drive forward the conversion of war time factory space and as the vehicle for developing the government's advanced, standard factory building programme. The company's remit was extended beyond South Wales following the scheduling of the development areas in and around Wrexham. The Wales and Monmouthshire Industrial Estates Ltd assumed the responsibility for the conversion of the Bridgend and Marchwiel (Wrexham) ordnance factories, a programme of 200,000 sq ft advance factory building to which was added the provision of some 10 'Grenfell' factories (named after D R Grenfell M.P.), whose report to government had successfully recommended a special programme designed to create jobs for disabled miners.[2]

Yet a huge question mark hung over what might be seen as a cosy consensus. Could it meet the awesome challenge of rapid demobilisation not only from the services but also from the huge war production machine built for the war and which had brought full employment for the first time in the century? The war production machine had taken over the Treforest trading estate, displacing virtually all pre war Jewish inward investors. It had, also, taken over most of the pre war factories built under the Special Areas Act and, of course, it had occupied the newly created royal ordnance factories at Bridgend, Hirwaun, Glascoed and Pembrey. The same programme had financed the agency factories such as ICI at Dowlais. War had boosted production and employment via government contracts in a number of pre war firms such as Polikoffs and Porth Textiles in the Rhondda. Major national companies had taken unprecedented factory space - Morris Motors at Llanelli, Lucas in Cwmbran.

The challenge of conversion was one for the whole area but also intensely local. Merthyr, Dowlais, Treorchy and the Rhondda, Aberdare and Mountain Ash, communities synonymous with the depression of the 30s, had tasted full employment for the first time in twenty five years. Fear of returning to the 'bad old days' of the twenties and thirties informed every letter and deputation. S.O. Davies, MP for Merthyr Tydfil, felt it necessary, in October 1945, to warn Cripps of a growing agitation locally over the serious employment situation. He had, initially, dissuaded local trade unions from a mass descent upon Whitehall but hoped the President of the Board of Trade would deliver alternative jobs for the rapidly growing dole queues. For, despite government power and will (within the first year of peace) unemployment rose steeply, from near full employment to 60,800 out of work in the area. That this represented less than half the pre war unemployment levels offered cold comfort to a new Labour government committed to delivering jobs fit for heroes and heroines.[3]

Treforest Revisited

The government faced the immediate test of re-converting the Treforest estate and the ROF factory complexes at Bridgend and Hirwaun. At Treforest, those first pre war Jewish inward investors had been expelled from the estate, considered as security risks. Officials now undertook detailed investigations to encourage their return. Some like Labin & Co making handbags and fancy leather goods, wished to return to a larger factory, to employ some 150 people. Burlington High Class glovers under the ownership of Mr Gluckstien, also agreed to return 'though as far away as possible from the Upper Boat power station and its dust!' Others, such as Gnome Photographers, had resettled in Cardiff and rejected the disruption of further move. Another company which had scarcely established itself at Treforest before the outbreak of war found a more congenial and satisfactory home further north in Merthyr Tydfil. O.P. Chocolates discovered the Taf Brewery site, which would allow space for some 100 jobs and ultimately 300. O.P. became one of the Merthyr borough's most significant post war employers.

Of the dispersed companies, 8 out of the 17 indicated a willingness to return to Treforest, with an employment potential of 900/1000 girls and 160 men. They, fortunately, shared the estate with those major war time players, BOAC, KLG Plugs and Simmonds Accessories. These predominant war time production companies remained, though neither they nor the Treforest Estate ever again reached war time peaks of employment when 100 tenants created 16,000 jobs. Post war reconstruction of Treforest offered some 10,000 jobs.[4]

Treforest estate was, of course, no longer the sole flagship of government financed industrial space. The reconstituted Wales and Mon. Estates company under the leadership of Sir Gerald Bruce and Eugene Brunning, carried the government's advance factory building into a host of communities - Pembroke Dock, Llanelli, Neath, Ferndale, Mountain Ash, Aberbargoed, Abercarn and Tredegar. Companies followed the new building programme, companies which became the industrial heart of local communities: Smith Watches at Ystradgynlais, Pullman Springs at Ammanford, Midland Metal Spinners at Neath. Another company, which had begun to drop its roots in 1938/9, Kayser Bondor at Dowlais, took over one of the new 'standard' factories built in Merthyr. Three huge new concerns, Lucas in Cwmbran (419,000 sq ft) Llanelli motors (320,000 sq ft) and Standard Telephones at Newport (200,000 sq ft) confirmed or established a significant role in the new South Wales economy. New industrial investment and new companies reached the extremities of the enlarged South Wales development area. In the west, at the ancient borough of Kidwelly, an American optical company took a standard factory to create 300 jobs. The 'Optical' became an integral part of the economy of this small south west Wales community.[5]

At the other extreme, a very different kind of industrial production found its way to Cwmbran, Monmouthshire. The milk machine manufacturing company, Alfa Laval, at its Brentford works had prospered within the closed domestic markets of the war. Shortage of farm labour and more stringent regulations regarding clean milk production had prompted a rapid increase in demand. Alfa Laval had, originally, applied for an extension of their own Brentford premises, claiming it to be vitally important to the national economy. The Ministry of Supply resisted such a request, arguing that the new capacity should be sited in 'an easier labour district'. They refuted the company's claim that skills would not be available. Milking machines had not been made in Britain before the war. Key workers must have acquired skills within the country, and, therefore, workers in other parts of the country could also be trained as quickly. Alfa Laval was first taken to view the Dowlais factories and others, at Ammanford and Ferndale before the company alighted upon a newly built factory at Cwmbran, originally intended for a clothing company. At a meeting of the distribution of industry panel in December 1947, clearance was given to Monmouthshire for this novel industrial production line.[6]

But the most awesome challenge for the new Whitehall lay in the conversion of the two great ROF factory complexes at Bridgend and Hirwaun, and the conversions of the war time production within the Rhondda, Aberdare and Merthyr valleys. Bridgend, in one sense, presented the easiest. Location of parts of the Woolwich arsenal at Bridgend had, after all, been made because of better access to the rest of the country. The Labour government's first ever report on development in Wales (1946) boasted that a variety of companies had already committed themselves to fill a large part of the 1.5 million sq ft available at

Bridgend. They included furniture and vacuum flask making, collar studs and links. One of the largest, Koray Ltd, were major manufacturing chemists, and polish manufacturers.[7]

A large number of ordnance workers, however, found little comfort in these alternative jobs or in the character of the new breed of employer attracted to the estate. In October 1945, the ROF factories Workers Association pleaded with Aneurin Bevan to intervene. They complained bitterly that Bridgend was 'being sacrificed to private enterprise, unless something can be done to keep it for state purposes!' They noted a recent Bevan speech spelling out the desperate national need for building commodities. Bridgend, the workers claimed, 'with its very large army of unemployed in the midst of plenty of cement, limestone, coal and clay' was surely the ideal site for such production. The factories were, instead, being turned over to promote private enterprise. If a Tory government were in power they might not have expected otherwise but with a Labour government! More immediately, ROF workers complained of the character of their new employers. 'The cockney element is sacking our people because they don't jump about quickly enough and our unions are not consulted as to the condition in any shape or form.' There is no evidence that Bevan either accepted the workers' invitation to visit or that he did anything to bring such grievances to the attentions of government.[8]

'Not Suitable For Industrial Development'

Converting Hirwaun presented a more fundamental challenge, Whitehall frankly thought, at first, the task of conversion an impossible mission. Post war use of the premises as an ordnance factory or by commercial firms was 'improbable'. The location was 'not suitable for industrial development other than that which has been accidentally created by the erection of ROF.' The official Whitehall committee in February 1945 recognised the serious labour problem of discharging more than 6,000 workers, but believed their needs better met by factory space in Aberdare, Merthyr Tydfil and Treorchy.

The fear of Hirwaun workers, inevitably, reached the ears of local politicians. S.O. Davies conveyed them to Cripps and Dalton in April 1945. 'Depressing reviews are in circulation among the employees, largely associated with the greater part of the factory now engaged with the production of the 25 pound shell'. Internal memoranda confirmed the workers' gloomiest rumours. A workforce of some 6000 in May 1945 would fall to 1800 by 30 June. While as a result of 'the agitation' a certain amount of additional work could be diverted to Hirwaun, that would only postpone the deadlines by a month or so. Dalton replied to S.O. Davies in mollifying terms while, behind the scenes, frantic efforts were to be made to convert the massive factories of nearly a million sq ft through a 99 year lease given to the Wales and Monmouthshire Estates Company.

Hirwaun's development was bedevilled by the poor state of the buildings and a perception by many employers that this was a god forsaken corner to which they had to be dragged. Ironically, the successful development of the first major employer, Allied Radios (Sobells) initially complicated the possible attraction of a second significant company, Murphy Radios. Officials doubted whether another radio company in the vicinity would be advisable. Murphys, too, were less than enthusiastic. In November 1943, the company had sought clearance for 200,000 sq ft within a 50 mile radius of London. A little later, the company's options extended to Lowestoft or Bognor before grudgingly considering South Wales, and, as something of a last resort, Hirwaun, where in 1947 they eventually took 45,000 sq ft to employ some 300, of which a half would be male. They occupied the factory originally let to a company, Truvox, which had already come and left the estate.

Murphys continued to complain about the unsatisfactory labour, the appalling climate and the transport arrangements. In 1949 they intimated that they would not stay another winter, and intensifying pressure upon officials, sought a building licence to develop in Welwyn Garden City. Regional officials held their nerve. While acknowledging the uncertainty of a number of the tenants' intentions which caused continuing instability, they strove to bring to the estate at least one other major employer and, in 1950, found one.

The Dunlop company had decided to drop its plan to produce in Birmingham its new product, latex, and sought 260,000 sq ft at Hirwaun. Regional officials pleaded with the Treasury to endorse the necessary expenditure. Hirwaun, they explained, had for some time been causing considerable anxiety because many of the tenants had not been prepared to settle down on a long term basis, and had refused to sign their leases. The arrival of Dunlop offering 750 male jobs and 100 women, would secure 'the nucleus of permanent employment on the estate'. 'We shall now be able to deal much more firmly with the other firms unwilling to commit themselves'. They forecast that the Dunlop project would prove to be the turning point in the affairs of 'this very difficult area'. It certainly had the desirable effect upon Murphys who promptly agreed a new 21 year lease upon their premises.[9]

The Standard Advance Factory

New companies reaching South Wales were not confined to the former ROF factories. The standard advance factory building programme proved one of the simplest and most effective vehicles for carrying companies into traditional mining communities from Maesteg to Mountain Ash. In Mountain Ash, the 33,000 sq ft units brought to the town in 1949, a firm that created jobs for two generations. A.B. Metal Products making electrical accessories and switches found their great west road site at Feltham threatened by the proposed Heathrow Airport extension. The prospect of AB taking the prize advance factory did not initially enthuse regional officers. Reflecting a growing political anxiety, they jibbed at granting premium space to a company where labour requirement was primarily female. Unless the company could formulate a scheme employing at least 50% males, it would be preferable that it looked elsewhere. Colwyn Bay offered seasonal labour! However, under intense pressure to relocate, the company revamped its application to meet the demands of an equal ratio of male to female jobs, offering in total some 400 jobs. The company attracted a £75,000 loan from D.A.T.A.C. to make a wider range of electrical goods, including a musical whiskey pourer! Business flourished, especially exports to the United States, Argentina, Holland and Switzerland. The labour force rose to 450, receiving qualified praise from the London management. 'The men were better than those in London, the women not so good.'[10]

The London management of the other company which found its way to the Aberdare valley, however, raised the hackles of the local workforce. Sterling Textiles, makers of needles and pressed felts, jute and hair, registered an interest in the other remaining Mountain Ash advance factory. Managing director W.P. Franklin made a series of escalating offers of jobs during the course of 1947 from 100 to 250, of which 175 would be male. A later decision to close completely their Ponders End premises, led to a revised estimate of 400 to 500 jobs in 50,000 sq ft at two Mountain Ash factories. Such exaggerated job numbers never really materialised. In part, expansion was regularly impeded by the rationing of the jute raw materials. Board of Trade officials were sensitive to the political repercussions and representations from local members of parliament. The firm employed some 85 men, of whom 45 were disabled. Officials confessed that 'raw material difficulties were causing stoppages and much discontent in the Valleys'. We want to avoid adding Mountain Ash to the list of disgruntled districts if this is at all possible'

Officials succeeded in assuaging the company's raw material needs. Disgruntled sentiments came from a different quarter. On the eve of granting Sterling Textiles a lease to the second advance factory, regional officials feared 'a good deal of agitation in trade union circles, if the firm were allowed to take possession.' Managing Director Franklin held 'strong views about the labour he employs.' 'He feels he should be at liberty to employ or discharge whatever workers he thinks fit.' He was 'prone to take on non union labour' and did not regard himself as being bound by union rates of pay - refusing to discuss labour problems with union officials.'[11]

New products, and new production also reached the Rhondda. The new pre war companies, Porth Textiles and Polikoffs, had adapted production for war time purposes and survived. Polikoffs remained a source of irritation and concern to Nuffield trustees, left with the task of overseeing the large pre war loans made to the company; but Polikoffs continued to become one of the Rhondda's most significant post war employers. One other major company dropped its roots in Treorchy. Dalton, as war time President of the Board of Trade, had fumed over the obstructive tactics of the powerful Powell Duffryn Coal company in trying to prevent alternative manufacturing facilities being built over the coal seams in the community. Exigencies of war had overridden such objections. Under the aegis of the ministry of aircraft production (MAP), a large 150,000 sq ft factory had been erected for HMV. to make specialist valves. Now the company applied for an immediate conversion of this precious industrial space to manufacture a considerable proportion of their peacetime production of domestic appliances, radio, television and gramophones. The distribution of industry panel agreed this change of use from war production.[12]

Prams, Toys And Light Bulbs

The consumer boom of pre war Britain had been led by the rapid pace of electrification of domestic households, from 730,000 to 9 million between the wars. Under the inventive genius of Julius Thorn, Thorn lighting had prospered at its greater London Edmonton plant. Not surprisingly, the company became one of the earliest companies to seek post war expansion. Case No. 153 before the official committee on the distribution of industry panel (May 1945) envisaged a 50,000 sq ft factory at Merthyr, financed by the trading estate company in a total investment of £85,000 to create 200 jobs, rising to 500, making electric lamps and domestic electrical appliances. The project deemed 'particularly important for the location and diversification of industry point of view' was rapidly endorsed. While the new factory rose on the site of the old Cyfarthfa iron works, Thorn took space at Hirwaun. Originally intended as a temporary measure, the Hirwaun factory became a permanent part of Thorn's production presence in the valleys. The new Merthyr factory concentrated upon lamp production while the Hirwaun premises produced the 'Mary Ann' electric irons, vacuum cleaners and 'Ferguson' radios.[13]

Thorn were attracted by the offer of a purpose built new factory. The second major arrival to the borough eagerly sought occupation of pre war premises also erected on the site of the disused Cyfarthfa iron works. Originally intended for British Sewing Machines, the factory had been requisitioned for other production, and had housed Merthyr's largest war time company, Rotax/Lucas, employing at the height of the war more than 2,000. The immediate closure of Rotax had equally heightened the borough's fears of a return to mass unemployment, fears that began to be allayed as a queue of companies sought the Rotax lease. Almost on a first come basis, regional officials committed the factory for the production of prams, toys and towed targets by the Lines Brothers.

Walter Lines had first made contact with ministry officials in January 1944, in search of space between 50,000 and 200,000 sq ft to expand but also to replace space destroyed by enemy action at their London suburban factory. A visit by one of South Wales' key officials, Eugene Brunning, prompted the Lines Brothers' interest in the area. By October 1944, the company had further redefined its needs for a very different product, towed anti-aircraft targets. This kind of production almost led the company to a different location in the Newport area, close to the Richard Thomas steelworks. However, in June 1945, the Lines brothers had discovered the vacant Rotax factory and dangled before Sir Philip Warter and other ministry officials the prospects of 1500 jobs if early entry could be effected. Relationships between the company and Whitehall, nevertheless, became fraught. An impatient Walter Lines complained bitterly about delays attributed to the Wales and Monmouthshire Estates Company. Why, he asked, should the company become involved? 'We shall surely require none of their management.' Why could they not be treated on the same lines as other large factories in the Midlands without the intermediary of an estates company? There followed a veiled threat. Walter Lines 'had been most careful not to criticise the department in any way to the press, despite being bothered considerably by them and the borough council'.

The local member of parliament, S.O. Davies, had, indeed, been bombarding Stafford Cripps, President of the Board of Trade, with demands for the 'speedy expedition of the transfer. 'Had prompt action been taken, a considerable number of my people would be in employment, whereas there were already 5,000 unemployed and increasing weekly'. Relations between company and bureaucracy remained fractious for many months. At the end of January 1946, a frantic, bitter letter from Lines expressed their exasperation. Machinery, which the company had wished to retain, had been removed. Despite these misunderstandings and resentments and the incompatible characters of the impatient entrepreneur and the meticulous bureaucrats, Lines brothers (later Triang) established themselves in the borough, another key piece in the Merthyr post war industrial reconstruction.[14]

'A Model Factory, A Symbol of Prosperity'

Prevarication over completing the deal with Lines had arisen from an attractive alternative industrial suitor of the Cyfarthfa factory. British Thermostats based at Sunbury on Thames, had played a significant role in the war time production of high grade aircraft and industrial thermo-static controls. The ministry of aircraft production had encouraged the company's dynamic, if rather difficult, managing director, Mr William Forrest Martin-Hurst, to take over the Rotax premises, only to find that Lines had pre-empted the space. Teddingtons Controls, a part of the parent company, had been seeking 50,000 sq ft to fulfil MAP contracts, employing 700 (50% female). After suggesting a sharing arrangement with Lines, a suggestion rejected by Whitehall as 'bad policy', Martin-Hurst agreed to go into the drill hall, Merthyr, 7000 sq ft with a nucleus of seven skilled workers while the industrial estates company developed a factory adjoining Rotax, which would allow for some 600 - 700 jobs and 25 - 30 key worker houses. An impatient Martin-Hurst opted for partial occupation by Christmas. He was to be a very disappointed man.

Teddingtons were in fact wooed out of Merthyr just across the borough boundary by the small but enterprising Vaynor and Penderyn council who, when approached for some key worker houses, sold Martin Hurst the idea of developing both factory and houses in Cefn Coed. Mr Martin-Hurst and Teddingtons' frustrations were only just beginning. An eighteen month delay nearly led to the loss of the company to the community. The company desperately needed the space to complete a reorganisation of their industrial production countrywide, to leave their Oldham and Northern Ireland factories. Under pressure, the ministry suggested yet another alternative, a move to Treforest. In rejecting this situation the company revealed its primary interest in Merthyr - the skilled ex Rotax workforce. In a letter to the Board of Trade headquarters Martin-Hurst spelt out his woes. While he found 'the labour extremely anxious to work, energetic and competent,' he was also finding a marked reluctance among his key workers at Sunbury to move to Merthyr because of the 'below standard accommodation and the educational facilities.' 'The rail services were bad, and the roads not good. The journey to Bristol by train was two and half hours, and three and half hours by car unless the ferry at Chepstow was used.' That too was crowded, runs hourly and 'on which it is not possible to make a reservation!' Could not the Board of trade allow the company to move the ROF factory at Poole in Dorset?

Once again, officials made reassuring noises about communications. A proposed trunk road from Cardiff to Birmingham would improve connections with the Midlands and, of course, conditions would improve 'dramatically' when the new Severn bridge was built. An aptly named man from the ministry, Mr Peppercorn, also pointed out that, whereas there was skilled labour in Merthyr, it had never been possible even under war time conditions to find the full amount of labour required in Poole. Officials frankly admitted to themselves that conditions of workers in the makeshift factory in Merthyr's drill hall were extremely difficult, and that had the company known about the various set backs they would never have moved.

Despite these seemingly huge obstacles, the company survived. By October 1947 it was back to the ministry requesting a 25,000 sq ft extension to accommodate a deal struck with the American company Standard Thompson to transfer its secret brazing technique in constructing oil and radiator coolers. A hundred men's jobs would be created. The American deal sadly fell through but by December 1948 the factory was bursting at the seams. Another 24,000 sq ft was needed to create another 150 jobs on top of the 572 already employed. By August the factory had grown to 95,000 sq ft and employed more than 1200. A mellowing Mr Martin-Hurst became a pillar of South Wales industrial society, chairman of the Merthyr industrial group of employers, and member of the governing body of the Church of Wales. The Western Mail described Teddingtons as more than 'a model factory, a symbol of prosperity.'[15]

'Our Pentrebach Child'

If Teddingtons became a symbol one other company, above all, came to represent the post war regeneration of the South Wales valleys. The coming of Hoover to Merthyr Tydfil was the greatest prize achieved by the accumulative political pressure placed upon Whitehall in 1945/6. Hoover was steered, if not directed, to the town because Whitehall, ministers and officials recognized that they had to deliver something significant to a community which personified the bad old 30s, or as an official had put it in 1944, 'a byword for all evils.' The guiding force was Sir Philip Warter, controller general at the Board of trade. Cripps had sent his chief official to Merthyr on 24th January 1946, within days of first meeting with Messrs Colston and Puckey of Hoover. As one official later observed, 'the firm is located in Merthyr at the request of Sir Philip Warter.' Colston and Puckey visited South Wales twice in March 1946 (8th and 18th) and were brought to Merthyr and Dowlais. To the chagrin of the South Wales Estates company they rejected the offer of Dowlais and promptly plumped for the Pentrebach site in the Merthyr valley.

An anguished letter from the Estates company explained why. 'Hoover were first shown the Dowlais site which they rejected owing to its uninspiring locality' and estates officials confessed 'it was certainly very grim there, but not much grimmer than Pentrebach ...' The real reason for the choice of Pentrebach emerged; in Dowlais the company 'would be tucked away in an obscure spot whereas at Pentrebach all the Cardiff, Merthyr traffic would pass the factory which would, therefore, have a high advertisement value.' Pentrebach was to be the South Wales equivalent of Hoover's famous presence on the great west road at Perivale. The estates company, however, feared from previous experience that the site, subject to subsidence, would prove expensive; and so it did.

The company was, however, in the driving seat. It had not wanted to make South Wales its first choice, hoping for a location in south west England close to ports and docks. The market for their new and revolutionary product - the washing machine - would be the USA. Charles Colston had gone to the United States to acquire, from Mr George Gibson, a new design and patent for a low priced washing machine that would fit into the average home. The company's application to a panel of the committee of the distribution of industry reflected a progressive expansion of production. The design and layout of the buildings permitted extensions to 'a masterplan', the initial building of some 6,000 sq ft costing £160,000 and employing 500 (300 men) to supplement the Perivale workforce of 5500 (it had been as high as 7500). An expansion of another 100,000 sq ft was envisaged, lifting the workforce to 1500 and employing 130 to 150 during construction.

There were the inevitable frictions and quarrels between company and officials over costs and timescales. The ministry was 'bounced' by the company to give the go ahead before Treasury consent had been sought for a 'frantically expensive factory'. On 21st June 1946, Hoover's Mr Northover telephoned officials to inform them that he had arranged a ceremony of cutting the first sod for Wednesday 26th June. Horrified officials sought a fortnight's postponement, as the Treasury had not been told of the project. Mr Colston advised that the mayor, corporation, local MP and press had been lined up and he 'hesitated to think what the consequences would be if the ceremony now had to be put off at the insistence of the Board of Trade'. After hasty consultations with senior officials and Sir Philip Warter, local officials bowed to the inevitable. Any attempt to defer the sod cutting ceremony would have created 'every prospect of first class political trouble.'

A premature sod cutting ceremony was not to be the only tension and quarrel between company and ministry. Disputes broke out over the £30,000 tenants' 'extras'. The company incurred the regular wrath of ministry officials over breaches in the strict building licences, while, in turn, management complained of the delays and difficulties in the building of the factory. The threat of being expelled in November 1947 from their temporary storage premises, the Dowlais Engine Houses, brought the plaintive appeal from a senior company official:

'I am afraid that I can hardly agree with you that our
new factory is weather proof and thief proof. The sad
fact remains that it is neither. While our Pentrebach child
is certainly growing to full stature there are times when, as
at least one of its parents, I have wondered what sort
of offspring I have helped to bring into the world. Indeed,
on many occasions even its parentage has been in extreme doubt ...'

But the trials and tribulations were forgotten at the splendid grand opening of the 'Merthyr Project' (MP1) on 12th October 1948. The 'Pentrebach child' grew at an amazing pace. Between 1948 and 1953, MP2 and 3 were authorised to meet the incredible market response to the company's new product, the washing machine. Some of that excitement, of a new product for a new market produced in one of the most traditional industrial communities, is caught in the memorandum of the company's maintenance superintendent, Mr Rogers:

'The increasing home demand, the expansion for exports
to countries abroad, and, in particular, our success in
discovering a new and valuable market in the USA
make it increasingly evident that the first building extension
is an interim step towards further expansion. In our
judgement demands for washing machines will soon require
the establishment at Merthyr of some 2,200 personnel. The volume
of production should be stepped up to something like eight
times the figure used in the calculations for the original Pentrebach
factory when the potential of the markets was practically unknown ...'

A project which began with an estimated employment of 500 had risen to
2500 by the mid fifties and reached its astonishing peak in the 1970s at
5,400. Hoover, Pentrebach, Merthyr Tydfil became a symbol of the
manufacturing regeneration of South Wales.[16]

'Simply a matter of internal arrangements'

If Hoover became such a symbol and a household name in South Wales, a
lesser known and, perhaps, forgotten company at Rhymney represented,
in a more vivid fashion, the character of the new post war state. James
Smith had been making uniforms and clothes in Derby since 1830. In
March 1945 approaches were made to the Board of Trade and the
Rhymney urban district council to build a factory on old Powell Duffryn
land. The project attracted the immediate support of the local member of
parliament, Aneurin Bevan, and, consequently, enthusiastic support of
Hugh Dalton, President of the Board of Trade. Officials were less
enamoured. They anticipated, with some justification, nightmarish
escalating costs arising from subsidence and old mine workings, while the
development highlighted a significant wider policy problem. A factory on
the site would sterilise precious coal reserves of 0.25 million tons, a point
the avaricious Powell Duffryn company was only too quick to press.

Valuation of sterilised coal reserves had all the makings of an interminable
argument and delay. The dilemmas were, in fact, swiftly resolved. A
minute from Sir Philip Warter spelled out an immediate answer. The
question of future workings and valuation of the minerals would be duly
settled after the nationalisation of the coal industry. 'It would then
become simply a matter of the internal arrangements of two government
departments'. There could not have been a simpler statement heralding
the emergence of the new state. Only ten years earlier, the powerful Sir
Warren Fisher, permanent secretary at the Treasury, had dismissed any
such role for the state in creating employment. There had been 'nothing
new, nothing heroic' to do on behalf of the unemployed of South Wales.

War had created a new state with powers unimaginable in 1935/6, though even before such a catalyst there had been a grudging acceptance that something more had to be done for the distressed areas. The relationship between South Wales and Whitehall was never to be the same.[17] Sir Warren Fisher and Sir Philip Warter personified the dramatic change in the role of Whitehall and the state. War created a state with powers unimaginable in 1935/36, powers which survived the war to create a new manufacturing society in South Wales.

1945-1951: Something will be Done

Cripps and Warter

1. For Sir Philip Warter's role, see Hugh Dalton, *Second world war diary*.

2. The reconversion of the Treforest Trading Estate, G. Percival, *The Government's Industrial Estates in Wales.*

3. S.O. Davies exchanges with Cripps, BT 177/1131.

Treforest

4. Post War Treforest records, BT 64/3510.

5. G.Percival, The Government's Industrial estates in Wales; individual company records are contained in the BT 177 series.

6. Alfa Laval company, BT 177/970.

7. Reports of Government Action in Wales and Monmouthshire, Cmnd. 6938, HC 1945-6.

8. The R.O.F Workers Association, BT 106/80, LAB 12/256.

'Not Suitable for Industrial Development'

9. Hirwaun estate records, BT 106/74, BT 104/65,74; S.O. Davies exchange with Cripps, BT 177/1131; Allied Radios, BT 177/982; Murphy Radios, BT 177/104; Dunlop, BT 177/1004.

The Standard Advanced Factory

10. AB Metal Products, BT 177/964.

11. Sterling Textiles, BT 177/1125.

12. Flex Fasteners, BT 177/1011; Polikoff BT 177/1110; The Advance Factory Programme, BT 177/1141, 1146, 1147, 1151, 1152.

Prams Toys and Light Bulbs

13. Thorn, BT 177/1119.

14. Lines Bros, BT 177/1131.

'A Model Factory A Symbol of Prosperity'

15. Teddingtons, BT 177/1074

'Our Pentrebach Child'

16. Hoover, BT 177/1018, 1019, 1020

'Simply a matter of internal arrangements'

17. James Smith, BT 177/106.

B.D.I.(A) 40 Region...8......   Case No...DIP/8/20........

OFFICIAL COMMITTEE ON THE DISTRIBUTION OF INDUSTRY

BUILDING PROJECT -

SUBMISSION TO REGIONAL DISTRIBUTION OF
INDUSTRY PANEL AND TO PANEL A FOR APPROVAL

---

1. Name of firm: Hoover Ltd.

2. Address of firm: Perivale, Greenford, Middlesex

3. New building proposed - state

   (a) whether an extension to existing
      works is proposed or entirely new   New building
      building:

   (b) estimated cost of the project

	Initial	Expansion	
(i) Site Clearance	£30,000	£40,000	) Trading
(ii) Building	£130,000	£120,000	) Estate
			) Finance
	£160,000	£160,000	)

      (iii) Plant   £40,000   N/A

   (c) Area of Building: 86,000 sq.ft. rising ultimately to 186,000 sq.ft.

   (d) average no. of building   First stage   Second stage
      workers required for month: 130   150

   (e) estimated time required for building: 12/18 months each stage

4. Location of project:
   (a) Town and County   Merthyr Tydfil, Glamorgan.
   (b) Site area   6/8 acres
   (c) Site position (preferably by reference
      to military grid ref. on 2½" scale map) Site No.4. Lower Pentre Bach.
   (d) Present Land use of site:

5. Whether the firm has been asked to consider
   locating the project in a Development Area: Development Area

6. Information available as to additional
   requirements of:-
   (a) Electricity   N/A
   (b) Gas   Particulars to be supplied later. Considerable quantities
                will be required for die-casting
   (c) Water   N/A
   (d) Sewage and Effluent Disposal   N/A

7. Nature of intended production: Domestic Washing Machines

8. Number of workers employed on production:

	Males	Females	Juveniles	Total
(a) Pre-war) at Middlesex	5,650	1,850	-	7,500
(b) Present)	3,300	2,200	-	5,500
(c) After completion of project	300	200	-	500
(d) Peak	900	600	-	1,500

NOTE. Employment figures relate to first stage of 86,000 sq.ft. only: no
      information has been supplied by firm in regard to labour needed for
      the second stage.

9. Other comments: Up to 50% of the output will be exported.
               Present factories will be retained.

The Hoover application to build in Pentrebach

i

The Hoover factory opening 12th October 1948

Postscript

The thirty years covered by this book represent some of the most traumatic years in Welsh history. At their beginning, South Wales was a vital and seemingly indispensable part of a powerful British economy, and a major player in the global economy, in modern terms a 'tiger economy'. Welsh iron and coal constituted the strength and sinews of the empire. Their production reached almost the four corners of the world. South Wales coal was a dominant force in the European energy market. The coal and iron products from one small community of Dowlais alone were truly international. As a constituent had reminded Mr. Oscar Guest MP, soldiers in the great war from Dowlais were conveyed out into the desert to face the Turks in trucks built at Dowlais, drawn by locomotives made in Dowlais and upon rails struck in Dowlais.

But in such a powerful, but narrow, domination of coal and iron lay also the seeds of destruction of such a community as Dowlais. Professor J Williams' challenging essay 'Was Wales Industrialised?' has underlined the fallibility of the South Wales economy. Its coal and iron had remained essentially primary products for export.

Although there were in 1911 more factories than mines, the overwhelming majority of urbanised communities were built around, and dependent upon, the pit and works, not the factory. The 'factory society' which brought varied skills and work opportunities to other parts of industrial Britain was noticeably absent in the South Wales valleys. It has already been noted that in the pleas and representations of the mid 30s, few called for new factories. Almost all sought salvation in the revival of the coal market and the alternative utilisation of coal products. The South Wales of the early 1930s had not been connected to the growing consumer production. Whitehall regularly bemoaned the limited skills of the South Wales valleys. Welsh steel went into new motor cars but the cars were made elsewhere. The wealth of the coalowners and ironmasters had not financed alternative forms of productive activity in the community.

Thus, when the crisis of the early 1920s struck, the area was poorly equipped to respond. At first, both centrally and locally, it was fondly hoped that this was just another cyclical down turn in fortunes which had been such a feature of the nineteenth century coal and iron trade. When, within a decade, the realisation grew that something rather more fundamental was occurring, no consensus existed on the action required to deal with the crisis. Except for the brief necessity of the great war, the state had played little or no role in determining the location and development of industrial production. It would have been a wholly novel concept that the state should, somehow, become directly involved in the creation of jobs. As the numerous minutes and memoranda quoted in this study simply demonstrate, those who governed Britain in the inter war period did not believe it was the responsibility of the state to do such a thing.

The natural and instinctive reaction of those in positions of power and influence had been to reject any form of intervention. The conditions by which a powerful South Wales economy had grown in the first place, the existence of key raw materials and the arrival and availability of a large labour force migrating from the countryside, no longer applied. No government had determined the original growth of South Wales and, therefore, no government could now reverse its decline. The mass arrival of workers from the land that created Merthyr Tydfil and Dowlais had been market driven. Now market forces should determine their exodus, modestly aided and abetted by an industrial transference board. Migration and transference constituted government policy. As Sir Arthur Robinson, permanent secretary and chairman of the imperial defence committee had brutally observed 'the plain truth was that this policy had to be directed to one object, removing that population as quickly as one could to where it can find industrial occupation'.

With or without government exhortation and assistance, a significant proportion of the healthy and able valleys workforce left. Small mining communities suffered staggering population losses of the order of 18 - 25% within a decade. These were decades which created a Welsh diaspora into the carmaking and consumer production towns of the midlands and the south east, such an important feature of the Welsh/British relationship.

The experience of the inter war years left a deep scar upon the South Wales consciousness but was also to leave a significant mark upon British government. The National government had no wish to be dragged into the wholly unpalatable activity of job creation. When Baldwin and Chamberlain felt the need, initially, to concede the appointment of investigators, and subsequently, a commissioner of the special areas with a budget, it was conceived in very limited terms. Chamberlain revealingly explained it to ministerial colleagues as essentially complementary and supplementary to the primary objective of transference. Government should endeavour to make life as comfortable for older long term unemployed; 'the unemployable residuum should be kept as contented and happy as circumstances permitted'. The main thrust of government economic policy, 2% interest rates and protection delivered a general improvement for three quarters of Britain and delivered to National government in November 1935 another substantial election victory.

Yet a twelve month later the same government, ideologically committed to non intervention, introduced a second Special Areas bill which breached all fundamental principles hitherto promoted and preached. The significance of the 1937 Special Areas (Amendment) Act has to be evaluated within the particular political and official context of the time. The hostility from officials, the strength of the language of the memoranda of objections confirms the seriousness with which they considered the bill to be a breach of fundamental policy principles. In legislating for the financing of the private sector industrial job creation, they believed the government had crossed a rubicon. Ministers and officials became drawn into a detailed involvement with company decision making in the production of such things as silk stockings, aluminium, cables and glass. Whitehall and its advisers deliberated on loan applications in a manner which bears an uncanny resemblance to the post war industrial advisory boards. The case studies indicate that the Special Areas Amendment Act foreshadowed post war regional industrial policy more significantly than it has hitherto been accepted.

Chamberlain, of course, was no convert to the cause of big government. He clearly hated the ground he had been forced to give in the autumn of 1936. He repeatedly laid emphasis upon the experimental and temporary nature of the policy. His hand written minute in November 1936 had conveyed, in very personal terms, his ambivalence and distaste for the whole idea as well as a strong dose of scepticism about its efficacy. He anxiously sounded out ministerial colleagues in 1939 about scrapping the commission and transferring certain residual functions to his own creation, the Unemployment Assistance Board. He found them too nervous to agree to such a politically contentious move.

Thus, the Second Special Areas Act constituted no change of heart but, certainly, a change of policy. But why was such a change conceded? This account illustrates the particular nature of the British parliamentary and political processes. Despite commanding majorities, Baldwin and Chamberlain felt the instant peculiar pressures that constant parliamentary accountability brings. Rumblings in the cabinet, growing unease among government back benchers, a highly critical commissioner's report, which had to be published at a most politically inconvenient time, and, then, the unexpected foray by the King into the distressed areas turned what should have been a routine House of Commons occasion into a major parliamentary confrontation.

The King's motive for undertaking his South Wales tour has been the subject of considerable speculation, especially seen in the light of his subsequent ambivalent attitudes to Hitler and fascism. The evidence publicly available does not validate any extreme interpretation of his actions in November 1936. They were a part of his personal populist instincts that had been manifest during his service as Prince of Wales. On his return from South Wales he spent more time sipping champagne with Chips Channon than pleading the cause of the unemployed of the valleys. It was his proposed marriage, and not the special areas policy that led to the fatal breach between king and government. The intervention, nevertheless, made a contribution to the change in policy. Its timing added to the pressure upon Chamberlain. The Chancellor's decision to rush a copy of his speech across to the Palace on the eve of the King's tour was no act of courtesy, but a reflection of his apprehension about the political impact of the visit.

It was not, however, the Palace but the palace of Westminster that ultimately forced Chamberlain's hand. Parliamentary accountability played its part in the change of policy. Chamberlain felt that he could not go 'naked' into the Commons. The pressure from the hunger marchers, public sympathy, government backbenchers and the commission for the special areas had transmitted itself to the Commons. The influence of the Commons on events is often derided or taken for granted. It is worthwhile reminding ourselves of a very contrasting set of events unfolding in Germany during the identical 6/7 year period 1929 to 1936. In both countries, unemployment placed intolerable pressures upon political structures. Hitler rose to power constitutionally and electorally but, with the tacit consent of a large majority, proceeded to dismantle the democratic structures. The Reichstag went up in flames. An enabling act bestowed huge autocratic emergency power upon Chancellor Hitler to deal with the crisis of mass unemployment. Chancellor Chamberlain enjoyed no such power, would not have sought it, and would not have been granted it by a House of Commons. Hundreds of thousands of unemployed people in the distressed areas felt betrayed by government and did take to the streets. Britain, of course, had not suffered the dire indignation and humiliation of defeat in war; but levels of violence and the threat of violence were taken very seriously by the authorities.* Cabinet discussions in October 1936 reveal such ministerial nervousness. Yet the political and parliamentary processes acted sufficiently as a conduit to prevent hunger marchers becoming revolutionaries. Parliament survived the test of more than 3 million out of work.**

War, and the prospect of war, transformed the unemployment position, thus preventing any easy, meaningful evaluation of the 'temporary' 'experimental' employment measure of 1937/38. War revalued the unemployed. Yet, the experiences of government of the late thirties and bitter memories of the plight of the unemployed hung over war time coalition government policies. Compelled to consider post war reconstruction as early as 1942, the war cabinet acknowledged the political impossibility of dismantling war time controls which might address regional unemployment.

Alongside Butler's Education Act and the white paper on employment, the Coalition government's Distribution of Industry Act ensured power and a post war role for Whitehall and its newly created regional industrial administration. This regional administration proved to be one of the lasting legacies of the war.

Recent assessments have tended to devalue the effectiveness of post war regional policy, drawing attention to the continuing regional economic and employment disparities and the fragile character of regional economics, dependent upon 'the branch factory'. But any comparisons between 'the situation in Merthyr Tydfil', 1936, and Merthyr Tydfil, 1956 demonstrate the enormous practical influence of regional employment policy upon the fortunes of that community. The contrast in the situation was striking: 1935, 12,000 unemployed representing 65% of the insured population: 1955 less that 1,000 and 2.7%.

The county borough's working population grew and changed character. Whereas in 1938 the ratio of men to women in employment had been 11:1 by the mid 1950s the ratio was 2:1, 16,000 men and more then 6,600 women. Coalmining, representing 44% in 1931, had fallen to 15%. Manufacturing had replaced coal and metal as the mainstay of the local economy, rising from 11% pre-war to 41% of the working population in 1951. Thorn, Hoover, OP Chocolate offered an alternative to the four major pits. Many men shuttled between pit and factory. The remnants of the coal industry, at Taf Merthyr, Deep Navigation, Trelewis and Merthyr Vale collieries ensured one generation of valleys' miners reasonable well paid and regular employment. The Guest/BSC works enjoyed a revival tied to powerful expansion of the Port Talbot works. Employment at the Dowlais works reached a post war peak in 1958 of more than a thousand.

Merthyr County Borough Council regained a degree of confidence and stability to play its part in post war regeneration. Its local government 'status' as a county borough, considered in 1936 as too great a burden, was unchallenged until the England and Wales local government reform of the 1970s. Unburdened of public assistance to the unemployed, it began the painstaking and, at times painful, task of reconstructing some of its oldest communities, Penydarren and Dowlais, with a large and expensive council house building programme. Housing had to be given a special degree of urgency, not only because of the age and state of much of the housing stock. Virtually the total absence of any building between the wars was to be one of the most damaging and poignant consequences of the thirties depression. Whereas much of inter war Britain enjoyed one of the greatest private house building booms in its history, none were built in Merthyr, breaking a long tradition of working class owner occupation, and converting a significant percentage of the post war population to depend upon 'council housing'.

Regional policy, of course, proved to be no panacea, or total security against economic fluctuations. Surviving war time production at ICI, BSA and Teddingtons eventually closed. Merthyr's population decline was not wholly arrested. Between 1951 and 1961 a population of 61,142 fell to 59,039, a 3% loss during a period when Glamorgan's grew by 2% and England and Wales' by 5.3%. Yet it was not the appalling 20% of the inter war years. A growing dependence on factory consumer durables production also made Merthyr vulnerable to credit squeezes, leading to periodic short time working. Industrial relations often reflected swings and moods of the market place, evidenced by the disputes at the Hoover plant in 1960 and 1965 and a prolonged unofficial strike in 1969.

But Merthyr's economic problems had become comparative rather than the absolute destitution experienced during the thirties, cyclical as much as structural. Reasonable regular employment also established, at least for one generation, different employment terms and conditions, occupational pensions, contributory benefits and right to redundancy, sick and unemployment pay. They were to prove an important safety net when, for the third time in the century, the county borough faced the challenge of the recession and the structural changes of the 1980s, when the final connection between iron and Dowlais was broken with the closure of the BSC works, when the four collieries were closed as well as Thorn Lighting, and Hoover shrank from more that 5,500 to less than a thousand. Sadly, many of the deprivation indices, GDP per capita, health statistics, percentages of those suffering from long term illness, economic activity rates, still marked out Merthyr Tydfil and neighbouring valley communities.

One will not know until the release of the cabinet records of the 1980s whether the 'situation in Merthyr Tydfil' of the 1980s reached the cabinet as it had done in 1936. One doubts it. The absolute destitution of the thirties which had led to the implosion of valley coal communities was not repeated during the 1980s, for the action of governments and the introduction of a welfare state propped up local communities. A relevant, if currently unfashionable, message emerges from this study. It was the power of the state which transformed the South Wales economy after the disasters of the inter war years. In an age when the emphasis is upon individual or community 'empowerment' and when the global economy is regularly mooted to demonstrate the limitation of national governments, it is salutary to be reminded that, for at least one generation and more, it was state 'empowerment' which proved to be the salvation of South Wales and Merthyr Tydfil

* For a detailed account of conflict in labour disputes: Jane Morgan: Conflict and Order, the police and labour disputes in England and Wales, 1900 - 1939 (Clarendon Press, 1987.)

**For the best discussion on 'The revolution that never was ' J Stevenson and Chris Cook, Britain in the Depression, (Longman:1994).

A Note on Sources

As the chapter footnotes indicate this study has drawn primarily upon the Whitehall departmental records at the Public Record Office (PRO)

An excellent and essential guide to the records has been published: Records of Interest to Social Scientists 1919 - 1939: Employment and Unemployment (PRO, Handbooks No 18).

The book draws upon both Cabinet and cabinet committee minutes and memoranda. The chief cabinet source materials are contained in the Cabinet committee on Unemployment established in 1934 to receive the Investigators' reports on the distressed area and, subsequently, the commissioners' reports: CAB27/577-579.

One other major Whitehall cabinet committee considered some aspects of employment in the distressed areas, the committee for Imperial Defence (CID) and its Defence Policy requirements committees (DPR) and, particularly, the Billingham Sub committee.

Four major Whitehall departments dealt primarily with distressed or special areas policy and administration: Treasury, Ministry of Labour, Housing and Local Government, and Board of Trade. Three other departments contributed, Ministry of Agriculture, Fisheries and Food, Ministry of Health and Ministry of Transport. The War Office became involved in the debates on the location of the armaments industry. The relevant records and references are identified below:

The Treasury (T)
The Chancellor of Exchequer's office; Miscellaneous papers

T172/1827, 1828 Special Areas: establishment notes on operation, public works policy and history of government assistance 1934 - 1937.
T172/1850: Depressed areas deputation from Welsh MPs 14.5 1936.

Chancellor of Exchequer's office: Budget and Finance Papers
T171/317-319, 324, 328-338, bill papers relating the Special Areas Reconstruction (Agreement) Bill, 1936.

Supply files:
T161/714/S39260/02/1,2: Special Areas Bill, 1934.

T161/669/539853/1,2: Work of Special Commissioners 1934-1938.

T161/779/S41961; S41961/01; Special Areas Amendment bill, 1937.
T161/777/S416421: Special Areas: proposal for remission of income tax and local rates 1936/7.

T161/930/S41848/1-3: Special Areas, and Special Areas Reconstruction Association, 1935-1936.
T161/940/S44092/1-3; 941/S44323: Loans to industry in Special and other Areas, Use of Special Area Reconstruction Association and Nuffield Trust.

The Ministry of Labour
Employment
LAB 8/10-13: various provisions relating to Special Areas, 1936-1937.
LAB 8/18-19 Appointment of commissioner 1934-1939.
LAB 8/71 Special Areas: land settlement programme 1934-1938.
LAB 8/205 Special Areas: state provided inducement to attract industries.
LAB 8/208/209, 211 papers relating to scale and nature of financial inducements for attracting industry to Special Areas, 1937.

Establishments
LAB 12/58 Office of Commission of Special Areas, staffing 1934-1940

Training
LAB 18/28, 29 Special Areas correspondence between Prime Minister, Treasury and Ministry of Health, 1934-1935.
LAB 18/34-37 Development of Trading Estates.
LAB 18/38 Representations, Correspondence with Prime Minister over unemployment 1935.

Ministry of Housing and Local Government (HLG)

Unemployment: Special Areas

HLG30/10 Special Areas Amendment bill, 1936 - 1937.
HLG30/13 Appointment of Commissioner 1934-1935.
HLG30/20/24: Merthyr Tydfil and Report of Commission.
HLG30/41,53 relating to Merthyr Tydfil. HLG30/49-51 Investigators' survey of depressed areas, 1934.

The Board of Trade (BT)
Commissioner for Special Areas

Establishment and development of trading estates 1934-1957; BT104/5-9; Merthyr Tydfil, clearance of Dowlais site.
BT32-40; South Wales and Monmouthshire Trading Estates.

Industries and Manufacturers Department:

BT64/11/1 1981: Special Areas comment upon proposal to Commissioner for the establishment of trading estates 1936.

Chief Industrial Adviser's Department

BT56/37-40: Miscellaneous Papers relating to surveys of depressed areas and establishment of trading estates.

Departmental Committees

BT55/14/15: Departmental observations of Sir Wyndham Portal's report and correspondence with Portal.

Ministry of Agriculture, Fisheries and Food (MAF)

Land Correspondence and papers;
MAF48/94,279-280 Special Areas, provision of small holdings

Welsh Department: Correspondence and papers
MAF 70/85,86 Special Areas: development of small holdings 1935-1936.

Ministry of Health
MH 61/1-9: Commission for the Special Areas files and correspondence.
MH 79/304: Distress in Mining Areas during Winter 1928/9.

Ministry of Transport(MT)

Highways: Correspondence and Papers
MT 39/18, BD 30/74 Severn barrage road and railway schemes, 1920-1924.
BD 30/13, BD 28/470 MT 95/164: Severn bridge papers.

War Office.
WO 33/1366, WO185/12b: Discussion on the relocation of the Woolwich Arsenal.

I have drawn upon one other non departmental Whitehall source, the personal papers of the Prime Minister, the PREM series, and particularly PREM 30/69/680.

Non Whitehall primary sources include the records of the Nuffield Trust, Nuffield College, gathered into company boxes dealing with grants and loans to companies in the distressed areas: the Bank of England records relating to the work of the Special Areas Reconstruction Association (S.A.R.A); BOE; SMT 2/16-29.

I have also kindly received the gracious permission of Her Majesty the Queen to quote sources of reference from the Royal Archives, RA.PS/GV1/01182.

Finally, I have drawn briefly upon one other significant primary source, the Neville Chamberlain papers at Birmingham University.

The period has, inevitably, attracted a large number of academics. The most comprehensive bibliographies for the period can be found in two of the best studies; W.R. Garside, *British Unemployment 1919-1939, A Study in Public Policy* (Cambridge University Press, 1990) and R. Lowe, *Adjusting to Democracy, the Role of Ministry of Labour in British Politics, 1916 - 1939* (Oxford 1986). I drew heavily upon one other published source for the introductory chapter, P Williamson, *National Crisis and the National Government British politics, the Economy and Empire, 1926-1932* (Cambridge University Press, 1992). A thought provoking set of essays can be found in J Stevenson and Chris Cook, *Britain in the Depression*, (Longman 1994). Other secondary and printed sources are acknowledged within the chapter footnotes.

The Welsh scene is brilliantly covered by Kenneth O Morgan, *Birth of a Nation, Wales 1880 - 1980*, (University of Wales Press, 1982). An excellent summary of the Glamorgan economy during the period, can be found in Colin Baber and Denis Thomas, *The Glamorgan Economy 1914 - 1945, Glamorgan County History vol 5*, ed. J. J. John and Glanmor Williams (University of Wales press), while Hywel Francis' and David Smith's, *The Fed, a history of the South Wales Miners in the twentieth century* (Lawrence and Wishart, London 1980) remains indispensable.

A

A.B. Metal Products, 179
Aberbargoed, 176
Abercarn, 176
Abercrave collieries, 140
Aberdare, 19, 62, 67, 85, 98, 109, 123, 133, 138, 144, 155, 159, 165, 174, 176, 177, 179
Abertillery, 25, 28, 42, 109
Adler family, 127, 143
Alexander Gibbs and Partners, 74
Alfa Laval, 176, 188
Allied Radios, 178, 188
Ammanford, 138, 169, 176
Anglo Irish Coal for Cattle Deal, 51

B

B.I.D.C., 92
Baldock, 128
Baldwin, Stanley, 16, 24, 27, 34, 36, 43, 75, 77, 81, 84, 87, 102, 103, 104, 121, 122, 152, 191, 192
Bank of England, 45
Bank of England, 34, 35, 78, 81, 92, 95, 106, 111, 112, 129, 200
Bankers Industrial Development Corporation, 92
Barker, George, 18, 28
Barking, 88
Barlow report, 161
Barry, 73, 109
Beddau, 67
Bedwellty, 25, 29, 39, 40
Benedict, Richard, 130
Berry, Seymour, 85
Betterton, Sir Henry, 36, 41, 43, 44, 50, 76
Bevan, Aneurin, 18, 19, 56, 57, 77, 81, 99, 104, 107, 177, 186
Bevin, Ernest, 62
Billingham, 71, 90, 146, 147, 151, 152, 154, 197
Blackburn, 16, 148
Blaenavon, 49, 97, 109, 140, 144, 157, 158
Blaina, 25, 46, 67
Blue Circle, 63
BOAC, 157, 158, 165, 175
Board of Education, 29

Board of Trade, 41, 60, 73, 74, 76, 92, 124, 125, 126, 132, 133, 136, 137, 156, 158, 160, 163, 169, 170, 171, 173, 175, 179, 180, 181, 182, 185, 186, 197, 199
Bognor, 178
Bolton, 79
Boverton Co-operative, 68
Brecon, 68, 69
Breconshire, 15, 46
Brentford, 176
Bridgend, 26, 67, 109, 136, 147, 148, 149, 150, 154, 155, 159, 165, 171, 174, 175, 176, 177
Bristol Aeroplane Company, 150
Bristow, Colonel, 136
British Aluminium company, 137
British Coated Board Mill, 138, 144
British Matches, 95
British Oxygen company, 90
British Portland Cement, 63
British Sewing Machine, 129
British Small Arms, 157
British Thermostats, 182
Brown Lennox, 135, 144, 165
Brown, Ernest, 85, 94, 96, 97, 99, 138, 152
Brunning, Eugene, 170, 175, 181
Brynamman, 117
Brynmawr, 15, 46, 57, 109, 157, 170
BSA, 157, 195
BSM, 129, 130
Buckland, Lord, 26
Burlington High Class glovers, 175

C

C.I.D, 146, 147, 149
Cardiff, 11, 17, 39, 41, 45, 46, 47, 73, 74, 76, 109, 114, 120, 122, 124, 126, 127, 138, 143, 144, 163, 165, 168, 170, 175, 183, 184
Carmarthenshire, 117
Casey, Bishop of Bloomfontein, 91
Cefn Coed, 182
Central Electricity Board, 36, 88
Chamberlain, Neville, viii, 22, 23, 24, 25, 30, 33, 35, 36, 37, 40, 42, 43, 44, 49, 50, 53, 54, 55, 56, 59, 62, 63, 65, 66, 68, 70, 71, 74, 75, 76, 80, 81, 83, 86, 87, 91, 92, 93, 94, 95, 96, 97, 101, 102, 103, 104, 107, 108, 110, 111, 114, 115, 118, 119, 128,

141, 147, 150, 152, 153, 154, 191, 192, 193, 200

Chancellor, 21, 22, 28, 29, 35, 36, 43, 53, 54, 63, 64, 70, 71, 72, 76, 85, 93, 94, 95, 97, 100, 102, 108, 110, 115, 118, 127, 137, 145, 147, 150, 153, 193, 197

Chepstow, 183

Chirk, 146

Chorley, 147, 148

Churchill, Winston, 28, 29, 40, 104, 167

Clarry, Reginald, 19, 86, 118

Colonel Bristow, 136

Colston and Puckey of Hoover, 184

Colwyn Bay, 179

commissioner, 43, 53, 54, 55, 56, 57, 58, 59, 62, 63, 64, 65, 67, 68, 70, 74, 77, 80, 83, 84, 85, 86, 94, 95, 102, 108, 109, 114, 115, 117, 118, 119, 121, 122, 124, 131, 146, 156, 161, 191, 192, 198

Committee for Imperial Defence, viii, 146, 148

Conservative government, 25

Cos-sors, 169

Cowbridge, 26, 68

Cranshaw, 134

Crawshay, 13, 66, 68, 69, 75, 80, 121, 122, 156

Credit for Industry Ltd, 49, 84, 91, 92

Cripps, Sir Stafford, 173, 181

Cross, Eugene, 159

Crystal, Sir George, 89

Cumberland, 37, 43

Cwmbran, 49, 75, 131, 133, 140, 157, 174, 176

Cyfarthfa, 13, 66, 75, 121, 129, 130, 157, 160, 180, 181, 182

Czechoslovakia, 128

D

D.A.T.A.C, 170, 179

Dagenham, 88, 150

Daggar, George, 42

Dalton, Hugh, 20, 116, 120, 160, 168, 186, 188

Davies, SO, 11, 56, 175, 177, 178, 181, 188

Devereux, 137

Dinas, 130

Distribution of Industry, v, 168, 169, 170, 172, 194

Dorset, 183

Dowlais, iv, v, vii, ix, 11, 14, 15, 26, 47, 66, 75, 89, 97, 99, 100, 102, 107, 108, 121,

122, 123, 128, 130, 131, 141, 142, 143, 146, 148, 151, 152, 154, 157, 160, 164, 174, 176, 184, 185, 190, 191, 194, 195, 199

Duncan, Sir Andrew, 36, 77

Dunlop company, 178

E

East Glamorgan hospital, 67

Ebbw Vale, iv, 15, 25, 28, 46, 47, 48, 50, 75, 76, 78, 81, 109

Edmund de Stein, 93

Ely Paper Mills, 138

Ernest Brown, 85, 107

Evans, James, 25, 31, 32, 33

F

Factory and Storage Premises, 170

Falmouth Committee, 151

Fed, 17, 18, 20, 29, 30, 33, 38, 200

Feltham, 179

Ferguson' radios, 181

Ferndale, 109, 176

Firth, Lady, 77

Firth, Sir William, 76, 77, 78, 81

Fisher, Warren, 21, 22, 23, 25, 39, 50, 95, 128, 141, 186, 187

Fisons, 151

Flex Fasteners, 130, 165, 188

Ford, 150

Forestry Commission, 69

Franklin, W P, 179

Full Fashioned Hosiery, 128

G

Garnant, 117, 138

Garth Works, 125

Gilfach Goch, 67

GKN, 13, 16, 26, 46, 47, 85

Glanammon, 117

Gloucestershire, 73, 127

Gnome, 175

Goatmill Road, 14, 121

Goodenday, 128

Governor, Bank of England, 92, 93, 94, 112, 114, 137

Governor, Bank of England, 112

Great Western Railway, 45, 72

greater London Edmonton plant, 180

Greenwood, Arthur, 162

Griffiths, James, 117, 138
Griffiths, James, 62
Guest, vii, 14, 16, 99, 107, 121, 122, 123,
    190, 194
GWR, 73

H

Hacking, Douglas, 145
Hailsham, 146
Hall Telephones, 123, 127, 128, 142, 157
Hall, George, 18, 19, 62, 98, 106, 123, 134
Hardinge, Major, 97, 98, 99, 106, 107
Hartlepool, 79
Hartshorn, Vernon, 33
Heathrow Airport, 179
Hensol Castle, 67
Hereford, 148, 155
Hertfordshire, 128
High Duty Alloy Ltd, 137
Hill Plymouth, 13
Hirwaun, 155, 159, 165, 171, 174, 175, 176,
    177, 178, 180, 188
HMV, 180
Hollings, 121
Home Office, 124, 125
Hopkins, Sir Richard, 22, 23, 39, 71, 81, 92,
    96, 97, 102, 114, 117, 128, 141, 145,
    154, 159
Huddersfield, 153
Hudson, 57, 62

I

ICI, 46, 47, 71, 90, 95, 126, 146, 147, 151,
    152, 153, 154, 158, 164, 173, 174, 195
Imperial policy group, 90, 91, 99
Inland Revenue, 22, 96, 106, 110
Inskip, Sir Thomas, 90, 101, 149, 155
Iron and Coal, 26

J

Jarrow, vii, 75, 78, 83
Jarvie, Mr Gibson, 50, 84, 91, 92, 93, 112
Jarvie, Mr Gibson, 112
Jenkins, Ald. Arthur, 68
Jewish entrepreneurs, 123, 124
John, Will, 18, 57
Jones, Garro, 160
Jowitt, Sir William, 160, 162, 163

K

Kayser, 121, 129, 141, 143, 157, 164, 169,
    176
Keynes, 22, 71
Keynesian, 19, 22, 24, 35
Kidwelly, 170, 176
King Edward VIII, vii, 83, 97, 99, 107
Koray Ltd, 177
Kunert, 127, 128

L

Labin & Co, 175
Labour party, 17, 18, 20, 23, 27, 33, 34, 35,
    36, 78, 116, 169
Lancashire, 57, 92, 114, 115, 147, 150
latex, 178
Leiner, Arnold, 126
Lennox Boyd, 90
Lines Brothers, 181
Lines, Walter, 181
Llandaf, Bishop of, 17, 18, 38, 94, 105
Llandovery, 69
Llanelli, 76, 166, 170, 174, 176
Llantarnam, 131
Llantwit Major, 148
Lloyd George, 17, 18, 19, 20, 21, 23, 33, 52,
    57, 68, 70, 71, 87, 116, 162, 163, 167,
    168
Lloyd George, Megan, 167
Local Government, vii, 197, 198
Lord Nuffield, 143
Lowestoft, 178
Lowry, Sir Arthur, 31
Lucas, 127, 129, 141, 157, 174, 176, 181
Lyttleton, Oliver, 155

M

MacDonald, Ramsay, 24, 60
Macmillan, 22, 38, 57, 58, 64, 118
Maesteg, 109, 147, 165, 179
Mainwaring, W, 18, 99, 100, 113, 169
Maitland, Sir Arthur Steel, 30
MAP, 157, 180, 182
Marchwiel, 174
Marks and Spencer, 95, 127, 130
Marquand, Prof, 52, 70, 73, 114, 116, 120
Martin-Hurst, William Forrest, 182, 183
Mary Ann, 181
Merthyr, iv, vii, viii, ix, 10, 11, 13, 14, 15,
    16, 18, 26, 31, 32, 37, 38, 39, 46, 48, 49,

56, 62, 66, 67, 68, 81, 83, 88, 89, 90, 91,
  99, 101, 102, 103, 105, 108, 109, 110,
  121, 122, 123, 127, 128, 129, 130, 133,
  138, 141, 146, 148, 149, 151, 152, 154,
  157, 159, 160, 164, 169, 170, 171, 174,
  175, 176, 177, 180, 181, 182, 183, 184,
  185, 186, 191, 194, 195, 198, 199
Merthyr Express, 105
Merthyr Vale, 13, 194
Minister for Co-ordination of Defence, 90, 149
Minister for Labour, 17, 36, 71, 76
Minister for Production, 155
Minister for War Production, 160
Minister of Health, 30, 36, 88, 90, 98, 101
Ministry of Aircraft Production, 157
Ministry of Health, 21, 25, 29, 31, 110, 197,
  198, 199
Ministry of Housing, vii, 198
Ministry of Labour, 21, 23, 26, 39, 43, 44,
  64, 80, 85, 100, 105, 108, 124, 145, 148,
  151, 156, 159, 160, 197, 198, 200
Ministry of Supply, 156, 159, 160, 170, 176
Ministry of Town and Country Planning, 161
Ministry of Transport, 72, 197, 199
Monmouthshire, 15, 16, 17, 18, 46, 51, 72,
  73, 75, 76, 84, 110, 118, 121, 131, 140,
  149, 166, 170, 174, 176, 178, 181, 188,
  199
Montague Norman, 92, 94, 112
Morrell, Enoch, 18, 30
Morris Motors, 174
Morris-Jones, Sir Henry, 162
Mosley, Oswald, 33, 45
Mossend, 152
Mountain Ash, 109, 164, 174, 176, 179
MP1, 185
Murphy Radios, 178, 188
Mynydd, 49

N

Nantyglo, 15, 25, 67, 109
National Government, 33, 40, 42, 82, 200
National Unemployed Workers Movement, 36
Neath, 17, 26, 109, 138, 159, 165, 169, 176
New Crown Forgings, 158
Newport, 17, 19, 51, 73, 86, 87, 109, 114,
  118, 128, 165, 168, 170, 176, 181
Nixons, 13
Nobel, 149
North East, 37, 43, 74, 112, 113, 146, 168
north Glamorgan, 15
Northover, 185

Nuffield, 114, 119, 120, 124, 126, 127, 128,
  129, 131, 132, 134, 135, 136, 138, 139,
  140, 141, 143, 144, 157, 163, 170, 180,
  198, 200
Nuffield, Lord, 111, 131
NUUWM, 122
NUWM, 36

O

O.P. Chocolates, 175
Ocean, 13, 68, 131, 169, 172
Ocean Colliery company, 131
Oldham, 16, 79, 148, 182
Optical, 176

P

Padmore, Sir Thomas, 128, 139
Panteg, 75
Paton, RR, 125
Pembrey, 149, 150, 153, 154, 174
Pembroke, 109, 149, 170, 176
Pembrokeshire, 48, 60
Penarth, 73, 86
Pentrebach, v, 184, 185, 186, 189
Penybont, 67
PEP, 14
Peppercorn, 183
Perivale, 184
Phillips, Sir Thomas, 85
Phillips, Sir Thomas, 151
Pilkington Glass company, 132
Political and Economic Planning, 14, 38
Pontlottyn, 67, 109
Pontypridd, 26, 29, 75, 109, 135, 147, 164,
  165
Poole, 183
Port Talbot, 46, 109, 137, 147, 150, 165,
  166, 194
Portal, Sir Wyndham, 43, 44, 45, 46, 47, 48,
  49, 50, 51, 52, 58, 60, 62, 70, 76, 81, 88,
  91, 94, 98, 105, 106, 108, 112, 113, 114,
  124, 126, 128, 129, 130, 131, 132, 133,
  134, 135, 137, 138, 139, 140, 141, 144,
  163, 168, 174, 199
Porth, 109, 121, 130, 147, 165, 174, 180
Porth Textiles, 121, 130, 174, 180
Powell Duffryn, 16, 17, 26, 85, 158, 180, 186
Preston, 79, 148
Prince of Wales, 32, 33, 193
Princess of Wales, 168, 172
Pullman Springs, 176

Q

Queensferry, 146, 147

R

R.O.F, 159, 165, 188
Reith, Lord, 163
Revenue, 22, 96, 110
Rhandirmwyn, 69
Rheola, 138, 166
Rhondda, 10, 15, 16, 18, 39, 57, 67, 99, 113, 121, 130, 131, 164, 165, 174, 176, 180
Rhymney, 14, 15, 25, 46, 97, 99, 104, 107, 186
Richard Thomas and Co, 16, 76, 78
Robert Byass & Co, 166
Robinson, Sir Arthur, 30, 40, 148, 154, 191
Rootes, 150
Rotax, 127, 129, 141, 157, 160, 164, 181, 182
Ruabon, 146
Runciman, Walter, 41
Rushcliffe, 56
Rushcliffe, Lord, 55

S

S.A.R.A, iv, 49, 86, 87, 91, 93, 94, 95, 97, 106, 111, 113, 114, 119, 120, 124, 125, 126, 127, 128, 129, 130, 132, 133, 134, 136, 138, 140, 141, 143, 170, 200
S.M.T., 92
Salford, 79
Sankey, Lord, 162
Saunders Valves, 131, 133, 143, 158
Scotland, 32, 37, 50, 78, 95, 146, 151, 152, 161, 162
Scottish reconstruction advisory council, 161
Scunthorpe, 151
Secretary of State for Wales, v, 166, 167, 168, 172
Security Management Trust, 92
Senghenydd, 46
Severn Bridge, 58, 72, 74, 81, 87, 95, 199
Severn tunnel, 72
Sieff, Issac, 127, 128
Sieff, Michael, 130
Simmonds Accessories, 157, 165, 175
Simpson, Mrs, 103
Skinner, EDF, 92, 93, 112, 113, 129
Slough, 37, 74
Smith Watches, 176

Snowden, 33
Sobells, 178
South Wales, iv, v, vii, 10, 11, 13, 15, 16, 17, 18, 19, 22, 24, 25, 26, 28, 29, 30, 31, 32, 37, 38, 40, 41, 42, 43, 44, 45, 46, 47, 48, 49, 50, 51, 52, 58, 59, 60, 62, 64, 66, 67, 68, 69, 70, 71, 72, 73, 74, 75, 76, 77, 78, 80, 81, 83, 84, 85, 86, 87, 88, 91, 94, 96, 97, 98, 100, 101, 102, 103, 104, 105, 107, 109, 112, 113, 114, 116, 118, 120, 121, 122, 123, 124, 126, 130, 131, 132, 133, 134, 135, 136, 137, 139, 140, 141, 142, 143, 144, 145, 147, 148, 149, 150, 151, 153, 155, 156, 157, 158, 159, 161, 164, 165, 166, 168, 169, 170, 171, 173, 174, 176, 178, 179, 181, 183, 184, 186, 190, 191, 193, 196, 199, 200
South Wales Miners Federation, 17
South Wales' Forgemasters, 135
Special Areas Act, 46, 72, 73, 119, 140, 168, 174, 192
Special Areas Act (1937), 46
Special Areas Amendment Act, viii, 192
Special Areas amendment bill, 117, 120
Special Areas Reconstruction Association, 49, 91, 93, 94, 111, 124, 198, 200
St Athan, 148
St Martin's, 146
Standard Telephones, 176
Stanley, Oliver, 57, 58, 64, 65, 80, 85
Stanley, Oliver, 51, 62, 64
Sterling Textiles, 179, 180, 188
Stevens, Dr, 89
Stewart, Sir Malcolm, iv, 59, 61, 62, 63, 64, 65, 66, 67, 68, 70, 72, 74, 75, 77, 80, 81, 83, 84, 85, 92, 94, 95, 96, 97, 100, 102, 103, 106, 108, 109, 110, 111, 124, 136, 146, 154, 161
Stewart, Sir Malcolm, 64
Stockport, 79
Stockton, 79
Sunbury on Thames, 182
Sunderland, 79
Swansea, 46, 168, 169, 170
Swiss Aluminium company, 137, 138

T

Taf Fechan, 13
Taffs Wells, 125, 135
Teddingtons Controls, 182
Teesside, 57, 71
Thomas, Aeron, 94, 113

Thomas, Percy, 156, 159
Thorn lighting, 180
Thorn, Julius, 180
Times, 27, 28, 40, 42, 43, 45, 53, 60, 81,
   100, 104, 113, 116
Tirpentwys, 49
Tonypandy, 20, 48, 109, 165
Trafford Park, 74, 150
Transference Board, 22, 25, 27
Treasury, viii, 21, 22, 23, 25, 27, 31, 34, 35,
   36, 37, 39, 50, 53, 56, 60, 64, 65, 68, 69,
   71, 72, 81, 86, 87, 92, 93, 94, 95, 96,
   103, 106, 107, 109, 110, 111, 113, 114,
   117, 119, 120, 121, 124, 127, 128, 129,
   131, 132, 133, 134, 135, 136, 137, 138,
   139, 140, 141, 145, 150, 153, 154, 157,
   170, 178, 185, 186, 197, 198
Treasury loan scheme, 111, 113, 114, 139
Tredegar, 25, 109, 176
Treforest, iv, v, 73, 75, 81, 109, 121, 123,
   125, 126, 127, 130, 138, 139, 142, 143,
   152, 156, 157, 162, 165, 171, 174, 175,
   182, 188
Treharris, 13
Treorchy, 109, 130, 165, 169, 174, 177, 180
Triangs, 182

U

UAB, 41, 42, 55, 56, 61, 62, 80, 85
UDT, 92, 93
Unemployment Assistance Board, 17, 23, 41,
   42, 55, 59, 62, 76, 192
Unemployment Grants Committee, 24, 35, 41
United Dominion Trust, 92
Upper Boat, 152, 175
Usher, 133

V

Vaynor and Penderyn, 170, 182
Viponds, 49

W

Weir, Lord, 36, 87, 146, 151
Welsh advisory reconstruction council, 166
Welsh Associated Collieries, 49
Welsh Board of Health, 52
Welsh Land Trust, 68, 80
Welsh Metals, 134, 135, 144, 157
Welsh Parliamentary Party, 19, 86, 87, 105,
   162, 167, 173
Welsh Regional Production Board, 155
Welwyn Garden City, 178
Western Mail, 81, 122, 123, 183
Weston, Garfield, 131
white paper on full employment, 169
White Waltham, 150
Wiggins Teape, 45, 139
Wilkinson, Eleanor, 78
Wise AK, 90
Wolfe, Hubert, 85
Woolton, Lord, 170
Woolwich arsenal, 53, 84, 145, 146, 147, 176
Woolworth, 95, 130
Worldwin pistons, 130
Wrexham, 146, 174

Y

Young, Hilton, 36
Ystrad, 67
Ystradgynlais, 169, 170, 176